Advanced Analytics with Spark

Sandy Ryza, Uri Laserson, Sean Owen, and Josh Wills

Beijing · Boston · Farnham · Sebastopol · Tokyo

Advanced Analytics with Spark

by Sandy Ryza, Uri Laserson, Sean Owen, and Josh Wills

Printed in the United States of America.

Published by O'Reilly Media, Inc., 1005 Gravenstein Highway North, Sebastopol, CA 95472.

O'Reilly books may be purchased for educational, business, or sales promotional use. Online editions are also available for most titles (*http://safaribooksonline.com*). For more information, contact our corporate/institutional sales department: 800-998-9938 or *corporate@oreilly.com*.

Editor: Marie Beaugureau	**Indexer:** Judy McConville
Production Editor: Kara Ebrahim	**Interior Designer:** David Futato
Copyeditor: Kim Cofer	**Cover Designer:** Ellie Volckhausen
Proofreader: Rachel Monaghan	**Illustrator:** Rebecca Demarest

April 2015:   First Edition

Revision History for the First Edition
2015-03-27:   First Release
2015-08-07:   Second Release

See *http://oreilly.com/catalog/errata.csp?isbn=9781491912768* for release details.

978-1-491-91276-8

[LSI]

Table of Contents

Foreword

Ever since we started the Spark project at Berkeley, I've been excited about not just building fast parallel systems, but helping more and more people make use of large-scale computing. This is why I'm very happy to see this book, written by four experts in data science, on advanced analytics with Spark. Sandy, Uri, Sean, and Josh have been working with Spark for a while, and have put together a great collection of content with equal parts explanations and examples.

The thing I like most about this book is its focus on examples, which are all drawn from real applications on real-world data sets. It's hard to find one, let alone ten examples that cover big data and that you can run on your laptop, but the authors have managed to create such a collection and set everything up so you can run them in Spark. Moreover, the authors cover not just the core algorithms, but the intricacies of data preparation and model tuning that are needed to really get good results. You should be able to take the concepts in these examples and directly apply them to your own problems.

Big data processing is undoubtedly one of the most exciting areas in computing today, and remains an area of fast evolution and introduction of new ideas. I hope that this book helps you get started in this exciting new field.

—*Matei Zaharia, CTO at Databricks*
and Vice President, Apache Spark

Preface

Sandy Ryza

I don't like to think I have many regrets, but it's hard to believe anything good came out of a particular lazy moment in 2011 when I was looking into how to best distribute tough discrete optimization problems over clusters of computers. My advisor explained this newfangled Spark thing he had heard of, and I basically wrote off the concept as too good to be true and promptly got back to writing my undergrad thesis in MapReduce. Since then, Spark and I have both matured a bit, but one of us has seen a meteoric rise that's nearly impossible to avoid making "ignite" puns about. Cut to two years later, and it has become crystal clear that Spark is something worth paying attention to.

Spark's long lineage of predecessors, running from MPI to MapReduce, makes it possible to write programs that take advantage of massive resources while abstracting away the nitty-gritty details of distributed systems. As much as data processing needs have motivated the development of these frameworks, in a way the field of big data has become so related to these frameworks that its scope is defined by what these frameworks can handle. Spark's promise is to take this a little further—to make writing distributed programs feel like writing regular programs.

Spark will be great at giving ETL pipelines huge boosts in performance and easing some of the pain that feeds the MapReduce programmer's daily chant of despair ("why? whyyyyy?") to the Hadoop gods. But the exciting thing for me about it has always been what it opens up for complex analytics. With a paradigm that supports iterative algorithms and interactive exploration, Spark is finally an open source framework that allows a data scientist to be productive with large data sets.

I think the best way to teach data science is by example. To that end, my colleagues and I have put together a book of applications, trying to touch on the interactions between the most common algorithms, data sets, and design patterns in large-scale analytics. This book isn't meant to be read cover to cover. Page to a chapter that looks like something you're trying to accomplish, or that simply ignites your interest.

What's in This Book

The first chapter will place Spark within the wider context of data science and big data analytics. After that, each chapter will comprise a self-contained analysis using Spark. The second chapter will introduce the basics of data processing in Spark and Scala through a use case in data cleansing. The next few chapters will delve into the meat and potatoes of machine learning with Spark, applying some of the most common algorithms in canonical applications. The remaining chapters are a bit more of a grab bag and apply Spark in slightly more exotic applications—for example, querying Wikipedia through latent semantic relationships in the text or analyzing genomics data.

Using Code Examples

Supplemental material (code examples, exercises, etc.) is available for download at *https://github.com/sryza/aas*.

This book is here to help you get your job done. In general, if example code is offered with this book, you may use it in your programs and documentation. You do not need to contact us for permission unless you're reproducing a significant portion of the code. For example, writing a program that uses several chunks of code from this book does not require permission. Selling or distributing a CD-ROM of examples from O'Reilly books does require permission. Answering a question by citing this book and quoting example code does not require permission. Incorporating a significant amount of example code from this book into your product's documentation does require permission.

We appreciate, but do not require, attribution. An attribution usually includes the title, author, publisher, and ISBN. For example: "*Advanced Analytics with Spark* by Sandy Ryza, Uri Laserson, Sean Owen, and Josh Wills (O'Reilly). Copyright 2015 Sandy Ryza, Uri Laserson, Sean Owen, and Josh Wills, 978-1-491-91276-8."

If you feel your use of code examples falls outside fair use or the permission given above, feel free to contact us at *permissions@oreilly.com*.

Safari® Books Online

 *Safari Books Online* is an on-demand digital library that delivers expert content in both book and video form from the world's leading authors in technology and business.

Technology professionals, software developers, web designers, and business and creative professionals use Safari Books Online as their primary resource for research, problem solving, learning, and certification training.

Safari Books Online offers a range of plans and pricing for enterprise, government, education, and individuals.

Members have access to thousands of books, training videos, and prepublication manuscripts in one fully searchable database from publishers like O'Reilly Media, Prentice Hall Professional, Addison-Wesley Professional, Microsoft Press, Sams, Que, Peachpit Press, Focal Press, Cisco Press, John Wiley & Sons, Syngress, Morgan Kaufmann, IBM Redbooks, Packt, Adobe Press, FT Press, Apress, Manning, New Riders, McGraw-Hill, Jones & Bartlett, Course Technology, and hundreds more. For more information about Safari Books Online, please visit us online.

How to Contact Us

Please address comments and questions concerning this book to the publisher:

O'Reilly Media, Inc.
1005 Gravenstein Highway North
Sebastopol, CA 95472
800-998-9938 (in the United States or Canada)
707-829-0515 (international or local)
707-829-0104 (fax)

We have a web page for this book, where we list errata, examples, and any additional information. You can access this page at *http://bit.ly/advanced-spark*.

To comment or ask technical questions about this book, send email to *bookquestions@oreilly.com*.

For more information about our books, courses, conferences, and news, see our website at *http://www.oreilly.com*.

Find us on Facebook: *http://facebook.com/oreilly*

Follow us on Twitter: *http://twitter.com/oreillymedia*

Watch us on YouTube: *http://www.youtube.com/oreillymedia*

Acknowledgments

It goes without saying that you wouldn't be reading this book if it were not for the existence of Apache Spark and MLlib. We all owe thanks to the team that has built and open sourced it, and the hundreds of contributors who have added to it.

We would like to thank everyone who spent a great deal of time reviewing the content of the book with expert eyes: Michael Bernico, Ian Buss, Jeremy Freeman, Chris Fregly, Debashish Ghosh, Juliet Hougland, Jonathan Keebler, Frank Nothaft, Nick Pentreath, Kostas Sakellis, Marcelo Vanzin, and Juliet Hougland again. Thanks all! We owe you one. This has greatly improved the structure and quality of the result.

I (Sandy) also would like to thank Jordan Pinkus and Richard Wang for helping me with some of the theory behind the risk chapter.

Thanks to Marie Beaugureau and O'Reilly, for the experience and great support in getting this book published and into your hands.

CHAPTER 1

Analyzing Big Data

Sandy Ryza

> *[Data applications] are like sausages. It is better not to see them being made.*
> —Otto von Bismarck

- Build a model to detect credit card fraud using thousands of features and billions of transactions.
- Intelligently recommend millions of products to millions of users.
- Estimate financial risk through simulations of portfolios including millions of instruments.
- Easily manipulate data from thousands of human genomes to detect genetic associations with disease.

These are tasks that simply could not be accomplished 5 or 10 years ago. When people say that we live in an age of "big data," they mean that we have tools for collecting, storing, and processing information at a scale previously unheard of. Sitting behind these capabilities is an ecosystem of open source software that can leverage clusters of commodity computers to chug through massive amounts of data. Distributed systems like Apache Hadoop have found their way into the mainstream and have seen widespread deployment at organizations in nearly every field.

But just as a chisel and a block of stone do not make a statue, there is a gap between having access to these tools and all this data, and doing something useful with it. This is where "data science" comes in. As sculpture is the practice of turning tools and raw material into something relevant to nonsculptors, data science is the practice of turning tools and raw data into something that nondata scientists might care about.

Often, "doing something useful" means placing a schema over it and using SQL to answer questions like "of the gazillion users who made it to the third page in our registration process, how many are over 25?" The field of how to structure a data warehouse and organize information to make answering these kinds of questions easy is a rich one, but we will mostly avoid its intricacies in this book.

Sometimes, "doing something useful" takes a little extra. SQL still may be core to the approach, but to work around idiosyncrasies in the data or perform complex analysis, we need a programming paradigm that's a little bit more flexible and a little closer to the ground, and with richer functionality in areas like machine learning and statistics. These are the kinds of analyses we are going to talk about in this book.

For a long time, open source frameworks like R, the PyData stack, and Octave have made rapid analysis and model building viable over small data sets. With fewer than 10 lines of code, we can throw together a machine learning model on half a data set and use it to predict labels on the other half. With a little more effort, we can impute missing data, experiment with a few models to find the best one, or use the results of a model as inputs to fit another. What should an equivalent process look like that can leverage clusters of computers to achieve the same outcomes on huge data sets?

The right approach might be to simply extend these frameworks to run on multiple machines, to retain their programming models and rewrite their guts to play well in distributed settings. However, the challenges of distributed computing require us to rethink many of the basic assumptions that we rely on in single-node systems. For example, because data must be partitioned across many nodes on a cluster, algorithms that have wide data dependencies will suffer from the fact that network transfer rates are orders of magnitude slower than memory accesses. As the number of machines working on a problem increases, the probability of a failure increases. These facts require a programming paradigm that is sensitive to the characteristics of the under-lying system: one that discourages poor choices and makes it easy to write code that will execute in a highly parallel manner.

Of course, single-machine tools like PyData and R that have come to recent promi-nence in the software community are not the only tools used for data analysis. Scien-tific fields like genomics that deal with large data sets have been leveraging parallel computing frameworks for decades. Most people processing data in these fields today are familiar with a cluster-computing environment called HPC (high-performance computing). Where the difficulties with PyData and R lie in their inability to scale, the difficulties with HPC lie in its relatively low level of abstraction and difficulty of use. For example, to process a large file full of DNA sequencing reads in parallel, we must manually split it up into smaller files and submit a job for each of those files to the cluster scheduler. If some of these fail, the user must detect the failure and take care of manually resubmitting them. If the analysis requires all-to-all operations like sorting the entire data set, the large data set must be streamed through a single node, or the scientist must resort to lower-level distributed frameworks like MPI, which are difficult to program without extensive knowledge of C and distributed/networked systems. Tools written for HPC environments often fail to decouple the in-memory data models from the lower-level storage models. For example, many tools only know how to read data from a POSIX filesystem in a single stream, making it difficult to make tools naturally parallelize, or to use other storage backends, like databases. Recent systems in the Hadoop ecosystem provide abstractions that allow users to treat a cluster of computers more like a single computer—to automatically split up files and distribute storage over many machines, to automatically divide work into smaller tasks and execute them in a distributed manner, and to automatically recover from failures. The Hadoop ecosystem can automate a lot of the hassle of working with large data sets, and is far cheaper than HPC.

The Challenges of Data Science

A few hard truths come up so often in the practice of data science that evangelizing these truths has become a large role of the data science team at Cloudera. For a system that seeks to enable complex analytics on huge data to be successful, it needs to be informed by, or at least not conflict with, these truths.

First, the vast majority of work that goes into conducting successful analyses lies in preprocessing data. Data is messy, and cleansing, munging, fusing, mushing, and many other verbs are prerequisites to doing anything useful with it. Large data sets in particular, because they are not amenable to direct examination by humans, can require computational methods to even discover what preprocessing steps are required. Even when it comes time to optimize model performance, a typical data pipeline requires spending far more time in feature engineering and selection than in choosing and writing algorithms.

For example, when building a model that attempts to detect fraudulent purchases on a website, the data scientist must choose from a wide variety of potential features: any fields that users are required to fill out, IP location info, login times, and click logs as users navigate the site. Each of these comes with its own challenges in converting to vectors fit for machine learning algorithms. A system needs to support more flexible transformations than turning a 2D array of doubles into a mathematical model.

Second, *iteration* is a fundamental part of the data science. Modeling and analysis typically require multiple passes over the same data. One aspect of this lies *within* machine learning algorithms and statistical procedures. Popular optimization procedures like stochastic gradient descent and expectation maximization involve repeated scans over their inputs to reach convergence. Iteration also matters within the data scientist's own workflow. When data scientists are initially investigating and trying to get a feel for a data set, usually the results of a query inform the next query that should run. When building models, data scientists do not try to get it right in one try. Choosing the right features, picking the right algorithms, running the right significance tests, and finding the right hyperparameters all require experimentation. A framework that requires reading the same data set from disk each time it is accessed adds delay that can slow down the process of exploration and limit the number of things we get to try.

Third, the task isn't over when a well-performing model has been built. If the point of data science is making data useful to nondata scientists, then a model stored as a list of regression weights in a text file on the data scientist's computer has not really accomplished this goal. Uses of data recommendation engines and real-time fraud detection systems culminate in data applications. In these, models become part of a production service and may need to be rebuilt periodically or even in real time.

For these situations, it is helpful to make a distinction between analytics in the *lab* and analytics in the *factory*. In the lab, data scientists engage in exploratory analytics. They try to understand the nature of the data they are working with. They visualize it and test wild theories. They experiment with different classes of features and auxiliary sources they can use to augment it. They cast a wide net of algorithms in the hopes that one or two will work. In the factory, in building a data application, data scientists engage in operational analytics. They package their models into services that can inform real-world decisions. They track their models' performance over time and obsess about how they can make small tweaks to squeeze out another percentage point of accuracy. They care about SLAs and uptime. Historically, exploratory analytics typically occurs in languages like R, and when it comes time to build production applications, the data pipelines are rewritten entirely in Java or C++.

Of course, everybody could save time if the original modeling code could be actually used in the app for which it is written, but languages like R are slow and lack integration with most planes of the production infrastructure stack, and languages like Java and C++ are just poor tools for exploratory analytics. They lack Read-Evaluate-Print Loop (REPL) environments for playing with data interactively and require large amounts of code to express simple transformations. A framework that makes modeling easy but is also a good fit for production systems is a huge win.

Introducing Apache Spark

Enter Apache Spark, an open source framework that combines an engine for distributing programs across clusters of machines with an elegant model for writing programs atop it. Spark, which originated at the UC Berkeley AMPLab and has since been contributed to the Apache Software Foundation, is arguably the first open source software that makes distributed programming truly accessible to data scientists.

One illuminating way to understand Spark is in terms of its advances over its predecessor, MapReduce. MapReduce revolutionized computation over huge data sets by offering a simple model for writing programs that could execute in parallel across hundreds to thousands of machines. The MapReduce engine achieves near linear scalability—as the data size increases, we can throw more computers at it and see jobs complete in the same amount of time—and is resilient to the fact that failures that occur rarely on a single machine occur all the time on clusters of thousands. It breaks up work into small *tasks* and can gracefully accommodate task failures without compromising the job to which they belong.

Spark maintains MapReduce's linear scalability and fault tolerance, but extends it in three important ways. First, rather than relying on a rigid map-then-reduce format, its engine can execute a more general directed acyclic graph (DAG) of operators. This means that, in situations where MapReduce must write out intermediate results to the distributed filesystem, Spark can pass them directly to the next step in the pipeline. In this way, it is similar to *Dryad* (*http://research.microsoft.com/en-us/projects/dryad/*), a descendant of MapReduce that originated at Microsoft Research. Second, it complements this capability with a rich set of transformations that enable users to express computation more naturally. It has a strong developer focus and streamlined API that can represent complex pipelines in a few lines of code.

Third, Spark extends its predecessors with in-memory processing. Its Resilient Distributed Dataset (RDD) abstraction enables developers to materialize any point in a processing pipeline into memory across the cluster, meaning that future steps that want to deal with the same data set need not recompute it or reload it from disk. This capability opens up use cases that distributed processing engines could not previously approach. Spark is well suited for highly iterative algorithms that require multiple passes over a data set, as well as reactive applications that quickly respond to user queries by scanning large in-memory data sets.

Perhaps most importantly, Spark fits well with the aforementioned hard truths of data science, acknowledging that the biggest bottleneck in building data applications is not CPU, disk, or network, but analyst productivity. It perhaps cannot be overstated how much collapsing the full pipeline, from preprocessing to model evaluation, into a single programming environment can speed up development. By packaging an expressive programming model with a set of analytic libraries under a REPL, it avoids the round trips to IDEs required by frameworks like MapReduce and the challenges of subsampling and moving data back and forth from HDFS required by frameworks like R. The more quickly analysts can experiment with their data, the higher likelihood they have of doing something useful with it.

With respect to the pertinence of munging and ETL, Spark strives to be something closer to the Python of big data than the Matlab of big data. As a general-purpose computation engine, its core APIs provide a strong foundation for data transformation independent of any functionality in statistics, machine learning, or matrix algebra. Its Scala and Python APIs allow programming in expressive general-purpose languages, as well as access to existing libraries.

Spark's in-memory caching makes it ideal for iteration both at the micro and macro level. Machine learning algorithms that make multiple passes over their training set can cache it in memory. When exploring and getting a feel for a data set, data scientists can keep it in memory while they run queries, and easily cache transformed versions of it as well without suffering a trip to disk.

Last, Spark spans the gap between systems designed for exploratory analytics and systems designed for operational analytics. It is often quoted that a data scientist is someone who is better at engineering than most statisticians and better at statistics than most engineers. At the very least, Spark is better at being an operational system than most exploratory systems and better for data exploration than the technologies commonly used in operational systems. It is built for performance and reliability from the ground up. Sitting atop the JVM, it can take advantage of many of the operational and debugging tools built for the Java stack.

Spark boasts strong integration with the variety of tools in the Hadoop ecosystem. It can read and write data in all of the data formats supported by MapReduce, allowing it to interact with the formats commonly used to store data on Hadoop like Avro and Parquet (and good old CSV). It can read from and write to NoSQL databases like HBase and Cassandra. Its stream processing library, Spark Streaming, can ingest data continuously from systems like Flume and Kafka. Its SQL library, SparkSQL, can interact with the Hive Metastore, and a project that is in progress at the time of this writing seeks to enable Spark to be used as an underlying execution engine for Hive, as an alternative to MapReduce. It can run inside YARN, Hadoop's scheduler and resource manager, allowing it to share cluster resources dynamically and to be managed with the same policies as other processing engines like MapReduce and Impala.

Of course, Spark isn't all roses and petunias. While its core engine has progressed in maturity even during the span of this book being written, it is still young compared to MapReduce and hasn't yet surpassed it as the workhorse of batch processing. Its specialized subcomponents for stream processing, SQL, machine learning, and graph processing lie at different stages of maturity and are undergoing large API upgrades. For example, MLlib's pipelines and transformer API model is in progress while this book is being written. Its statistics and modeling functionality comes nowhere near that of single machine languages like R. Its SQL functionality is rich, but still lags far behind that of Hive.

About This Book

The rest of this book is not going to be about Spark's merits and disadvantages. There are a few other things that it will not be either. It will introduce the Spark programming model and Scala basics, but it will not attempt to be a Spark reference or provide a comprehensive guide to all its nooks and crannies. It will not try to be a machine learning, statistics, or linear algebra reference, although many of the chapters will provide some background on these before using them.

Instead, it will try to help the reader get a *feel* for what it's like to use Spark for complex analytics on large data sets. It will cover the entire pipeline: not just building and evaluating models, but cleansing, preprocessing, and exploring data, with attention paid to turning results into production applications. We believe that the best way to teach this is by example, so, after a quick chapter describing Spark and its ecosystem, the rest of the chapters will be self-contained illustrations of what it looks like to use Spark for analyzing data from different domains.

When possible, we will attempt not to just provide a "solution," but to demonstrate the full data science workflow, with all of its iterations, dead ends, and restarts. This book will be useful for getting more comfortable with Scala, more comfortable with Spark, and more comfortable with machine learning and data analysis. However, these are in service of a larger goal, and we hope that most of all, this book will teach you how to approach tasks like those described at the beginning of this chapter. Each chapter, in about 20 measly pages, will try to get as close as possible to demonstrating how to build one of these pieces of data applications.

CHAPTER 2

Introduction to Data Analysis with Scala and Spark

Josh Wills

If you are immune to boredom, there is literally nothing you cannot accomplish.
—David Foster Wallace

Data cleansing is the first step in any data science project, and often the most important. Many clever analyses have been undone because the data analyzed had fundamental quality problems or underlying artifacts that biased the analysis or led the data scientist to see things that weren't really there.

Despite its importance, most textbooks and classes on data science either don't cover data cleansing or only give it a passing mention. The explanation for this is simple: cleansing data is really boring. It is the tedious, dull work that you have to do before you can get to the really cool machine learning algorithm that you've been dying to apply to a new problem. Many new data scientists tend to rush past it to get their data into a minimally acceptable state, only to discover that the data has major quality issues after they apply their (potentially computationally intensive) algorithm and get a nonsense answer as output.

Everyone has heard the saying "garbage in, garbage out." But there is something even more pernicious: getting reasonable-looking answers from a reasonable-looking data set that has major (but not obvious at first glance) quality issues. Drawing significant conclusions based on this kind of mistake is the sort of thing that gets data scientists fired.

One of the most important talents that you can develop as a data scientist is the ability to discover interesting and worthwhile problems in every phase of the data analytics lifecycle. The more skill and brainpower that you can apply early on in an analysis project, the stronger your confidence will be in your final product.

Of course, it's easy to say all that; it's the data science equivalent of telling children to eat their vegetables. It's much more fun to play with a new tool like Spark that lets us build fancy machine learning algorithms, develop streaming data processing engines, and analyze web-scale graphs. So what better way to introduce you to working with data using Spark and Scala than a data cleansing exercise?

Scala for Data Scientists

Most data scientists have a favorite tool, like R or Python, for performing interactive data munging and analysis. Although they're willing to work in other environments when they have to, data scientists tend to get very attached to their favorite tool, and are always looking to find a way to carry out whatever work they can using it. Introducing them to a new tool that has a new syntax and a new set of patterns to learn can be challenging under the best of circumstances.

There are libraries and wrappers for Spark that allow you to use it from R or Python. The Python wrapper, which is called PySpark, is actually quite good, and we'll cover some examples that involve using it in one of the later chapters in the book. But the vast majority of our examples will be written in Scala, because we think that learning how to work with Spark in the same language in which the underlying framework is written has a number of advantages for you as a data scientist:

It reduces performance overhead.
   Whenever we're running an algorithm in R or Python on top of a JVM-based language like Scala, we have to do some work to pass code and data across the different environments, and oftentimes, things can get lost in translation. When you're writing your data analysis algorithms in Spark with the Scala API, you can be far more confident that your program will run as intended.

It gives you access to the latest and greatest.
   All of Spark's machine learning, stream processing, and graph analytics libraries are written in Scala, and the Python and R bindings can get support for this new functionality much later. If you want to take advantage of all of the features that Spark has to offer (without waiting for a port to other language bindings), you're going to need to learn at least a little bit of Scala, and if you want to be able to extend those functions to solve new problems you encounter, you'll need to learn a little bit more.

It will help you understand the Spark philosophy.
   Even when you're using Spark from Python or R, the APIs reflect the underlying philosophy of computation that Spark inherited from the language in which it was developed—Scala. If you know how to use Spark in Scala, even if you primarily use it from other languages, you'll have a better understanding of the system and will be in a better position to "think in Spark."

There is another advantage to learning how to use Spark from Scala, but it's a bit more difficult to explain because of how different it is from any other data analysis tool. If you've ever analyzed data that you pulled from a database in R or Python, you're used to working with languages like SQL to retrieve the information you want, and then switching into R or Python to manipulate and visualize the data you've retrieved. You're used to using one language (SQL) for retrieving and manipulating lots of data stored in a remote cluster and another language (Python/R) for manipulating and visualizing information stored on your own machine. If you've been doing it for long enough, you probably don't even think about it anymore.

With Spark and Scala, the experience is different, because you're using the same language for *everything*. You're writing Scala to retrieve data from the cluster via Spark. You're writing Scala to manipulate that data locally on your own machine. And then —and this is the really neat part—you can send Scala code into the cluster so that you can perform the exact same transformations that you performed locally on data that is still stored in the cluster. It's difficult to express how transformative it is to do all of your data munging and analysis in a single environment, regardless of where the data itself is stored and processed. It's the sort of thing that you have to experience for yourself to understand, and we wanted to be sure that our examples captured some of that same magic feeling that we felt when we first started using Spark.

The Spark Programming Model

Spark programming starts with a data set or few, usually residing in some form of distributed, persistent storage like the Hadoop Distributed File System (HDFS). Writing a Spark program typically consists of a few related steps:

- Defining a set of transformations on input data sets.
- Invoking actions that output the transformed data sets to persistent storage or return results to the driver's local memory.
- Running local computations that operate on the results computed in a distributed fashion. These can help you decide what transformations and actions to undertake next.

Understanding Spark means understanding the intersection between the two sets of abstractions the framework offers: storage and execution. Spark pairs these abstractions in an elegant way that essentially allows any intermediate step in a data processing pipeline to be cached in memory for later use.

Record Linkage

The problem that we're going to study in this chapter goes by a lot of different names in the literature and in practice: entity resolution, record deduplication, merge-and-purge, and list washing. Ironically, this makes it difficult to find all of the research papers on this topic across the literature in order to get a good overview of solution techniques; we need a data scientist to deduplicate the references to this data cleansing problem! For our purposes in the rest of this chapter, we're going to refer to this problem as *record linkage*.

The general structure of the problem is something like this: we have a large collection of records from one or more source systems, and it is likely that some of the records refer to the same underlying entity, such as a customer, a patient, or the location of a business or an event. Each of the entities has a number of attributes, such as a name, an address, or a birthday, and we will need to use these attributes to find the records that refer to the same entity. Unfortunately, the values of these attributes aren't perfect: values might have different formatting, or typos, or missing information that means that a simple equality test on the values of the attributes will cause us to miss a significant number of duplicate records. For example, let's compare the business listings shown in Table 2-1.

Table 2-1. The challenge of record linkage

Name	Address	City	State	Phone
Josh's Coffee Shop	1234 Sunset Boulevard	West Hollywood	CA	(213)-555-1212
Josh Cofee	1234 Sunset Blvd West	Hollywood	CA	555-1212
Coffee Chain #1234	1400 Sunset Blvd #2	Hollywood	CA	206-555-1212
Coffee Chain Regional Office	1400 Sunset Blvd Suite 2	Hollywood	California	206-555-1212

The first two entries in this table refer to the same small coffee shop, even though a data entry error makes it look as if they are in two different cities (West Hollywood versus Hollywood). The second two entries, on the other hand, are actually referring to different business locations of the same chain of coffee shops that happen to share a common address: one of the entries refers to an actual coffee shop, and the other one refers to a local corporate office location. Both of the entries give the official phone number of corporate headquarters in Seattle.

This example illustrates everything that makes record linkage so difficult: even though both pairs of entries look similar to each other, the criteria that we use to make the duplicate/not-duplicate decision is different for each pair. This is the kind of distinction that is easy for a human to understand and identify at a glance, but is difficult for a computer to learn.

Getting Started: The Spark Shell and SparkContext

We're going to use a sample data set from the UC Irvine Machine Learning Repository, which is a fantastic source for a variety of interesting (and free) data sets for research and education. The data set we'll be analyzing was curated from a record linkage study that was performed at a German hospital in 2010, and it contains several million pairs of patient records that were matched according to several different criteria, such as the patient's name (first and last), address, and birthday. Each matching field was assigned a numerical score from 0.0 to 1.0 based on how similar the strings were, and the data was then hand-labeled to identify which pairs represented the same person and which did not. The underlying values of the fields themselves that were used to create the data set were removed to protect the privacy of the patients, and numerical identifiers, the match scores for the fields, and the label for each pair (match versus nonmatch) were published for use in record linkage research.

From the shell, let's pull the data from the repository:

```
$ mkdir linkage
$ cd linkage/
$ curl -L -o donation.zip http://bit.ly/1Aoywaq
$ unzip donation.zip
$ unzip 'block_*.zip'
```

If you have a Hadoop cluster handy, you can create a directory for the block data in HDFS and copy the files from the data set there:

```
$ hadoop fs -mkdir linkage
$ hadoop fs -put block_*.csv linkage
```

The examples and code in this book assume you have Spark 1.2.1 available. Releases can be obtained from the Spark project site (*http://spark.apache.org/downloads.html*). Refer to the Spark documentation (*http://spark.apache.org/docs/latest/*) for instructions on setting up a Spark environment, whether on a cluster or simply on your local machine.

Now we're ready to launch the `spark-shell`, which is a REPL (read-eval-print loop) for the Scala language that also has some Spark-specific extensions. If you've never seen the term REPL before, you can think of it as something similar to the R environment: it's a place where you can define functions and manipulate data in the Scala programming language.

If you have a Hadoop cluster that runs a version of Hadoop that supports YARN, you can launch the Spark jobs on the cluster by using the value of `yarn-client` for the Spark master:

```
$ spark-shell --master yarn-client
```

However, if you're just running these examples on your personal computer, you can launch a local Spark cluster by specifying local[N], where N is the number of threads to run, or * to match the number of cores available on your machine. For example, to launch a local cluster that uses eight threads on an eight-core machine:

```
$ spark-shell --master local[*]
```

The examples will work the same way locally. You will simply pass paths to local files, rather than paths on HDFS beginning with hdfs://. Note that you will still need to cp block_*.csv into your chosen local directory rather than use the directory containing files you unzipped earlier, because it contains a number of other files besides the *.csv* data files.

The rest of the examples in this book will not show a --master argument to spark-shell, but you will typically need to specify this argument as appropriate for your environment.

You may need to specify additional arguments to make the Spark shell fully utilize your resources. For example, when running Spark with a local master, you can use --driver-memory 2g to let the single local process use 2 gigabytes of memory. YARN memory configuration is more complex, and relevant options like --executor-memory are explained in the Spark on YARN documentation (*http://bit.ly/1BVpP9J*).

After running one of these commands, you will see a lot of log messages from Spark as it initializes itself, but you should also see a bit of ASCII art, followed by some additional log messages and a prompt:

```
Welcome to
      ____              __
     / __/__  ___ _____/ /__
    _\ \/ _ \/ _ `/ __/  '_/
   /___/ .__/\_,_/_/ /_/\_\   version 1.2.1
      /_/

Using Scala version 2.10.4
  (Java HotSpot(TM) 64-Bit Server VM, Java 1.7.0_67)
Type in expressions to have them evaluated.
Type :help for more information.
Spark context available as sc.
scala>
```

If this is your first time using the Spark shell (or any Scala REPL, for that matter), you should run the :help command to list available commands in the shell. :history and :h? can be helpful for finding the names that you gave to variables or functions that you wrote during a session but can't seem to find at the moment. :paste can help you correctly insert code from the clipboard—something you may well want to do while following along with the book and its accompanying source code.

In addition to the note about `:help`, the Spark log messages indicated that "Spark context available as sc." This is a reference to the `SparkContext`, which coordinates the execution of Spark jobs on the cluster. Go ahead and type `sc` at the command line:

```
sc
...
res0: org.apache.spark.SparkContext =
  org.apache.spark.SparkContext@DEADBEEF
```

The REPL will print the string form of the object, and for the `SparkContext` object, this is simply its name plus the hexadecimal address of the object in memory (`DEAD BEEF` is a placeholder; the exact value you see here will vary from run to run.)

It's good that the `sc` variable exists, but what exactly do we do with it? `SparkContext` is an object, and as an object, it has methods associated with it. We can see what those methods are in the Scala REPL by typing the name of a variable, followed by a period, followed by tab:

```
sc.[\t]
...
accumulable                  accumulableCollection
accumulator                  addFile
addJar                       addSparkListener
appName                      asInstanceOf
broadcast                    cancelAllJobs
cancelJobGroup               clearCallSite
clearFiles                   clearJars
clearJobGroup                defaultMinPartitions
defaultMinSplits             defaultParallelism
emptyRDD                     files
getAllPools                  getCheckpointDir
getConf                      getExecutorMemoryStatus
getExecutorStorageStatus     getLocalProperty
getPersistentRDDs            getPoolForName
getRDDStorageInfo            getSchedulingMode
hadoopConfiguration          hadoopFile
hadoopRDD                    initLocalProperties
isInstanceOf                 isLocal
jars                         makeRDD
master                       newAPIHadoopFile
newAPIHadoopRDD              objectFile
parallelize                  runApproximateJob
runJob                       sequenceFile
setCallSite                  setCheckpointDir
setJobDescription            setJobGroup
startTime                    stop
submitJob                    tachyonFolderName
textFile                     toString
union                        version
wholeTextFiles
```

The SparkContext has a long list of methods, but the ones that we're going to use most often allow us to create *Resilient Distributed Datasets*, or *RDDs*. An RDD is Spark's fundamental abstraction for representing a collection of objects that can be distributed across multiple machines in a cluster. There are two ways to create an RDD in Spark:

- Using the SparkContext to create an RDD from an external data source, like a file in HDFS, a database table via JDBC, or a local collection of objects that we create in the Spark shell.

- Performing a transformation on one or more existing RDDs, like filtering records, aggregating records by a common key, or joining multiple RDDs together.

RDDs are a convenient way to describe the computations that we want to perform on our data as a sequence of small, independent steps.

Resilient Distributed Datasets

An RDD is laid out across the cluster of machines as a collection of *partitions*, each including a subset of the data. Partitions define the unit of parallelism in Spark. The framework processes the objects within a partition in sequence, and processes multiple partitions in parallel. One of the simplest ways to create an RDD is to use the parallelize method on SparkContext with a local collection of objects:

```
val rdd = sc.parallelize(Array(1, 2, 2, 4), 4)
...
rdd: org.apache.spark.rdd.RDD[Int] = ...
```

The first argument is the collection of objects to parallelize. The second is the number of partitions. When the time comes to compute the objects within a partition, Spark fetches a subset of the collection from the driver process.

To create an RDD from a text file or directory of text files residing in a distributed filesystem like HDFS, we can pass the name of the file or directory to the textFile method:

```
val rdd2 = sc.textFile("hdfs:///some/path.txt")
...
rdd2: org.apache.spark.rdd.RDD[String] = ...
```

When you're running Spark in local mode, the textFile method can access paths that reside on the local filesystem. If Spark is given a directory instead of an individual file, it will consider all of the files in that directory as part of the given RDD. Finally, note that no actual data has been read by Spark or loaded into memory yet, either on our client machine or the cluster. When the time comes to compute the objects within a partition, Spark reads a section (also known as a *split*) of the input

---

file, and then applies any subsequent transformations (filtering, aggregation, etc.) that we defined via other RDDs.

Our record linkage data is stored in a text file, with one observation on each line. We will use the `textFile` method on `SparkContext` to get a reference to this data as an RDD:

```
val rawblocks = sc.textFile("linkage")
...
rawblocks: org.apache.spark.rdd.RDD[String] = ...
```

There are a few things happening on this line that are worth going over. First, we're declaring a new variable called `rawblocks`. As we can see from the shell, the `raw blocks` variable has a type of `RDD[String]`, even though we never specified that type information in our variable declaration. This is a feature of the Scala programming language called *type inference*, and it saves us a lot of typing when we're working with the language. Whenever possible, Scala figures out what type a variable has based on its context. In this case, Scala looks up the return type from the `textFile` function on the `SparkContext` object, sees that it returns an `RDD[String]`, and assigns that type to the `rawblocks` variable.

Whenever we create a new variable in Scala, we must preface the name of the variable with either `val` or `var`. Variables that are prefaced with `val` are immutable, and cannot be changed to refer to another value once they are assigned, whereas variables that are prefaced with `var` can be changed to refer to different objects of the same type. Watch what happens when we execute the following code:

```
rawblocks = sc.textFile("linkage")
...
<console>: error: reassignment to val

var varblocks = sc.textFile("linkage")
varblocks = sc.textFile("linkage")
```

Attempting to reassign the linkage data to the `rawblocks` `val` threw an error, but reassigning the `varblocks` `var` is fine. Within the Scala REPL, there is an exception to the reassignment of `vals`, because we are allowed to redeclare the same immutable variable, like the following:

```
val rawblocks = sc.textFile("linakge")
val rawblocks = sc.textFile("linkage")
```

In this case, no error is thrown on the second declaration of `rawblocks`. This isn't typically allowed in normal Scala code, but it's fine to do in the shell, and we will make extensive use of this feature throughout the examples in the book.

The REPL and Compilation

In addition to its interactive shell, Spark also supports compiled applications. We typically recommend using *Maven* (*http://maven.apache.org*) for compiling and managing dependencies. The GitHub repository included with this book holds a self-contained Maven project setup under the *simplesparkproject/* directory to help you with getting started.

With both the shell and compilation as options, which should you use when testing out and building a data pipeline? It is often useful to start working entirely in the REPL. This enables quick prototyping, faster iteration, and less lag time between ideas and results. However, as the program builds in size, maintaining a monolithic file of code become more onerous, and Scala interpretation eats up more time. This can be exacerbated by the fact that, when you're dealing with massive data, it is not uncommon for an attempted operation to cause a Spark application to crash or otherwise render a SparkContext unusable. This means that any work and code typed in so far becomes lost. At this point, it is often useful to take a hybrid approach. Keep the frontier of development in the REPL, and, as pieces of code harden, move them over into a compiled library. You can make the compiled JAR available to spark-shell by passing it to the --jars property. When done right, the compiled JAR only needs to be rebuilt infrequently, and the REPL allows for fast iteration on code and approaches that still need ironing out.

What about referencing external Java and Scala libraries? To compile code that references external libraries, you need to specify the libraries inside the project's Maven configuration (*pom.xml*). To run code that accesses external libraries, you need to include the JARs for these libraries on the classpath of Spark's processes. A good way to make this happen is to use Maven to package a JAR that includes all of your application's dependencies. You can then reference this JAR when starting the shell by using the --jars property. The advantage of this approach is the dependencies only need to be specified once: in the Maven *pom.xml*. Again, the *simplesparkproject/* directory in the GitHub repository shows you how to accomplish this.

SPARK-5341 also tracks development on the capability to specify Maven repositories directly when invoking spark-shell and have the JARs from these repositories automatically show up on Spark's classpath.

Bringing Data from the Cluster to the Client

RDDs have a number of methods that allow us to read data from the cluster into the Scala REPL on our client machine. Perhaps the simplest of these is first, which returns the first element of the RDD into the client:

```
rawblocks.first
...
res: String = "id_1","id_2","cmp_fname_c1","cmp_fname_c2",...
```

The first method can be useful for sanity checking a data set, but we're generally interested in bringing back larger samples of an RDD into the client for analysis. When we know that an RDD only contains a small number of records, we can use the collect method to return all of the contents of an RDD to the client as an array. Because we don't know how big the linkage data set is just yet, we'll hold off on doing this right now.

We can strike a balance between first and collect with the take method, which allows us to read a given number of records into an array on the client. Let's use take to get the first 10 lines from the linkage data set:

```
val head = rawblocks.take(10)
...
head: Array[String] = Array("id_1","id_2","cmp_fname_c1",...

head.length
...
res: Int = 10
```

Actions

The act of creating an RDD does not cause any distributed computation to take place on the cluster. Rather, RDDs define logical data sets that are intermediate steps in a computation. Distributed computation occurs upon invoking an *action* on an RDD. For example, the count action returns the number of objects in an RDD:

```
rdd.count()
14/09/10 17:36:09 INFO SparkContext: Starting job: count ...
14/09/10 17:36:09 INFO SparkContext: Job finished: count ...
res0: Long = 4
```

The collect action returns an Array with all the objects from the RDD. This Array resides in local memory, not on the cluster:

```
rdd.collect()
14/09/29 00:58:09 INFO SparkContext: Starting job: collect ...
14/09/29 00:58:09 INFO SparkContext: Job finished: collect ...
res2: Array[(Int, Int)] = Array((4,1), (1,1), (2,2))
```

Actions need not only return results to the local process. The saveAsTextFile action saves the contents of an RDD to persistent storage, such as HDFS:

```
rdd.saveAsTextFile("hdfs:///user/ds/mynumbers")
14/09/29 00:38:47 INFO SparkContext: Starting job:
saveAsTextFile ...
14/09/29 00:38:49 INFO SparkContext: Job finished:
saveAsTextFile ...
```

The action creates a directory and writes out each partition as a file within it. From the command line outside of the Spark shell:

```
hadoop fs -ls /user/ds/mynumbers

-rw-r--r--   3 ds supergroup          0 2014-09-29 00:38 myfile.txt/_SUCCESS
-rw-r--r--   3 ds supergroup          4 2014-09-29 00:38 myfile.txt/part-00000
-rw-r--r--   3 ds supergroup          4 2014-09-29 00:38 myfile.txt/part-00001
```

Remember that textFile can accept a directory of text files as input, meaning that a future Spark job could refer to mynumbers as an input directory.

The raw form of data that is returned by the Scala REPL can be somewhat hard to read, especially for arrays that contain more than a handful of elements. To make it easier to read the contents of an array, we can use the foreach method in conjunction with println to print out each value in the array on its own line:

```
head.foreach(println)
...
"id_1","id_2","cmp_fname_c1","cmp_fname_c2","cmp_lname_c1","cmp_lname_c2",
  "cmp_sex","cmp_bd","cmp_bm","cmp_by","cmp_plz","is_match"
37291,53113,0.833333333333333,?,1,?,1,1,1,1,0,TRUE
39086,47614,1,?,1,?,1,1,1,1,1,TRUE
70031,70237,1,?,1,?,1,1,1,1,1,TRUE
84795,97439,1,?,1,?,1,1,1,1,1,TRUE
36950,42116,1,?,1,1,1,1,1,1,1,TRUE
42413,48491,1,?,1,?,1,1,1,1,1,TRUE
25965,64753,1,?,1,?,1,1,1,1,1,TRUE
49451,90407,1,?,1,?,1,1,1,1,0,TRUE
39932,40902,1,?,1,?,1,1,1,1,1,TRUE
```

The foreach(println) pattern is one that we will frequently use in this book. It's an example of a common functional programming pattern, where we pass one function (println) as an argument to another function (foreach) in order to perform some action. This kind of programming style will be familiar to data scientists who have worked with R and are used to processing vectors and lists by avoiding for loops and instead using higher-order functions like apply and lapply. Collections in Scala are similar to lists and vectors in R in that we generally want to avoid for loops and instead process the elements of the collection using higher-order functions.

Immediately, we see a couple of issues with the data that we need to address before we begin our analysis. First, the CSV files contain a header row that we'll want to filter out from our subsequent analysis. We can use the presence of the "id_1" string in the row as our filter condition, and write a small Scala function that tests for the presence of that string inside of the line:

```
def isHeader(line: String) = line.contains("id_1")
isHeader: (line: String)Boolean
```

Like Python, we declare functions in Scala using the keyword def. Unlike Python, we have to specify the types of the arguments to our function; in this case, we have to indicate that the line argument is a String. The body of the function, which uses the contains method for the String class to test whether or not the characters "id_1" appear anywhere in the string, comes after the equals sign. Even though we had to specify a type for the line argument, note that we did not have to specify a return type for the function, because the Scala compiler was able to infer the type based on its knowledge of the String class and the fact that the contains method returns true or false.

Sometimes, we will want to specify the return type of a function ourselves, especially for long, complex functions with multiple return statements, where the Scala compiler can't necessarily infer the return type itself. We might also want to specify a return type for our function in order to make it easier for someone else reading our code later to be able to understand what the function does without having to reread the entire method. We can declare the return type for the function right after the argument list, like this:

```
def isHeader(line: String): Boolean = {
  line.contains("id_1")
}
isHeader: (line: String)Boolean
```

We can test our new Scala function against the data in the head array by using the filter method on Scala's Array class and then printing the results:

```
head.filter(isHeader).foreach(println)
...
"id_1","id_2","cmp_fname_c1","cmp_fname_c2","cmp_lname_c1",...
```

It looks like our isHeader method works correctly; the only result that was returned from applying it to the head array via the filter method was the header line itself. But of course, what we really want to do is get all of the rows in the data *except* the header rows. There are a few ways that we can do this in Scala. Our first option is to take advantage of the filterNot method on the Array class:

```
head.filterNot(isHeader).length
...
res: Int = 9
```

We could also use Scala's support for anonymous functions to negate the isHeader function from inside filter:

```
head.filter(x => !isHeader(x)).length
...
res: Int = 9
```

Anonymous functions in Scala are somewhat like Python's lambda functions. In this case, we defined an anonymous function that takes a single argument called x and passes x to the isHeader function and returns the negation of the result. Note that we did *not* have to specify any type information for the x variable in this instance; the Scala compiler was able to infer that x is a String from the fact that head is an Array[String].

There is nothing that Scala programmers hate more than typing, so Scala has lots of little features that are designed to reduce the amount of typing they have to do. For example, in our anonymous function definition, we had to type the characters x => in order to declare our anonymous function and give its argument a name. For simple anonymous functions like this one, we don't even have to do that; Scala will allow us to use an underscore (_) to represent the argument to the anonymous function, so that we can save four characters:

```
head.filter(!isHeader(_)).length
...
res: Int = 9
```

Sometimes, this abbreviated syntax makes the code easier to read because it avoids duplicating obvious identifiers. Sometimes, this shortcut just makes the code cryptic. The code listings use one or the other according to our best judgment.

Shipping Code from the Client to the Cluster

We just saw a wide variety of ways to write and apply functions to data in Scala. All of the code that we executed was done against the data inside the head array, which was contained on our client machine. Now we're going to take the code that we just wrote and apply it to the millions of linkage records contained in our cluster and represented by the rawblocks RDD in Spark.

Here's what the code looks like to do this; it should feel eerily familiar to you:

```
val noheader = rawblocks.filter(x => !isHeader(x))
```

The syntax that we used to express the filtering computation against the entire data set on the cluster is *exactly the same* as the syntax we used to express the filtering computation against the array of data in head on our local machine. We can use the first method on the noheader RDD to verify that the filtering rule worked correctly:

```
noheader.first
...
res: String = 37291,53113,0.833333333333333,?,1,?,1,1,1,1,0,TRUE
```

This is incredibly powerful. It means that we can interactively develop and debug our data-munging code against a small amount of data that we sample from the cluster, and then ship that code to the cluster to apply it to the entire data set when we're ready to transform the entire data set. Best of all, we never have to leave the shell. There really isn't another tool that gives you this kind of experience.

In the next several sections, we'll use this mix of local development and testing and cluster computation to perform more munging and analysis of the record linkage data, but if you need to take a moment to drink in the new world of awesome that you have just entered, we certainly understand.

Structuring Data with Tuples and Case Classes

Right now, the records in the head array and the noheader RDD are all strings of comma-separated fields. To make it a bit easier to analyze this data, we'll need to parse these strings into a structured format that converts the different fields into the correct data type, like an integer or double.

If we look at the contents of the head array (both the header line and the records themselves), we can see the following structure in the data:

- The first two fields are integer IDs that represent the patients that were matched in the record.
- The next nine values are (possibly missing) double values that represent match scores on different fields of the patient records, such as their names, birthdays, and location.
- The last field is a boolean value (TRUE or FALSE) indicating whether or not the pair of patient records represented by the line was a match.

Like Python, Scala has a built-in *tuple* type that we can use to quickly create pairs, triples, and larger collections of values of different types as a simple way to represent records. For the time being, let's parse the contents of each line into a tuple with four values: the integer ID of the first patient, the integer ID of the second patient, an array of nine doubles representing the match scores (with NaN values for any missing fields), and a boolean field that indicates whether or not the fields matched.

Unlike Python, Scala does not have a built-in method for parsing comma-separated strings, so we'll need to do a bit of the legwork ourselves. We can experiment with our parsing code in the Scala REPL. First, let's grab one of the records from the head array:

```
val line = head(5)
val pieces = line.split(',')
...
pieces: Array[String] = Array(36950, 42116, 1, ?,...
```

Note that we accessed the elements of the head array using parentheses instead of brackets; in Scala, accessing array elements is a function call, not a special operator. Scala allows classes to define a special function named apply that is called when we treat an object as if it were a function, so head(5) is the same thing as head.apply(5).

We broke up the components of `line` using the `split` function from Java's `String` class, returning an `Array[String]` that we named `pieces`. Now we'll need to convert the individual elements of `pieces` to the appropriate type using Scala's type conversion functions:

```
val id1 = pieces(0).toInt
val id2 = pieces(1).toInt
val matched = pieces(11).toBoolean
```

Converting the `id` variables and the `matched` boolean variable is pretty straightforward once we know about the appropriate `toXYZ` conversion functions. Unlike the `contains` method and `split` method that we worked with earlier, the `toInt` and `toBoolean` methods aren't defined on Java's `String` class. Instead, they are defined in a Scala class called `StringOps` that uses one of Scala's more powerful (and arguably somewhat dangerous) features: *implicit type conversion*. Implicits work like this: if you call a method on a Scala object, and the Scala compiler does not see a definition for that method in the class definition for that object, the compiler will try to convert your object to an instance of a class that *does* have that method defined. In this case, the compiler will see that Java's `String` class does not have a `toInt` method defined, but the `StringOps` class does, and that the `StringOps` class has a method that can convert an instance of the `String` class into an instance of the `StringOps` class. The compiler silently performs the conversion of our `String` object into a `StringOps` object, and then calls the `toInt` method on the new object.

Developers who write libraries in Scala (including the core Spark developers) really like implicit type conversion; it allows them to enhance the functionality of core classes like `String` that are otherwise closed to modification. For a user of these tools, implicit type conversions are more of a mixed bag, because they can make it difficult to figure out exactly where a particular class method is defined. Nonetheless, we're going to encounter implicit conversions throughout our examples, so it's best that we get used to them now.

We still need to convert the double-valued score fields—all nine of them. To convert them all at once, we can use the `slice` method on the Scala `Array` class to extract a contiguous subset of the array, and then use the `map` higher-order function to convert each element of the slice from a `String` to a `Double`:

```
val rawscores = pieces.slice(2, 11)
rawscores.map(s => s.toDouble)
...
java.lang.NumberFormatException: For input string: "?"
  at sun.misc.FloatingDecimal.readJavaFormatString(FloatingDecimal.java:1241)
  at java.lang.Double.parseDouble(Double.java:540)
  ...
```

Oops! We forgot about the "?" entry in the `rawscores` array, and the `toDouble` method in `StringOps` didn't know how to convert it to a `Double`. Let's write a function that will return a `NaN` value whenever it encounters a "?", and then apply it to our `rawscores` array:

```
def toDouble(s: String) = {
  if ("?".equals(s)) Double.NaN else s.toDouble
}
val scores = rawscores.map(toDouble)
scores: Array[Double] = Array(1.0, NaN, 1.0, 1.0, ...
```

There. Much better. Let's bring all of this parsing code together into a single function that returns all of the parsed values in a tuple:

```
def parse(line: String) = {
  val pieces = line.split(',')
  val id1 = pieces(0).toInt
  val id2 = pieces(1).toInt
  val scores = pieces.slice(2, 11).map(toDouble)
  val matched = pieces(11).toBoolean
  (id1, id2, scores, matched)
}
val tup = parse(line)
```

We can retrieve the values of individual fields from our tuple by using the positional functions, starting from _1, or via the `productElement` method, which starts counting from 0. We can also get the size of any tuple via the `productArity` method:

```
tup._1
tup.productElement(0)
tup.productArity
```

Although it is very easy and convenient to create tuples in Scala, addressing all of the elements of a record by position instead of by a meaningful name can make our code difficult to understand. What we would really like is a way of creating a simple record type that would allow us to address our fields by name, instead of by position. Fortunately, Scala provides a convenient syntax for creating these records, called *case classes*. A case class is a simple type of immutable class that comes with implementations of all of the basic Java class methods, like `toString`, `equals`, and `hashCode`, which makes them very easy to use. Let's declare a case class for our record linkage data:

```
case class MatchData(id1: Int, id2: Int,
  scores: Array[Double], matched: Boolean)
```

Now we can update our `parse` method to return an instance of our `MatchData` case class, instead of a tuple:

```
def parse(line: String) = {
  val pieces = line.split(',')
  val id1 = pieces(0).toInt
```

```
    val id2 = pieces(1).toInt
    val scores = pieces.slice(2, 11).map(toDouble)
    val matched = pieces(11).toBoolean
    MatchData(id1, id2, scores, matched)
}
val md = parse(line)
```

There are two things to note here: first, we do not need to specify the keyword new in front of MatchData when we create a new instance of our case class (another example of how much Scala developers hate typing). Second, our MatchData class comes with a built-in toString implementation that works great for every field except for the scores array.

We can access the fields of the MatchData case class by their names now:

```
md.matched
md.id1
```

Now that we have our parsing function tested on a single record, let's apply it to all of the elements in the head array, except for the header line:

```
val mds = head.filter(x => !isHeader(x)).map(x => parse(x))
```

Yep, that worked. Now, let's apply our parsing function to the data in the cluster by calling the map function on the noheader RDD:

```
val parsed = noheader.map(line => parse(line))
```

Remember that unlike the mds array that we generated locally, the parse function has not actually been applied to the data on the cluster yet. Once we make a call to the parsed RDD that requires some output, the parse function will be applied to convert each String in the noheader RDD into an instance of our MatchData class. If we make another call to the parsed RDD that generates a different output, the parse function will be applied to the input data *again*.

This isn't an optimal use of our cluster resources; after the data has been parsed once, we'd like to save the data in its parsed form on the cluster so that we don't have to re-parse it every time we want to ask a new question of the data. Spark supports this use case by allowing us to signal that a given RDD should be cached in memory after it is generated by calling the cache method on the instance. Let's do that now for the parsed RDD:

```
parsed.cache()
```

Caching

Although the contents of RDDs are transient by default, Spark provides a mechanism for persisting the data in an RDD. After the first time an action requires computing such an RDD's contents, they are stored in memory or disk across the cluster. The next time an action depends on the RDD, it need not be recomputed from its dependencies. Its data is returned from the cached partitions directly:

```
cached.cache()
cached.count()
cached.take(10)
```

The call to `cache` indicates that the RDD should be stored the next time it's computed. The call to `count` computes it initially. The `take` action returns the first 10 elements of the RDD as a local `Array`. When `take` is called, it accesses the cached elements of cached instead of recomputing them from their dependencies.

Spark defines a few different mechanisms, or `StorageLevel` values, for persisting RDDs. `rdd.cache()` is shorthand for `rdd.persist(StorageLevel.MEMORY)`, which stores the RDD as unserialized Java objects. When Spark estimates that a partition will not fit in memory, it simply will not store it, and it will be recomputed the next time it's needed. This level makes the most sense when the objects will be referenced frequently and/or require low-latency access, because it avoids any serialization overhead. Its drawback is that it takes up larger amounts of memory than its alternatives. Also, holding on to many small objects puts pressure on Java's garbage collection, which can result in stalls and general slowness.

Spark also exposes a `MEMORY_SER` storage level, which allocates large byte buffers in memory and serializes the RDD contents into them. When we use the right format (more on this in a bit), serialized data usually takes up two to five times less space than its raw equivalent.

Spark can use disk for caching RDDs as well. The `MEMORY_AND_DISK` and `MEMORY_AND_DISK_SER` are similar to the `MEMORY` and `MEMORY_SER` storage levels, respectively. For the latter two, if a partition will not fit in memory, it is simply not stored, meaning that it must be recomputed from its dependencies the next time an action uses it. For the former, Spark spills partitions that will not fit in memory to disk.

Deciding when to cache data can be an art. The decision typically involves trade-offs between space and speed, with the specter of garbage collecting looming overhead to occasionally confound things further. In general, RDDs should be cached when they are likely to be referenced by multiple actions and are expensive to regenerate.

Aggregations

Thus far in the chapter, we've focused on the similar ways that we process data that is on our local machine as well as on the cluster using Scala and Spark. In this section, we'll start to explore some of the differences between the Scala APIs and the Spark ones, especially as they relate to grouping and aggregating data. Most of the differences are about efficiency: when we're aggregating large data sets that are distributed across multiple machines, we're more concerned with transmitting information efficiently than we are when all of the data that we need is available in memory on a single machine.

To illustrate some of the differences, let's start by performing a simple aggregation over our `MatchData` on both our local client and on the cluster with Spark in order to calculate the number of records that are matches versus the number of records that are not. For the local `MatchData` records in the `mds` array, we'll use the `groupBy` method to create a Scala `Map[Boolean, Array[MatchData]]`, where the key is based on the `matched` field in the `MatchData` class:

```
val grouped = mds.groupBy(md => md.matched)
```

Once we have the values in the `grouped` variable, we can get the counts by calling the `mapValues` method on `grouped`, which is like a `map` method that only operates on the values in the `Map` object, and get the `size` of each array:

```
grouped.mapValues(x => x.size).foreach(println)
```

As we can see, all of the entries in our local data are matches, so the only entry returned from the map is the tuple (`true,9`). Of course, our local data is just a sample of the overall data in the linkage data set; when we apply this grouping to the overall data, we expect to find lots of nonmatches.

When we are performing aggregations on data in the cluster, we always have to be mindful of the fact that the data we are analyzing is stored across multiple machines, and so our aggregations will require moving data over the network that connects the machines. Moving data across the network requires a lot of computational resources: including determining which machines each record will be transferred to, serializing the data, compressing it, sending it over the wire, decompressing and then deserializing the results, and finally, performing computations on the aggregated data. To do this quickly, it is important that we try to minimize the amount of data that we move around; the more filtering that we can do to the data before performing an aggregation, the faster we will get an answer to our question.

Creating Histograms

Let's start out by creating a simple histogram to count how many of the `MatchData` records in `parsed` have a value of `true` or `false` for the `matched` field. Fortunately, the `RDD[T]` class defines an action called `countByValue` that performs this kind of computation very efficiently and returns the results to the client as a `Map[T,Long]`. Calling `countByValue` on a projection of the `matched` field from `MatchData` will execute a Spark job and return the results to the client:

```
val matchCounts = parsed.map(md => md.matched).countByValue()
```

Whenever we create a histogram or other grouping of values in the Spark client, especially when the categorical variable in question contains a large number of values, we want to be able to look at the contents of the histogram sorted in different ways, such as by the alphabetical ordering of the keys, or by the numerical counts of the values in ascending or descending order. Although our `matchCounts` `Map` only contains the keys `true` and `false`, let's take a brief look at how to order its contents in different ways.

Scala's `Map` class does not have methods for sorting its contents on the keys or the values, but we can convert a `Map` into a Scala `Seq` type, which does provide support for sorting. Scala's `Seq` is similar to Java's `List` interface, in that it is an iterable collection that has a defined length and the ability to look up values by index:

```
val matchCountsSeq = matchCounts.toSeq
```

Scala Collections

Scala has an extensive library of collections, including lists, sets, maps, and arrays. You can easily convert from one collection type to another using methods like `toList`, `toSet`, and `toArray`.

Our `matchCountsSeq` sequence is made up of elements of type (`String`, `Long`), and we can use the `sortBy` method to control which of the indices we use for sorting:

```
matchCountsSeq.sortBy(_._1).foreach(println)
...
(false,5728201)
(true,20931)

matchCountsSeq.sortBy(_._2).foreach(println)
...
(true,20931)
(false,5728201)
```

By default, the `sortBy` function sorts numeric values in ascending order, but it's often more useful to look at the values in a histogram in descending order. We can reverse the sort order of any type by calling the `reverse` method on the sequence before we print it out:

```
matchCountsSeq.sortBy(_._2).reverse.foreach(println)
...
(false,5728201)
(true,20931)
```

When we look at the match counts across the entire data set, we see a significant imbalance between positive and negative matches; less than 0.4% of the input pairs actually match. The implication of this imbalance for our record linkage model is profound: it's likely that any function of the numeric match scores we come up with will have a significant false positive rate (i.e., many pairs of records will look like matches even though they actually are not).

Summary Statistics for Continuous Variables

Spark's `countByValue` action is a great way to create histograms for relatively low cardinality categorical variables in our data. But for continuous variables, like the match scores for each of the fields in the patient records, we'd like to be able to quickly get a basic set of statistics about their distribution, like the mean, standard deviation, and extremal values like the maximum and minimum.

For instances of `RDD[Double]`, the Spark APIs provide an additional set of actions via implicit type conversion, in the same way we saw that the `toInt` method is provided for the `String` class. These implicit actions allow us to extend the functionality of an RDD in useful ways when we have additional information about how to process the values it contains.

Pair RDDs

In addition to the `RDD[Double]` implicit actions, Spark supports implicit type conversion for the `RDD[Tuple2[K, V]]` type that provides methods for performing per-key aggregations like `groupByKey` and `reduceByKey`, as well as methods that enable joining multiple RDDs that have keys of the same type.

One of the implicit actions for `RDD[Double]`, `stats`, will provide us with exactly the summary statistics about the values in the RDD that we want. Let's try it now on the first value in the `scores` array inside of the `MatchData` records in the `parsed` RDD:

```
parsed.map(md => md.scores(0)).stats()
StatCounter = (count: 5749132, mean: NaN, stdev: NaN, max: NaN, min: NaN)
```

Unfortunately, the missing NaN values that we are using as placeholders in our arrays are tripping up Spark's summary statistics. Even more unfortunate, Spark does not currently have a nice way of excluding and/or counting up the missing values for us, so we have to filter them out manually using the isNaN function from Java's Double class:

```
import java.lang.Double.isNaN
parsed.map(md => md.scores(0)).filter(!isNaN(_)).stats()
StatCounter = (count: 5748125, mean: 0.7129, stdev: 0.3887, max: 1.0, min: 0.0)
```

If we were so inclined, we could get all of the statistics for the values in the scores array this way, using Scala's Range construct to create a loop that would iterate through each index value and compute the statistics for the column, like so:

```
val stats = (0 until 9).map(i => {
  parsed.map(md => md.scores(i)).filter(!isNaN(_)).stats()
})

stats(1)
...
StatCounter = (count: 103698, mean: 0.9000, stdev: 0.2713, max: 1.0, min: 0.0)

stats(8)
...
StatCounter = (count: 5736289, mean: 0.0055, stdev: 0.0741, max: 1.0, min: 0.0)
```

Creating Reusable Code for Computing Summary Statistics

Although this approach gets the job done, it's pretty inefficient; we have to reprocess all of the records in the parsed RDD nine times to calculate all of the statistics. As our data sets get larger and larger, the cost of reprocessing all of the data over and over again goes up and up, even when we are caching intermediate results in memory to save on some of the processing time. When we're developing distributed algorithms with Spark, it can really pay off to invest some time in figuring out how we can compute all of the answers we might need in as few passes over the data as possible. In this case, let's figure out a way to write a function that will take in any RDD[Array[Double]] we give it and return to us an array that includes both the count of missing values for each index and a StatCounter object with the summary statistics of the nonmissing values for each index.

Whenever we expect that some analysis task we need to perform will be useful again and again, it's worth spending some time to develop our code in a way that makes it easy for other analysts to use the solution we come up in their own analyses. To do this, we can write Scala code in a separate file that we can then load into the Spark shell for testing and validation, and we can then share that file with others once we know that it works.

This is going to require a jump in code complexity. Instead of dealing in individual method calls and functions of a line or two, we need to create proper Scala classes and APIs, and that means using more complex language features.

For our missing value analysis, our first task is to write an analogue of Spark's StatCounter class that correctly handles missing values. In a separate shell on your client machine, open a file named *StatsWithMissing.scala*, and copy the following class definitions into the file. We'll walk through the individual fields and methods defined here after the code:

```scala
import org.apache.spark.util.StatCounter

class NAStatCounter extends Serializable {
  val stats: StatCounter = new StatCounter()
  var missing: Long = 0

  def add(x: Double): NAStatCounter = {
    if (java.lang.Double.isNaN(x)) {
      missing += 1
    } else {
      stats.merge(x)
    }
    this
  }

  def merge(other: NAStatCounter): NAStatCounter = {
    stats.merge(other.stats)
    missing += other.missing
    this
  }

  override def toString = {
    "stats: " + stats.toString + " NaN: " + missing
  }
}

object NAStatCounter extends Serializable {
  def apply(x: Double) = new NAStatCounter().add(x)
}
```

Our NAStatCounter class has two member variables: an immutable StatCounter instance named stats, and a mutable Long variable named missing. Note that we're marking this class as Serializable because we will be using instances of this class inside Spark RDDs, and our job will fail if Spark cannot serialize the data contained inside an RDD.

The first method in the class, add, allows us to bring a new Double value into the statistics tracked by the NAStatCounter, either by recording it as missing if it is NaN or adding it to the underlying StatCounter if it is not. The merge method incorporates the statistics that are tracked by another NAStatCounter instance into the current instance. Both of these methods return this so that they can be easily chained together.

Finally, we override the toString method on our NAStatCounter class so that we can easily print out its contents in the Spark shell. Whenever we override a method from a parent class in Scala, we need to prefix the method definition with the override keyword. Scala allows a much richer set of method override patterns than Java does, and the override keyword helps Scala keep track of which method definition should be used for any given class.

Along with the class definition, we define a *companion object* for NAStatCounter. Scala's object keyword is used to declare a singleton that can provide helper methods for a class, analogous to the static method definitions on a Java class. In this case, the apply method provided by the companion object creates a new instance of the NAStatCounter class and adds the given Double value to the instance before returning it. In Scala, apply methods have some special syntactic sugar that allows us to call them without having to type them out explicitly; for example, these two lines do exactly the same thing:

```
val nastats = NAStatCounter.apply(17.29)
val nastats = NAStatCounter(17.29)
```

Now that we have our NAStatCounter class defined, let's bring it into the Spark shell by closing and saving the *StatsWithMissing.scala* file and using the load command:

```
:load StatsWithMissing.scala
...
Loading StatsWithMissing.scala...
import org.apache.spark.util.StatCounter
defined class NAStatCounter
defined module NAStatCounter
warning: previously defined class NAStatCounter is not a companion to object
NAStatCounter. Companions must be defined together; you may wish to use
:paste mode for this.
```

We get a warning about our companion object not being valid in the incremental compilation mode that the shell uses, but we can verify that a few examples work as we expect:

```
val nas1 = NAStatCounter(10.0)
nas1.add(2.1)
val nas2 = NAStatCounter(Double.NaN)
nas1.merge(nas2)
```

Let's use our new `NAStatCounter` class to process the scores in the `MatchData` records within the `parsed` RDD. Each `MatchData` instance contains an array of scores of type `Array[Double]`. For each entry in the array, we would like to have an `NAStatCounter` instance that tracks how many of the values in that index are NaN along with the regular distribution statistics for the nonmissing values. Given an array of values, we can use the `map` function to create an array of `NAStatCounter` objects:

```
val arr = Array(1.0, Double.NaN, 17.29)
val nas = arr.map(d => NAStatCounter(d))
```

Every record in our RDD will have its own `Array[Double]`, which we can translate into an RDD where each record is an `Array[NAStatCounter]`. Let's go ahead and do that now against the data in the `parsed` RDD on the cluster:

```
val nasRDD = parsed.map(md => {
  md.scores.map(d => NAStatCounter(d))
})
```

We now need an easy way to aggregate multiple instances of `Array[NAStatCounter]` into a single `Array[NAStatCounter]`. We can combine two arrays of the same length using `zip`. This produces a new `Array` of the corresponding pairs of elements in the two arrays. Think of a zipper pairing up two corresponding strips of teeth into one fastened strip of interlocked teeth. This can be followed by a `map` method that uses the `merge` function on the `NAStatCounter` class to combine the statistics from both objects into a single instance:

```
val nas1 = Array(1.0, Double.NaN).map(d => NAStatCounter(d))
val nas2 = Array(Double.NaN, 2.0).map(d => NAStatCounter(d))
val merged = nas1.zip(nas2).map(p => p._1.merge(p._2))
```

We can even use Scala's `case` syntax to break the pair of elements in the zipped array into nicely named variables, instead of using the `_1` and `_2` methods on the `Tuple2` class:

```
val merged = nas1.zip(nas2).map { case (a, b) => a.merge(b) }
```

To perform this same merge operation across all of the records in a Scala collection, we can use the `reduce` function, which takes an associative function that maps two arguments of type `T` into a single return value of type `T` and applies it over and over again to all of the elements in a collection to merge all of the values together. Because the merging logic we wrote earlier is associative, we can apply it with the `reduce` method to a collection of `Array[NAStatCounter]` values:

```
val nas = List(nas1, nas2)
val merged = nas.reduce((n1, n2) => {
  n1.zip(n2).map { case (a, b) => a.merge(b) }
})
```

The RDD class also has a reduce action that works the same way as the reduce method we used on the Scala collections, only applied to all of the data that is distributed across the cluster, and the code we use in Spark is identical to the code we just wrote for the List[Array[NAStatCounter]]:

```
val reduced = nasRDD.reduce((n1, n2) => {
  n1.zip(n2).map { case (a, b) => a.merge(b) }
})
reduced.foreach(println)
...
stats: (count: 5748125, mean: 0.7129, stdev: 0.3887,
max: 1.0, min: 0.0) NaN: 1007
stats: (count: 103698, mean: 0.9000, stdev: 0.2713,
max: 1.0, min: 0.0) NaN: 5645434
stats: (count: 5749132, mean: 0.3156, stdev: 0.3342, max: 1.0, min: 0.0) NaN: 0
stats: (count: 2464, mean: 0.3184, stdev: 0.3684,
max: 1.0, min: 0.0) NaN: 5746668
stats: (count: 5749132, mean: 0.9550, stdev: 0.2073, max: 1.0, min: 0.0) NaN: 0
stats: (count: 5748337, mean: 0.2244, stdev: 0.4172, max: 1.0, min: 0.0) NaN: 795
stats: (count: 5748337, mean: 0.4888, stdev: 0.4998, max: 1.0, min: 0.0) NaN: 795
stats: (count: 5748337, mean: 0.2227, stdev: 0.4160, max: 1.0, min: 0.0) NaN: 795
stats: (count: 5736289, mean: 0.0055, stdev: 0.0741,
max: 1.0, min: 0.0) NaN: 12843
```

Let's encapsulate our missing value analysis code into a function in the *StatsWithMissing.scala* file that allows us to compute these statistics for any RDD[Array[Double]] by editing the file to include this block of code:

```
import org.apache.spark.rdd.RDD

def statsWithMissing(rdd: RDD[Array[Double]]): Array[NAStatCounter] = {
  val nastats = rdd.mapPartitions((iter: Iterator[Array[Double]]) => {
    val nas: Array[NAStatCounter] = iter.next().map(d => NAStatCounter(d))
    iter.foreach(arr => {
      nas.zip(arr).foreach { case (n, d) => n.add(d) }
    })
    Iterator(nas)
  })
  nastats.reduce((n1, n2) => {
    n1.zip(n2).map { case (a, b) => a.merge(b) }
  })
}
```

Note that instead of calling the map function to generate an Array[NAStatCounter] for each record in the input RDD, we're calling the slightly more advanced mapParti tions function, which allows us to process *all* of the records within a partition of the input RDD[Array[Double]] via an Iterator[Array[Double]]. This allows us to create a single instance of Array[NAStatCounter] for each partition of the data and then update its state using the Array[Double] values that are returned by the given itera- tor, which is a more efficient implementation. Indeed, our statsWithMissing method is now very similar to how the Spark developers implemented the `stats` method for instances of type `RDD[Double]`.

Simple Variable Selection and Scoring

With the `statsWithMissing` function, we can analyze the differences in the distribution of the arrays of scores for both the matches and the nonmatches in the `parsed` RDD:

```
val statsm = statsWithMissing(parsed.filter(_.matched).map(_.scores))
val statsn = statsWithMissing(parsed.filter(!_.matched).map(_.scores))
```

Both the `statsm` and `statsn` arrays have identical structure, but they describe different subsets of our data: `statsm` contains the summary statistics on the `scores` array for matches, while `statsn` does the same thing for nonmatches. We can use the differences in the values of the columns for matches and nonmatches as a simple bit of analysis to help us come up with a scoring function for discriminating matches from nonmatches purely in terms of these match scores:

```
statsm.zip(statsn).map { case(m, n) =>
  (m.missing + n.missing, m.stats.mean - n.stats.mean)
}.foreach(println)
...
((1007, 0.2854...), 0)
((5645434,0.09104268062279874), 1)
((0,0.6838772482597568), 2)
((5746668,0.8064147192926266), 3)
((0,0.03240818525033484), 4)
((795,0.7754423117834044), 5)
((795,0.5109496938298719), 6)
((795,0.7762059675300523), 7)
((12843,0.9563812499852178), 8)
```

A good feature has two properties: it tends to have significantly different values for matches and nonmatches (so the difference between the means will be large) and it occurs often enough in the data that we can rely on it to be regularly available for any pair of records. By this measure, Feature 1 isn't very useful: it's missing a lot of the time, and the difference in the mean value for matches and nonmatches is relatively small—0.09, for a score that ranges from 0 to 1. Feature 4 also isn't particularly helpful. Even though it's available for any pair of records, the difference in means is just 0.03.

Features 5 and 7, on the other hand, are excellent: they almost always occur for any pair of records, and there is a very large difference in the mean values (over 0.77 for both features.) Features 2, 6, and 8 also seem beneficial: they are generally available in the data set and the difference in mean values for matches and nonmatches are substantial.

Features 0 and 3 are more of a mixed bag: Feature 0 doesn't discriminate all that well (the difference in the means is only 0.28), even though it's usually available for a pair of records, while Feature 3 has a large difference in the means, but it's almost always missing. It's not quite obvious under what circumstances we should include these features in our model based on this data.

For now, we're going to use a simple scoring model that ranks the similarity of pairs of records based on the sums of the values of the obviously good features: 2, 5, 6, 7, and 8. For the few records where the values of these features are missing, we'll use 0 in place of the NaN value in our sum. We can get a rough feel for the performance of our simple model by creating an RDD of scores and match values and evaluating how well the score discriminates between matches and nonmatches at various thresholds:

```
def naz(d: Double) = if (Double.NaN.equals(d)) 0.0 else d
case class Scored(md: MatchData, score: Double)
val ct = parsed.map(md => {
  val score = Array(2, 5, 6, 7, 8).map(i => naz(md.scores(i))).sum
  Scored(md, score)
})
```

Using a high threshold value of 4.0, meaning that the average of the five features was 0.8, we filter out almost all of the nonmatches while keeping over 90% of the matches:

```
ct.filter(s => s.score >= 4.0).map(s => s.md.matched).countByValue()
...
Map(false -> 637, true -> 20871)
```

Using the lower threshold of 2.0, we can ensure that we capture *all* of the known matching records, but at a substantial cost in terms of false positives:

```
ct.filter(s => s.score >= 2.0).map(s => s.md.matched).countByValue()
...
Map(false -> 596414, true -> 20931)
```

Even though the number of false positives is higher than we would like, this more generous filter still removes 90% of the nonmatching records from our consideration while including every positive match. Even though this is pretty good, it's possible to do even better; see if you can find a way to use some of the other values from the scores array (both missing and not) to come up with a scoring function that successfully identifies every true match at the cost of less than 100 false positives.

Where to Go from Here

If this chapter was your first time carrying out data preparation and analysis with Scala and Spark, we hope that you got a feel for what a powerful foundation these tools provide. If you have been using Scala and Spark for a while, we hope that you will pass this chapter along to your friends and colleagues as a way of introducing them to that power as well.

Our goal for this chapter was to provide you with enough Scala knowledge to be able to understand and carry out the rest of the examples in this book. If you are the kind of person who learns best through practical examples, your next step is to continue on to the next set of chapters, where we will introduce you to MLlib, the machine learning library designed for Spark.

As you become a seasoned user of Spark and Scala for data analysis, it's likely that you will reach a point where you begin to build tools and libraries that are designed to help other analysts and data scientists apply Spark to solve their own problems. At that point in your development, it would be helpful to pick up additional books on Scala, like *Programming Scala* by Dean Wampler and Alex Payne, and *The Scala Cookbook* by Alvin Alexander (both from O'Reilly).

CHAPTER 3

Recommending Music and the Audioscrobbler Data Set

Sean Owen

De gustibus non est disputandum.
(There's no accounting for taste.)

When somebody asks what it is I work on for a living, the direct answer of "data science" or "machine learning" sounds impressive but usually draws a blank stare. Fair enough; even actual data scientists seem to struggle to define what these mean—storing lots of data, computing, predicting something? Inevitably, I jump straight to a relatable example:

"OK, you know how Amazon will tell you about books like the ones you bought? Yes? Yes! It's like that."

Empirically, the recommender engine seems to be an example of large-scale machine learning that everyone already understands, and most people have seen Amazon's. It is a common denominator because recommender engines are everywhere, from social networks to video sites to online retailers. We can also directly observe them in action. We're aware that a computer is picking tracks to play on Spotify, in a way we don't necessarily notice that Gmail is deciding whether inbound email is spam.

The output of a recommender is more intuitively understandable than other machine learning algorithms. It's exciting, even. For all that we think that musical taste is so personal and inexplicable, recommenders do a surprisingly good job of identifying tracks we didn't know we would like.

Finally, for domains like music or movies where recommenders are usually deployed, it's comparatively easy to reason about why a recommended piece of music fits with someone's listening history. Not all clustering or classification algorithms match that description. For example, a support vector machine classifier is a set of coefficients, and it's hard even for practitioners to articulate what the numbers mean when they make predictions.

So, it seems fitting to kick off the next three chapters, which will explore key machine learning algorithms on Spark, with a chapter built around recommender engines, and recommending music in particular. It's an accessible way to introduce real-world use of Spark and MLlib, and some basic machine learning ideas that will be developed in subsequent chapters.

Data Set

This example will use a data set published by Audioscrobbler. Audioscrobbler was the first music recommendation system for last.fm, one of the first Internet streaming radio sites, founded in 2002. Audioscrobbler provided an open API for "scrobbling," or recording listeners' plays of artists' songs. last.fm used this information to build a powerful music recommender engine. The system reached millions of users because third-party apps and sites could provide listening data back to the recommender engine.

At that time, research on recommender engines was mostly confined to learning from rating-like data. That is, recommenders were usually viewed as tools that operated on input like "Bob rates Prince 3.5 stars."

The Audioscrobbler data set is interesting because it merely records plays: "Bob played a Prince track." A play carries less information than a rating. Just because Bob played the track doesn't mean he actually liked it. You or I may occasionally play a song by an artist we don't care for, or even play an album and walk out of the room.

However, listeners rate music far less frequently than they play music. A data set like this is therefore much larger, covers more users and artists, and contains more total information than a rating data set, even if each individual data point carries less information. This type of data is often called *implicit feedback* data because the user-artist connections are implied as a side effect of other actions, and not given as explicit ratings or thumbs-up.

A snapshot of a data set distributed by last.fm in 2005 can be found online as a compressed archive (*http://bit.ly/1KiJdOR*). Download the archive, and find within it several files. The main data set is in the *user_artist_data.txt* file. It contains about 141,000 unique users, and 1.6 million unique artists. About 24.2 million users' plays of artists are recorded, along with their count.

The data set also gives the names of each artist by ID in the *artist_data.txt* file. Note that when plays are scrobbled, the client application submits the name of the artist being played. This name could be misspelled or nonstandard, and this may only be detected later. For example, "The Smiths," "Smiths, The," and "the smiths" may appear as distinct artist IDs in the data set, even though they are plainly the same. So, the data set also includes *artist_alias.txt*, which maps artist IDs that are known misspellings or variants to the canonical ID of that artist.

The Alternating Least Squares Recommender Algorithm

We need to choose a recommender algorithm that is suitable for this implicit feedback data. The data set consists entirely of interactions between users and artists' songs. It contains no information about the users, or about the artists other than their names. We need an algorithm that learns without access to user or artist attributes. These are typically called collaborative filtering (*http://en.wikipedia.org/wiki/Collaborative_filtering*) algorithms. For example, deciding that two users may share similar tastes because they are the same age *is not* an example of collaborative filtering. Deciding that two users may both like the same song because they play many other same songs *is* an example.

This data set looks large, because it contains tens of millions of play counts. But in a different sense, it is small and skimpy, because it is sparse. On average, each user has played songs from about 171 artists—out of 1.6 million. Some users have listened to only one artist. We need an algorithm that could provide decent recommendations to even these users. After all, every single listener must have started with just one play at some point!

Finally, we need an algorithm that scales, both in its ability to build large models and to create recommendations quickly. Recommendations are typically required in near real time—within a second, not tomorrow.

This example will employ a member of a broad class of algorithms called latent-factor (*http://en.wikipedia.org/wiki/Factor_analysis*) models. They try to explain *observed interactions* between large numbers of users and products through a relatively small number of *unobserved, underlying reasons*. It is analogous to explaining why millions of people buy a particular few of thousands of possible albums by describing users and albums in terms of tastes for perhaps tens of genres, tastes that are not directly observable or given as data.

More specifically, this example will use a type of matrix factorization (*http://en.wikipedia.org/wiki/Non-negative_matrix_factorization*) model. Mathematically, these algorithms treat the user and product data as if it were a large matrix A, where the entry at row i and column j exists if user i has played artist j. A is sparse: most entries of A are 0, because only a few of all possible user-artist combinations actually appear in the data. They factor A as the matrix product of two smaller matrices, X and Y. They are very skinny—both have many rows because A has many rows and columns, but both have just a few columns (k). The k columns correspond to the latent factors that are being used to explain the interaction data.

The factorization can only be approximate because k is small, as shown in Figure 3-1.

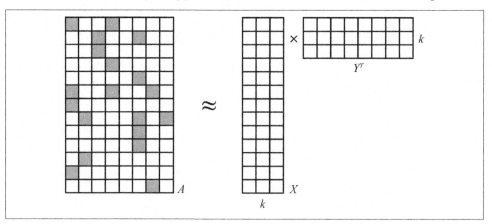

Figure 3-1. Matrix factorization

These algorithms are sometimes called matrix completion algorithms, because the original matrix A may be quite sparse, but the product XY^T is dense. Very few, if any, entries are 0, and therefore the model is only an approximation to A. It is a model in the sense that it produces ("completes") a value for even the many entries that are missing (that is, 0) in the original A.

This is a case where, happily, the linear algebra maps directly and elegantly to intuition. These two matrices contain a row for each user and each artist, respectively. The rows have few values—k. Each value corresponds to a latent feature in the model. So the rows express how much users and artists associate with these latent features, which might correspond to tastes or genres. And it is simply the product of a user-feature and feature-artist matrix that yields a complete estimation of the entire, dense user-artist interaction matrix.

The bad news is that $A = XY^T$ generally has no solution at all, because X and Y aren't large enough (technically speaking, too low rank (*http://bit.ly/1ALoQFK*)) to perfectly represent A. This is actually a good thing. A is just a tiny sample of all interactions that *could* happen. In a way, we believe A is a terribly spotty, and therefore hard-to-explain, view of a simpler underlying reality that is well explained by just some small number of factors, k of them. Think of a jigsaw puzzle depicting a cat. The final puzzle is simple to describe: a cat. When you're holding just a few pieces, however, the picture you see is quite difficult to describe.

XY^T should still be as close to A as possible. After all, it's all we've got to go on. It will not and should not reproduce it exactly. The bad news again is that this can't be solved directly for both the best X and best Y at the same time. The good news is that it's trivial to solve for the best X if Y is known, and vice versa. But, neither is known beforehand!

Fortunately, there are algorithms that can escape this catch-22 and find a decent solution. More specifically still, the example in this chapter will use the Alternating Least Squares (*http://bit.ly/16ilZZV*) (ALS) algorithm to compute X and Y. This type of approach was popularized around the time of the Netflix Prize (*http://en.wikipe dia.org/wiki/Netflix_Prize*) by papers like "Collaborative Filtering for Implicit Feedback Datasets" (*http://bit.ly/1ALoX4q*) and "Large-scale Parallel Collaborative Filtering for the Netflix Prize" (*http://bit.ly/16im1AT*). In fact, Spark MLlib's ALS implementation draws on ideas from both of these papers.

Y isn't known, but it can be initialized to a matrix full of randomly chosen row vectors. Then simple linear algebra gives the best solution for X, given A and Y. In fact, it's trivial to compute each row i of X separately as a function of Y and of one row of A. Because it can be done separately, it can be done in parallel, and that is an excellent property for a large-scale computation:

$$A_i Y (Y^T Y)^{-1} = X_i$$

Equality can't be achieved exactly, so in fact the goal is to minimize $|A_i Y (Y^T Y)^{-1} - X_i|$, or the sum of squared differences between the two matrices' entries. This is where the "least squares" in the name comes from. In practice this is never solved by actually computing inverses, but faster and more directly via methods like the QR decomposition (*http://en.wikipedia.org/wiki/QR_decomposition*). This equation simply elaborates the theory of how the row vector is computed.

The same thing can be done to compute each Y_j from X. And again, to compute X from Y, and so on. This is where the "alternating" part comes from. There's just one small problem: Y was made up, and random! X was computed optimally, yes, but given a bogus solution for Y. Fortunately, if this process is repeated, X and Y do eventually converge to decent solutions.

When used to factor a matrix representing implicit data, there is a little more complexity to the ALS factorization. It is not factoring the input matrix A directly, but a matrix P of 0s and 1s, containing 1 where A contains a positive value and 0 elsewhere. The values in A are incorporated later as weights. This detail is beyond the scope of this book, but is not necessary to understand how to use the algorithm.

Finally, the ALS algorithm can take advantage of the sparsity of the input data as well. This, and its reliance on simple, optimized linear algebra and its data-parallel nature, make it very fast at large scale. This is much of the reason it is the topic of this chapter —that, and the fact that ALS is the only recommender algorithm currently implemented in Spark MLlib!

Preparing the Data

Copy all three data files into HDFS. This chapter will assume that the files are available at */user/ds/*. Start spark-shell. Note that this computation will take an unusually large amount of memory. If you are running locally, rather than on a cluster, for example, you will likely need to specify --driver-memory 6g to have enough memory to complete these computations.

The first step in building a model is to understand the data that is available, and parse or transform it into forms that are useful for analysis in Spark.

One small limitation of Spark MLlib's ALS implementation is that it requires numeric IDs for users and items, and further requires them to be nonnegative 32-bit integers. This means that IDs larger than about Integer.MAX_VALUE, or 2147483647, can't be used. Does this data set conform to this requirement already? Access the file as an RDD of Strings in Spark with SparkContext's textFile method:

```
val rawUserArtistData = sc.textFile("hdfs:///user/ds/user_artist_data.txt")
```

By default, the RDD will contain one partition for each HDFS block. Because this file consumes about 400 MB on HDFS, it will split into about three to six partitions given typical HDFS block sizes. This is normally fine, but machine learning tasks like ALS are likely to be more compute-intensive than simple text processing. It may be better to break the data into smaller pieces—more partitions—for processing. This can let Spark put more processor cores to work on the problem at once. You can supply a second argument to this method to specify a different and larger number of partitions. You might set this to match the number of cores in your cluster, for example.

Each line of the file contains a user ID, an artist ID, and a play count, separated by spaces. To compute statistics on the user ID, we split the line by space, and the first (0-indexed) value is parsed as a number. The stats() method returns an object containing statistics like maximum and minimum. And likewise for the artist IDs:

```
rawUserArtistData.map(_.split(' ')(0).toDouble).stats()
rawUserArtistData.map(_.split(' ')(1).toDouble).stats()
```

The computed statistics that are printed reveal that the maximum user and artist IDs are 2443548 and 10794401, respectively. These are comfortably smaller than 2147483647. No additional transformation will be necessary to use these IDs.

It will be useful later in this example to know the artist names corresponding to the opaque numeric IDs. This information is contained in *artist_data.txt*. This time, it contains the artist ID and name separated by a tab. However, a straightforward parsing of the file into (Int,String) tuples will fail:

```
val rawArtistData = sc.textFile("hdfs:///user/ds/artist_data.txt")
val artistByID = rawArtistData.map { line =>
  val (id, name) = line.span(_ != '\t')
```

```
    (id.toInt, name.trim)
  }
```

Here, span() splits the line by its first tab by consuming characters that aren't tabs. It then parses the first portion as the numeric artist ID, and retains the rest as the artist name (with whitespace—the tab—removed). A small number of the lines appear to be corrupted. They don't contain a tab, or they inadvertently include a newline character. These lines cause a NumberFormatException, and ideally, they would not map to anything at all.

However, the map() function must return exactly one value for every input, so it can't be used. It's possible to remove the lines that don't parse with filter(), but this would duplicate the parsing logic. The flatMap() function is appropriate when each element maps to zero, one, or more results, because it simply "flattens" these collections of zero or more results from each input into one big RDD. It works with Scala collections, but also with Scala's Option class. Option represents a value that might only optionally exist. It is like a simple collection of 1 or 0 values, corresponding to its Some and None subclasses. So, while the function in flatMap in the following code could just as easily return an empty List, or a List of one element, this is a reasonable place to instead use the simpler and clearer Some and None:

```
val artistByID = rawArtistData.flatMap { line =>
  val (id, name) = line.span(_ != '\t')
  if (name.isEmpty) {
    None
  } else {
    try {
      Some((id.toInt, name.trim))
    } catch {
      case e: NumberFormatException => None
    }
  }
}
```

The *artist_alias.txt* file maps artist IDs that may be misspelled or nonstandard to the ID of the artist's canonical name. It contains two IDs per line, separated by a tab. This file is relatively small, containing about 200,000 entries. It will be useful to collect it as a Map, mapping "bad" artist IDs to "good" ones, instead of just using it as an RDD of pairs of artist IDs. Again, some lines are missing the first artist ID, for some reason, and are skipped:

```
val rawArtistAlias = sc.textFile("hdfs:///user/ds/artist_alias.txt")
val artistAlias = rawArtistAlias.flatMap { line =>
  val tokens = line.split('\t')
  if (tokens(0).isEmpty) {
    None
  } else {
    Some((tokens(0).toInt, tokens(1).toInt))
```

```
      }
    }.collectAsMap()
```

The first entry, for instance, maps ID 6803336 to 1000010. We can look these up from the RDD containing artist names:

```
artistByID.lookup(6803336).head
artistByID.lookup(1000010).head
```

This entry evidently maps "Aerosmith (unplugged)" to "Aerosmith."

Building a First Model

Although the data set is in nearly the right form for use with Spark MLlib's ALS implementation, it requires two small extra transformations. First, the aliases data set should be applied to convert all artist IDs to a canonical ID, if a different canonical ID exists. Second, the data should be converted into `Rating` objects, which is the implementation's abstraction for user-product-value data. Despite the name, `Rating` is suitable for use with implicit data. Note also that MLlib refers to "products" throughout its API, and so will this example, but the "products" here are artists. The underlying model is not at all specific to recommending products, or for that matter, to recommending things to people:

```
import org.apache.spark.mllib.recommendation._

val bArtistAlias = sc.broadcast(artistAlias)

val trainData = rawUserArtistData.map { line =>
  val Array(userID, artistID, count) = line.split(' ').map(_.toInt)
  val finalArtistID =
    bArtistAlias.value.getOrElse(artistID, artistID) ❶
  Rating(userID, finalArtistID, count)
}.cache()
```

❶   Get artist's alias if it exists, else get original artist

The `artistAlias` mapping created earlier can be referenced directly in an RDD's `map()` function, even though it is a local `Map` on the driver. This works, because it will be copied automatically with every task. However, it is not tiny, consuming about 15 megabytes in memory and at least several megabytes in serialized form. Because many tasks execute in one JVM, it's wasteful to send and store so many copies of the data.

Instead, we create a broadcast variable (*http://bit.ly/1ALqojd*) called `bArtistAlias` for `artistAlias`. This makes Spark send and hold in memory just one copy for *each executor* in the cluster. When there are thousands of tasks, and many execute in parallel on each executor, this can save significant network traffic and memory.

Broadcast Variables

When Spark runs a stage, it creates a binary representation of all the information needed to run tasks in that stage, called the *closure* of the function that needs to be executed. This closure includes all the data structures on the driver referenced in the function. Spark distributes it to every executor on the cluster.

Broadcast variables are useful in situations where many tasks need access to the same (immutable) data structure. They extend normal handling of task closures to enable:

- Caching data as raw Java objects on each executor, so they need not be deserialized for each task
- Caching data across multiple jobs and stages

For example, consider a natural language processing application that relies on a large dictionary of English words. Broadcasting the dictionary allows transferring it to every executor only once:

```
val dict = ...
val bDict = sc.broadcast(dict)
...
def query(path: String) = {
  sc.textFile(path).map(l => score(l, bDict.value))
  ...
}
```

The call to `cache()` suggests to Spark that this RDD should be temporarily stored after being computed, and furthermore, kept in memory in the cluster. This is helpful because the ALS algorithm is iterative, and will typically need to access this data 10 times or more. Without this, the RDD could be repeatedly recomputed from the original data each time it is accessed! The Storage tab in the Spark UI will show how much of the RDD is cached and how much memory it uses, as shown in Figure 3-2. This one consumes almost 900 MB across the cluster.

Storage Level	Cached Partitions	Fraction Cached	Size in Memory
Memory Deserialized 1x Replicated	120	100%	886.8 MB

Figure 3-2. Storage tab in the Spark UI, showing cached RDD memory usage

Finally, we can build a model:

```
val model = ALS.trainImplicit(trainData, 10, 5, 0.01, 1.0)
```

This constructs `model` as a `MatrixFactorizationModel`. The operation will likely take minutes or more depending on your cluster. Compared to some machine learning models, whose final form may consist of just a few parameters or coefficients, this type of model is huge. It contains a feature vector of 10 values for each user and product in the model, and in this case there are more than 1.7 million of them. The model contains these large user-feature and product-feature matrices as RDDs of their own.

To see some feature vectors, try the following. Note that the feature vector is an `Array` of 10 numbers, and arrays don't naturally print in a readable form. This translates the vectors to readable form with `mkString()`, a method commonly used in Scala to join elements of a collection into a delimited string:

```
model.userFeatures.mapValues(_.mkString(", ")).first()

...

(4293,-0.3233030601963864, 0.31964527593541325,
    0.49025505511361034, 0.09000932568001832, 0.4429537767744912,
    0.4186675713407441, 0.8026858843673894, -0.4841300444834003,
    -0.12485901532338621, 0.19795451025931002)
```

The values in your results will be somewhat different. The final model depends on a randomly chosen initial set of feature vectors.

The other arguments to `trainImplicit()` are *hyperparameters* whose value can affect the quality of the recommendations that the model makes. These will be explained later. The more important first question is, is the model any good? Does it produce good recommendations?

Spot Checking Recommendations

We should first see if the artist recommendations make any intuitive sense, by examining a user, his or her plays, and recommendations for that user. Take, for example, user 2093760. Extract the IDs of artists that this user has listened to and print their names. This means searching the input for artist IDs for this user, and then filtering the set of artists by these IDs so you can collect and print the names in order:

```
val rawArtistsForUser = rawUserArtistData.map(_.split(' ')).
  filter { case Array(user,_,_) => user.toInt == 2093760 } ❶

val existingProducts =
  rawArtistsForUser.map { case Array(_,artist,_) => artist.toInt }.
  collect().toSet ❷

artistByID.filter { case (id, name) =>
```

```
    existingProducts.contains(id)
}.values.collect().foreach(println) ❸


...
David Gray
Blackalicious
Jurassic 5
The Saw Doctors
Xzibit
```

❶ Find lines whose user is 2093760

❷ Collect unique artists

❸ Filter in those artists, get just artist, and print

The artists look like a mix of mainstream pop and hip-hop. A Jurassic 5 fan? Remember, it's 2005. In case you're wondering, the Saw Doctors are a very Irish rock band popular in Ireland.

We can do something similar to make five recommendations for this user:

```
val recommendations = model.recommendProducts(2093760, 5)
recommendations.foreach(println)


...
Rating(2093760,1300642,0.02833118412903932)
Rating(2093760,2814,0.027832682960168387)
Rating(2093760,1037970,0.02726611004625264)
Rating(2093760,1001819,0.02716011293509426)
Rating(2093760,4605,0.027118271894797333)
```

The result consists of `Rating` objects with a (redundant) user ID, artist ID, and numeric value. Although also in a field called `rating`, it is not an estimated rating. For this type of ALS algorithm, it is an opaque value normally between 0 and 1, where higher values mean a better recommendation. It is not a probability, but can be thought of as an estimate of a 0/1 value indicating whether the user won't, or will, interact with the artist, respectively.

After extracting the artist IDs for the recommendations, we can look up artist names in a similar way:

```
val recommendedProductIDs = recommendations.map(_.product).toSet

artistByID.filter { case (id, name) =>
  recommendedProductIDs.contains(id)
}.values.collect().foreach(println)


...
Green Day
Linkin Park
```

```
Metallica
My Chemical Romance
System of a Down
```

The result is a mix of pop punk and metal. This doesn't look like a great set of recommendations, at first glance. While these are generally popular artists, they don't appear personalized to this user's listening habits.

Evaluating Recommendation Quality

Of course, that's just one subjective judgment about one user's results. It's hard for anyone but that user to quantify how good the recommendations are. Moreover, it's infeasible to have any human manually score even a small sample of the output to evaluate the results.

It's reasonable to assume that users tend to play songs from artists who are appealing, and not play songs from artists who aren't appealing. So, the plays for a user give a partial picture of what "good" and "bad" artist recommendations are. This is a problematic assumption, but about the best that can be done without any other data. For example, presumably user 2093760 likes many more artists than the five listed previously, and among the 1.7 million other artists not played, a few are of interest and not all are "bad" recommendations.

What if a recommender were evaluated on its ability to rank good artists high in a list of recommendations? This is one of several generic metrics that can be applied to a system that ranks things, like a recommender. The problem is that "good" is defined as "artists the user has listened to," and the recommender system has already received all of this information as input. It could trivially return the user's previously listened-to artists as top recommendations and score perfectly. This is not useful, especially because the recommender's role is to recommend artists that the user has never listened to.

To make this meaningful, some of the artist play data can be set aside and hidden from the ALS model building process. Then, this held-out data can be interpreted as a collection of good recommendations for each user, but one that the recommender has not already been given. The recommender is asked to rank all items in the model, and the ranks of the held-out artists are examined. Ideally, the recommender places all of them at or near the top of the list.

We can then compute the recommender's score by comparing all held-out artists' ranks to the rest. (In practice, we compute this by examining only a sample of all such pairs, because a potentially huge number of such pairs may exist.) The fraction of pairs where the held-out artist is ranked higher is its score. 1.0 is perfect, 0.0 is the worst possible score, and 0.5 is the expected value achieved from randomly ranking artists.

This metric is directly related to an information retrieval concept, called the Receiver Operating Characteristic (*http://bit.ly/18sUUQK*) (ROC) curve. The metric in the preceding paragraph equals the area under this ROC curve, and is indeed known as AUC, for Area Under the Curve. AUC may be viewed as the probability that a randomly chosen good recommendation ranks above a randomly chosen bad recommendation.

The AUC metric is also used in evaluation of classifiers. It is implemented, along with related methods, in the MLlib class `BinaryClassificationMetrics`. For recommenders, we will compute AUC *per user* and average the result. The resulting metric is slightly different, and might be called "mean AUC."

Other evaluation metrics that are relevant to systems that rank things are implemented in `RankingMetrics`. These include metrics like precision, recall, and mean average precision (*http://bit.ly/1ALr1cG*) (MAP). MAP is also frequently used and focuses more narrowly on the quality of the top recommendations. However, AUC will be used here as a common and broad measure of the quality of the entire model output.

In fact, the process of holding out some data to select a model and evaluate its accuracy is common practice in all of machine learning. Typically, data is divided into three subsets: training, cross-validation (CV), and test sets. For simplicity in this initial example, only two sets will be used: training and CV. This will be sufficient to choose a model. In Chapter 4, this idea will be extended to include the test set.

Computing AUC

An implementation of AUC is provided in the source code accompanying this book. It is complex and not reproduced here, but is explained in some detail in comments in the source code. It accepts the CV set as the "positive" or "good" artists for each user, and a prediction function. This function translates each user-artist pair into a prediction as a `Rating` containing the user, artist, and a number wherein higher values mean higher rank in the recommendations.

In order to use it, we must split the input data into a training and CV set. The ALS model will be trained on the training data set only, and the CV set will be used to evaluate the model. Here, 90% of the data is used for training and the remaining 10% for cross-validation:

```
import org.apache.spark.rdd._

def areaUnderCurve(
    positiveData: RDD[Rating],
    bAllItemIDs: Broadcast[Array[Int]],
    predictFunction: (RDD[(Int,Int)] => RDD[Rating])) = {
  ...
```

```
}
val allData = buildRatings(rawUserArtistData, bArtistAlias) ❶
val Array(trainData, cvData) = allData.randomSplit(Array(0.9, 0.1))
trainData.cache()
cvData.cache()

val allItemIDs = allData.map(_.product).distinct().collect() ❷
val bAllItemIDs = sc.broadcast(allItemIDs)

val model = ALS.trainImplicit(trainData, 10, 5, 0.01, 1.0)
val auc = areaUnderCurve(cvData, bAllItemIDs, model.predict)
```

❶ This function is defined in accompanying source code

❷ Remove duplicates, and collect to driver

Note that areaUnderCurve() accepts a *function* as its third argument. Here, the pre
dict() method from MatrixFactorizationModel is passed in, but it will shortly be
swapped out for an alternative.

The result is about 0.96. Is this good? It's certainly higher than the 0.5 that is expected
from making recommendations randomly. It's close to 1.0, which is the maximum
possible score. Generally, an AUC over 0.9 would be considered high.

This evaluation could be repeated with a different 90% as the training set. The resulting AUC values' average might be a better estimate of the algorithm's performance on
the data set. In fact, one common practice is to divide the data into k subsets of similar size, use $k - 1$ subsets together for training, and evaluate on the remaining subset.
We can repeat this k times, using a different set of subsets each time. This is called k-
fold cross-validation (*http://bit.ly/1BVTEa9*). This won't be implemented in examples
here, for simplicity, but some support for this technique exists in MLlib in its MLU
tils.kFold() helper function.

It's helpful to benchmark this against a simpler approach. For example, consider recommending the globally most-played artists to every user. This is not personalized,
but is simple and may be effective. Define this simple prediction function and evaluate its AUC score:

```
def predictMostListened(
    sc: SparkContext,
    train: RDD[Rating])(allData: RDD[(Int,Int)]) = {

  val bListenCount = sc.broadcast(
    train.map(r => (r.product, r.rating)).
      reduceByKey(_ + _).collectAsMap()
  )
  allData.map { case (user, product) =>
    Rating(
```

```
        user,
        product,
        bListenCount.value.getOrElse(product, 0.0)
      )
    }
  }

  val auc = areaUnderCurve(
    cvData, bAllItemIDs, predictMostListened(sc, trainData))
```

This is another interesting demonstration of Scala syntax, where the function appears to be defined to take two lists of arguments. Calling the function and supplying the first two arguments creates a *partially applied function*, which itself takes an argument (allData) in order to return predictions. The result of predictMostListened(sc, trainData) is a *function*.

The result is about 0.93. This suggests that nonpersonalized recommendations are already fairly effective according to this metric. It is good to see that the model built so far beats this simple approach. Can it be made better?

Hyperparameter Selection

So far, the hyperparameter values used to build the MatrixFactorizationModel were simply given without comment. They are not learned by the algorithm, and must be chosen by the caller. The arguments to ALS.trainImplicit() were:

rank = *10*
> The number of latent factors in the model, or equivalently, the number of columns k in the user-feature and product-feature matrices. In nontrivial cases, this is also their rank.

iterations = *5*
> The number of iterations that the factorization runs. More iterations take more time but may produce a better factorization.

lambda = *0.01*
> A standard overfitting parameter. Higher values resist overfitting, but values that are too high hurt the factorization's accuracy.

alpha = *1.0*
> Controls the relative weight of observed versus unobserved user-product interactions in the factorization.

rank, lambda, and alpha can be considered *hyperparameters* to the model. (iterations is more of a constraint on resources used in the factorization.) These are not values that end up in the matrices inside the MatrixFactorizationModel—those are simply its *parameters*, and are chosen by the algorithm. These hyperparameters are instead parameters to the process of building itself.

The values used in the preceding list are not necessarily optimal. Choosing good hyperparameter values is a common problem in machine learning. The most basic way to choose values is to simply try combinations of values and evaluate a metric for each of them, and choose the combination that produces the best value of the metric.

In the following example, eight possible combinations are tried: rank = 10 or 50, lambda = 1.0 or 0.0001, and alpha = 1.0 or 40.0. These values are still something of a guess, but are chosen to cover a broad range of parameter values. The results are printed in order by top AUC score:

```
val evaluations =
  for (rank    <- Array(10,  50);
       lambda <- Array(1.0, 0.0001);
       alpha  <- Array(1.0, 40.0)) ❶
  yield {
    val model = ALS.trainImplicit(trainData, rank, 10, lambda, alpha)
    val auc = areaUnderCurve(cvData, bAllItemIDs, model.predict)
    ((rank, lambda, alpha), auc)
  }

evaluations.sortBy(_._2).reverse.foreach(println) ❷


...
((50,1.0,40.0),0.9776687571356233)
((50,1.0E-4,40.0),0.9767551668703566)
((10,1.0E-4,40.0),0.9761931539712336)
((10,1.0,40.0),0.976154587705189)
((10,1.0,1.0),0.9683921981896727)
((50,1.0,1.0),0.9670901331816745)
((10,1.0E-4,1.0),0.9637196892517722)
((50,1.0E-4,1.0),0.9543377999707536)
```

❶ Read as a triply nested for loop

❷ Sort by second value (AUC), descending, and print

 The for syntax here is a way to write nested loops in Scala. It is like a loop over alpha inside a loop over lambda, inside a loop over rank.

Interestingly, the parameter alpha seems consistently better at 40 than 1. (For the curious, 40 was a value proposed as a default in one of the original ALS papers mentioned earlier.) This can be interpreted as indicating that the model is better off focusing far more on what the user did listen to than what he or she did not listen to.

A higher `lambda` looks slightly better too. This suggests the model is somewhat susceptible to overfitting, and so needs a higher `lambda` to resist trying to fit the sparse input given from each user too exactly. Overfitting will be revisited in more detail in Chapter 4.

The number of features doesn't make a clear difference; 50 appears in both the highest- and lowest-scoring combinations, although the scores do not vary by much in absolute terms anyway. This could indicate that the right number of features is actually higher than 50, and that these values are alike in being too small.

Of course, this process can be repeated for different ranges of values, or more values. It is a brute-force means of choosing hyperparameters. However, in a world where clusters with terabytes of memory and hundreds of cores are not uncommon, and with frameworks like Spark that can exploit parallelism and memory for speed, it becomes quite feasible.

It is not strictly required to understand what the hyperparameters mean, although it is helpful to know what normal ranges of values are like in order to start the search over a parameter space that is neither too large nor too tiny.

Making Recommendations

Proceeding for the moment with the best set of hyperparameters, what does a new model recommend for user 2093760?

```
50 Cent
Eminem
Green Day
U2
[unknown]
```

Anecdotally, this makes a bit more sense, with two hip-hop artists. [unknown] is plainly not an artist. Querying the original data set reveals that it occurs 429,447 times, putting it nearly in the top 100! This is some default value for plays without an artist, maybe supplied by a certain scrobbling client. It is not useful information and we should discard it from the input before starting again. It's an example of how the practice of data science is often iterative, with discoveries about the data occurring at every stage.

This model can be used to make recommendations for all users. This could be useful in a batch process that recomputes a model, and recomputes recommendations, for users every hour or even less, depending on the size of the data and speed of the cluster.

At the moment, however, Spark MLlib's ALS implementation does not support a method to recommend to all users. It is possible to recommend to one user at a time, although each will launch a short-lived distributed job that takes a few seconds. This may be suitable for rapidly recomputing recommendations for small groups of users. Here, recommendations are made to 100 users taken from the data, and printed:

```
val someUsers = allData.map(_.user).distinct().take(100) ❶
val someRecommendations =
  someUsers.map(userID => model.recommendProducts(userID, 5)) ❷
someRecommendations.map(
  recs => recs.head.user + " -> " + recs.map(_.product).mkString(", ") ❸
).foreach(println)
```

❶ Copy 100 (distinct) users to the driver

❷ map() is a local Scala operation here

❸ mkString joins a collection to a string with a delimiter

Here, the recommendations are just printed. They could just as easily be written to an external store like HBase (*http://hbase.apache.org*), which provides fast lookup at runtime.

Interestingly, this entire process could also be used to recommend *users* to *artists*. This could be used to answer questions like, "which 100 users are most likely to be interested in the new album by artist X"? Doing so would only require swapping the user and artist field when parsing the input:

```
rawUserArtistData.map { line =>
  ...
  val userID = tokens(1).toInt ❶
  val artistID = tokens(0).toInt ❷
  ...
}
```

❶ Read artist as "user"

❷ Read user as "artist"

Where to Go from Here

Naturally, it's possible to spend more time tuning the model parameters, and finding and fixing anomalies in the input like the [unknown] artist.

For example, a quick analysis of play counts reveals that user 2064012 played artist 4468 an astonishing 439,771 times! Artist 4468 is the implausibly successful alterna-metal band System of a Down (*http://en.wikipedia.org/wiki/System_of_a_Down*), who turned up earlier in recommendations. Assuming an average song length of 4 minutes, this is over 33 years of playing hits like "Chop Suey!" and "B.Y.O.B." Because the band started making records in 1998, this would require playing 4 or 5 tracks at once for 7 years. It must be spam, or a data error, and another example of the types of real-world data problems that a production system would have to address.

ALS is not the only possible recommender algorithm. At this time, it is the only one supported by Spark MLlib. However, MLlib also supports a variant of ALS for nonimplicit data. Its use is identical, except that the model is built with the method `ALS.train()`. This is appropriate when data is rating-like, rather than count-like. For example, it is appropriate when the data set is user ratings of artists on a 1–5 scale. The resulting `rating` field in `Rating` objects returned from the various recommendation methods then really is an estimated rating.

Later, other recommender algorithms may be available in Spark MLlib or other libraries.

In production, recommender engines often need to make recommendations in real time, because they are used in contexts like ecommerce sites where recommendations are requested frequently as customers browse product pages. Precomputing and storing recommendations in a NoSQL store, as mentioned previously, is a reasonable way to make recommendations available at scale. One disadvantage of this approach is that it requires precomputing recommendations for all users who might need recommendations soon, which is potentially any of them. For example, if only 10,000 of 1 million users visit a site in a day, precomputing all 1 million users' recommendations each day is 99% wasted effort.

It would be nicer to compute recommendations on the fly, as needed. While we can compute recommendations for one user using the `MatrixFactorizationModel`, this is necessarily a distributed operation that takes several seconds, because `MatrixFactorizationModel` is uniquely large and therefore actually a distributed data set. This is not true of other models, which afford much faster scoring. Projects like Oryx 2 (*https://github.com/OryxProject/oryx*) attempt to implement real-time on-demand recommendations with libraries like MLlib by efficiently accessing the model data in memory.

CHAPTER 4

Predicting Forest Cover with Decision Trees

Sean Owen

Prediction is very difficult, especially if it's about the future.
—Niels Bohr

In the late 19th century, the English scientist Sir Francis Galton was busy measuring things like peas and people. He found that large peas (and people) had larger-than-average offspring. This isn't surprising. However, the offspring were, on average, smaller than their parents. In terms of people: the child of a 7-foot-tall basketball player is likely to be taller than the global average, but still more likely than not to be less than 7 feet tall.

As almost a side effect of his study, Galton plotted child versus parent size and noticed there was a roughly linear relationship between the two. Large parent peas had large children, but slightly smaller than themselves; small parents had small children, but generally a bit larger than themselves. The line's slope was therefore positive but less than 1, and Galton described this phenomenon as we do today, as *regression to the mean*.

Although maybe not perceived this way at the time, this line was, to me, an early example of a predictive model. The line links the two values, and implies that the value of one suggests a lot about the value of the other. Given the size of a new pea, this relationship could lead to a more accurate estimate of its offsprings' size than simply assuming the offspring would be like the parent or like every other pea.

Fast Forward to Regression

More than a century of statistics later, and since the advent of modern machine learning and data science, we still talk about the idea of predicting a value from other values as regression (*http://en.wikipedia.org/wiki/Regression_analysis*), even though it has nothing to do with slipping back toward a mean value, or indeed moving backward at all. Regression techniques also relate to classification (*http://en.wikipedia.org/wiki/Statistical_classification*) techniques. Generally, *regression* refers to predicting a numeric quantity like size or income or temperature, while *classification* refers to predicting a label or category, like "spam" or "picture of a cat."

The common thread linking regression and classification is that both involve predicting one (or more) values given one (or more) other values. To do so, both require a body of inputs and outputs to learn from. They need to be fed both questions and known answers. For this reason they are known as types of supervised learning (*http://en.wikipedia.org/wiki/Supervised_learning*).

Classification and regression are the oldest and most well-studied types of predictive analytics. Most algorithms you will likely encounter in analytics packages and libraries are classification or regression techniques, like support vector machines, logistic regression, naïve Bayes, neural networks, and deep learning. Recommenders, the topic of Chapter 3, were comparatively more intuitive to introduce, but are also just a relatively recent and separate subtopic within machine learning.

This chapter will focus on a popular and flexible type of algorithm for both classification and regression: decision trees (*http://en.wikipedia.org/wiki/Decision_tree*), and its extension, random decision forests (*http://en.wikipedia.org/wiki/Random_forest*). The exciting thing about these algorithms is that, with respect to Mr. Bohr, they can help predict the future—or at least, predict the things we don't yet know for sure, like your likelihood to buy a car based on your online behavior, whether an email is spam given its words, or which acres of land are likely to grow the most crops given their location and soil chemistry.

Vectors and Features

To explain the choice of the data set and algorithm featured in this chapter, and to begin to explain how regression and classification operate, it is necessary to briefly define the terms that describe their input and output.

Consider predicting tomorrow's high temperature given today's weather. There is nothing wrong with this idea, but "today's weather" is a casual concept, and requires structuring before it can be fed into a learning algorithm.

It is really certain *features* of today's weather that may predict tomorrow's temperature, such as:

- Today's high temperature
- Today's low temperature
- Today's average humidity

- Whether it's cloudy, rainy, or clear today
- The number of weather forecasters predicting a cold snap tomorrow

These features are also sometimes called *dimensions*, *predictors*, or just *variables*. Each of these features can be quantified. For example, high and low temperatures are measured in degrees Celsius, humidity can be measured as a fraction between 0 and 1, and weather type can be labeled `cloudy`, `rainy`, or `clear`. The number of forecasters is, of course, an integer count. Today's weather might therefore be reduced to a list of values like `13.1,19.0,0.73,cloudy,1`.

These five features together, in order, are known as a *feature vector*, and can describe any day's weather. This usage bears some resemblance to use of the term *vector* in linear algebra, except that a vector in this sense can conceptually contain nonnumeric values, and even lack some values.

These features are not all of the same type. The first two features are measured in degrees Celsius, but the third is unitless, a fraction. The fourth is not a number at all, and the fifth is a number that is always a nonnegative integer.

For purposes of discussion, this book will talk about features in two broad groups only: *categorical* features and *numeric* features. Numeric features, here, are those that can be quantified by a number and have a meaningful ordering. For example, it's meaningful to say that today's high was 23C, and that this is larger than yesterday's high of 22C. All of the features mentioned previously are numeric, except the weather type. Terms like `clear` are not numbers, and have no ordering. It is meaningless to say that `cloudy` is larger than `clear`. This is a categorical feature, which instead takes on one of several discrete values.

Training Examples

A learning algorithm needs to train on data in order to make predictions. It requires a large number of inputs, and known correct outputs, from historical data. For example, in this problem, the learning algorithm would be given that, one day, the weather was between 12 and 16 degrees Celsius, with 10% humidity, clear, with no forecast of a cold snap, and the following day, the high temperature was 17.2 degrees. With enough of these *examples*, a learning algorithm might learn to predict the following day's high temperature with some accuracy.

Feature vectors provide an organized way to describe input to a learning algorithm (here: `12.5,15.5,0.10,clear,0`). The output, or *target*, of the prediction can also be thought of as a feature, here a numeric feature: `17.2`.

It's not uncommon to simply include the target as another feature in the feature vector. The entire training example might be thought of as `12.5,15.5,0.10,clear, 0,17.2`. The collection of all of these examples is known as the *training set*.

Note that regression problems are just those where the target is a numeric feature, and classification problems are those where the target is categorical. Not every regression or classification algorithm can handle categorical features, or categorical targets; some are limited to numeric features.

Decision Trees and Forests

It turns out that the family of algorithms known as *decision trees* can naturally handle both categorical and numeric features. They can be built in parallel easily. They are robust to outliers in the data, meaning that a few extreme and possibly erroneous data points may not affect predictions at all. They can consume data of different types and on different scales without the need for preprocessing or normalization, which is an issue that will reappear in Chapter 5.

Decision trees generalize into a more powerful algorithm, called *random decision forests*. Their flexibility makes these algorithms worthwhile to examine in this chapter, where Spark MLlib's `DecisionTree` and `RandomForest` implementation will be applied to a data set.

Decision tree–based algorithms have the further advantage of being comparatively intuitive to understand and reason about. In fact, we all probably use the same reasoning embodied in decision trees, implicitly, in everyday life. For example, I sit down to have morning coffee with milk. Before I commit to that milk and add it to my brew, I want to predict: is the milk spoiled? I don't know for sure. I might check if the use-by date has passed. If not, I predict no, it's not spoiled. If the date has passed, but that was three or fewer days ago, I take my chances and predict no, it's not spoiled. Otherwise, I sniff the milk. If it smells funny, I predict yes, and otherwise no.

This series of yes/no decisions that lead to a prediction are what decision trees embody. Each decision leads to one of two results, which is either a prediction or another decision, as shown in Figure 4-1. In this sense, it is natural to think of the process as a tree of decisions, where each internal node in the tree is a decision, and each leaf node is a final answer.

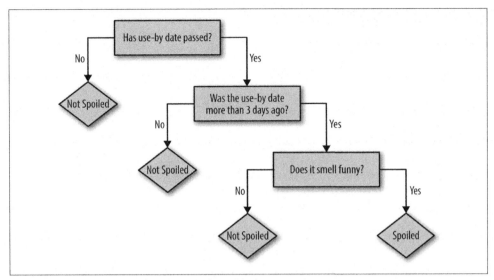

Figure 4-1. Decision tree: Is it spoiled?

The preceding rules were ones I learned to apply intuitively over years of bachelor life —they seemed like rules that were both simple and also usefully differentiated cases of spoiled and nonspoiled milk. These are also properties of a good decision tree.

That is a simplistic decision tree, and was not built with any rigor. To elaborate, consider another example. A robot has taken a job in an exotic pet store. It wants to learn, before the shop opens, which animals in the shop would make a good pet for a child. The owner lists nine pets that would and wouldn't be suitable before hurrying off. The robot compiles the information found in Table 4-1 from examining the animals.

Table 4-1. Exotic pet store "feature vectors"

Name	Weight (kg)	# Legs	Color	Good pet?
Fido	20.5	4	Brown	Yes
Mr. Slither	3.1	0	Green	No
Nemo	0.2	0	Tan	Yes
Dumbo	1390.8	4	Grey	No
Kitty	12.1	4	Grey	Yes
Jim	150.9	2	Tan	No

Name	Weight (kg)	# Legs	Color	Good pet?
Millie	0.1	100	Brown	No
McPigeon	1.0	2	Grey	No
Spot	10.0	4	Brown	Yes

Although a name is given, it will not be included as a feature. There is little reason to believe the name alone is predictive; "Felix" could name a cat or a poisonous tarantula, for all the robot knows. So, there are two numeric features (weight, number of legs) and one categorical feature (color) predicting a categorical target (is/is not a good pet for a child).

The robot might try to fit a simple decision tree to this training data to start, consisting of a single decision based on weight, as shown in Figure 4-2.

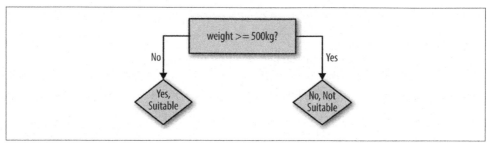

Figure 4-2. Robot's first decision tree

The logic of the decision tree is easy to read and make some sense of: 500kg animals certainly sound unsuitable as pets. This rule predicts the correct value in five of nine cases. A quick glance suggests that we could improve the rule by lowering the weight threshold to 100kg. This gets six of nine examples correct. The heavy animals are now predicted correctly; the lighter animals are only partly correct.

So, a second decision can be constructed to further refine the prediction for examples with weights less than 100kg. It would be good to pick a feature that changes some of the incorrect Yes predictions to No. For example, there is one small green animal, sounding suspiciously like a snake, that the robot could predict correctly by deciding on color, as in Figure 4-3.

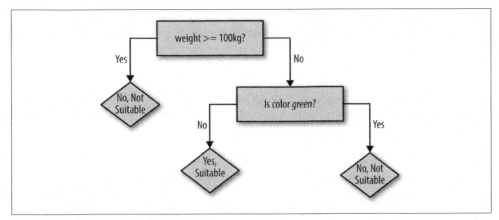

Figure 4-3. Robot's next decision tree

Now, seven of nine examples are correct. Of course, decision rules could be added until all nine were correctly predicted. The logic embodied in the resulting decision tree would probably sound implausible when translated into common speech: "If the animal's weight is less than 100kg, and its color is brown instead of green, and it has fewer than 10 legs, then yes it is a suitable pet." While perfectly fitting the given examples, a decision tree like this would fail to predict that a small, brown, four-legged wolverine is not a suitable pet. Some balance is needed to avoid this phenomenon, known as *overfitting*.

This is enough of an introduction to decision trees for us to begin using them with Spark. The remainder of the chapter will explore how to pick decision rules, how to know when to stop, and how to gain accuracy by creating a forest of trees.

Covtype Data Set

The data set used in this chapter is the well-known Covtype data set, available online (*http://bit.ly/1KiJRfg*) as a compressed CSV-format data file, *covtype.data.gz*, and accompanying info file, *covtype.info*.

The data set records the types of forest covering parcels of land in Colorado, USA. It's only coincidence that the data set concerns real-world forests! Each example contains several features describing each parcel of land, like its elevation, slope, distance to water, shade, and soil type, along with the known forest type covering the land. The forest cover type is to be predicted from the rest of the features, of which there are 54 in total.

This data set has been used in research, and even a Kaggle competition (*https://www.kaggle.com/c/forest-cover-type-prediction*). It is an interesting data set to explore in this chapter because it contains both categorical and numeric features. There are

581,012 examples in the data set, which does not exactly qualify as big data, but is large enough to be manageable as an example and still highlight some issues of scale.

Preparing the Data

Thankfully, the data is already in a simple CSV format and does not require much cleansing or other preparation to be used with Spark MLlib. Later, it will be of interest to explore some transformations of the data, but it can be used as is to start.

The *covtype.data* file should be extracted and copied into HDFS. This chapter will assume that the file is available at */user/ds/*. Start `spark-shell`.

The Spark MLlib abstraction for a feature vector is known as a `LabeledPoint`, which consists of a Spark MLlib `Vector` of features, and a target value, here called the *label*. The target is a `Double` value, and `Vector` is essentially an abstraction on top of many `Double` values. This suggests that `LabeledPoint` is only for numeric features. It can be used with categorical features, with appropriate encoding.

One such encoding is one-hot (*http://en.wikipedia.org/wiki/One-hot*) or 1-of-n encoding, in which one categorical feature that takes on *N* distinct values becomes *N* numeric features, each taking on the value 0 or 1. Exactly one of the *N* values has value 1, and the others are 0. For example, a categorical feature for weather that can be `cloudy`, `rainy`, or `clear` would become three numeric features, where `cloudy` is represented by `1,0,0`; `rainy` by `0,1,0`; and so on. These three numeric features might be thought of as `is_cloudy`, `is_rainy`, and `is_clear` features.

Another possible encoding simply assigns a distinct numeric value to each possible value of the categorical feature. For example, `cloudy` may become 1.0, `rainy` 2.0, and so on.

> Be careful when encoding a categorical feature as a single numeric feature. The original categorical values have no ordering, but when encoded as a number, they appear to. Treating the encoded feature as numeric leads to meaningless results because the algorithm is effectively pretending that `rainy` is somehow greater than, and two times larger than, `cloudy`. It's OK as long as the encoding's numeric value is not used as a number.

All of the columns contain numbers, but the Covtype data set does not consist solely of numeric features, at heart. The *covtype.info* file says that four of the columns are actually a one-hot encoding of a single categorical feature, called `Wilderness_Type`, with four values. Likewise, 40 of the columns are really one `Soil_Type` categorical feature. The target itself is a categorical value encoded as the values 1 to 7. The remaining features are numeric features in various units, like meters, degrees, or a qualitative "index" value.

We see both types of encodings of categorical features, then. It would have, perhaps, been simpler and more straightforward to not encode such features (and in two ways, no less), and instead simply include their values directly like "Rawah Wilderness Area." This may be an artifact of history; the data set was released in 1998. For performance reasons, or to match the format expected by libraries of the day, which were built more for regression problems, data sets often contain data encoded in these ways.

A First Decision Tree

To start, the data will be used as is. The `DecisionTree` implementation, like several in Spark MLlib, requires input in the form of `LabeledPoint` objects:

```
import org.apache.spark.mllib.linalg._
import org.apache.spark.mllib.regression._

val rawData = sc.textFile("hdfs:///user/ds/covtype.data")

val data = rawData.map { line =>
  val values = line.split(',').map(_.toDouble)
  val featureVector = Vectors.dense(values.init) ❶
  val label = values.last - 1 ❷
  LabeledPoint(label, featureVector)
}
```

❶ init returns all but last value; target is last column

❷ DecisionTree needs labels starting at 0; subtract 1

In Chapter 3, we built a recommender model right away on all of the available data. This created a recommender that could be sense-checked by anyone with some knowledge of music: looking at a user's listening habits and recommendations, we got some sense that it was producing good results. Here, that is not possible. We would have no idea how to make up a new 54-feature description of a new parcel of land in Colorado, or what kind of forest cover to expect from such a parcel.

Instead, we must jump straight to holding out some data for purposes of evaluating the resulting model. Before, the AUC metric was used to assess the agreement between held-out listening data and predictions from recommendations. The principle is the same here, although the evaluation metric will be different: *precision*. This time, the data will be split into the full three subsets: training, cross-validation (CV), and test. As you can see, 80% of the data is used for training, and 10% each for cross-validation and test:

```
val Array(trainData, cvData, testData) =
  data.randomSplit(Array(0.8, 0.1, 0.1))
trainData.cache()
cvData.cache()
testData.cache()
```

As with the `ALS` implementation, the `DecisionTree` implementation has several hyperparameters for which a value must be chosen. So, as before, the training and CV sets are used to choose a good setting of these hyperparameters for this data set. Here, the third set, the test set, is then used to produce an unbiased evaluation of the expected accuracy of a model built with those hyperparameters. The accuracy of the model on just the cross-validation set tends to be biased and slightly too optimistic. This chapter will take this extra step of evaluating the final model on the test set.

But first, try building a `DecisionTreeModel` on the training set, with some default arguments, and compute some metrics about the resulting model using the CV set:

```
import org.apache.spark.mllib.evaluation._
import org.apache.spark.mllib.tree._
import org.apache.spark.mllib.tree.model._
import org.apache.spark.rdd._

def getMetrics(model: DecisionTreeModel, data: RDD[LabeledPoint]):
    MulticlassMetrics = {
  val predictionsAndLabels = data.map(example =>
    (model.predict(example.features), example.label)
  )
  new MulticlassMetrics(predictionsAndLabels)
}

val model = DecisionTree.trainClassifier(
  trainData, 7, Map[Int,Int](), "gini", 4, 100)

val metrics = getMetrics(model, cvData)
```

Here, the use of `trainClassifier` instead of `trainRegressor` suggests that the target value within each `LabeledPoint` should be treated as a distinct category number, not a numeric feature value. (`trainRegressor` works similarly for regression problems, and will not be discussed separately in this chapter.)

At this time, we must specify the number of target values it will encounter: 7. The `Map` holds information about categorical features; this will be discussed later along with the meaning of "gini," the maximum depth of 4, and the maximum bin count of 100.

`MulticlassMetrics` computes standard metrics that in different ways measure the quality of the predictions from a classifier, which here has been run on the CV set. Ideally, the classifier should predict the correct target category for each example in the CV set. The metrics available here measure this sort of correctness, in different ways.

Its companion class, `BinaryClassificationMetrics`, contains similar evaluation metric implementations for the particular, common case of a categorical target with just two values. It can't be used directly here because the target takes on many values.

It may be helpful to look at the *confusion matrix* first:

```
metrics.confusionMatrix
```

```
...
14019.0  6630.0   15.0     0.0     0.0  1.0   391.0
5413.0   22399.0  438.0    16.0    0.0  3.0   50.0
0.0      457.0    2999.0   73.0    0.0  12.0  0.0
0.0      1.0      163.0    117.0   0.0  0.0   0.0
0.0      872.0    40.0     0.0     0.0  0.0   0.0
0.0      500.0    1138.0   36.0    0.0  48.0  0.0
1091.0   41.0     0.0      0.0     0.0  0.0   891.0
```

 Your values will be a little different. The process of building a decision tree includes some random choices that can lead to slightly different classifications.

Because there are seven target category values, this is a 7-×-7 matrix, where each row corresponds to an actual correct value, and each column to a predicted value, in order. The entry at row *i* and column *j* counts the number of times an example with true category *i* was predicted as category *j*. So, the correct predictions are the counts along the diagonal, and incorrect predictions are everything else. Counts are high along the diagonal, which is good. However, there are certainly a number of misclassifications, and, for example, category 5 is never predicted at all.

It's helpful to summarize the accuracy with a single number. An obvious place to start is to compute the fraction of all examples that were correctly predicted:

```
metrics.precision
```

```
...
0.7030630195577938
```

About 70% of examples were classified correctly. This is commonly called *accuracy*, and is called *precision* in Spark's `MulticlassMetrics`. This is a light overloading of the term.

Precision is actually a common metric for *binary* classification problems, where there are two category values, not several. In a binary classification problem, where there is some kind of `positive` and `negative` class, precision is the fraction of examples that the classifier marked `positive` that are actually `positive`. It is often accompanied by the metric *recall*. This is the fraction of all examples that are actually `positive` that the classifier marked `positive`.

For example, say there are 20 actually positive examples in a data set of 50 examples. The classifier marks 10 of the 50 as positive, and of those 10, 4 are actually positive (correctly classified). Precision is 4/10 = 0.4 and recall is 4/20 = 0.2 in this case.

We can apply these concepts to this multiclass problem by viewing each category independently as the `positive` class, and all else as `negative`. For example, to compute precision and recall for each category versus the rest:

```
(0 until 7).map(  ❶
  cat => (metrics.precision(cat), metrics.recall(cat))
).foreach(println)

...
(0.6805931840866961,0.6809492105763744)
(0.7297560975609756,0.7892237892589596)
(0.6376224968044312,0.8473952434881087)
(0.5384615384615384,0.3917910447761194)
(0.0,0.0)
(0.7083333333333334,0.0293778801843318)
(0.6956168831168831,0.42828585707146427)
```

❶ `DecisionTreeModel` numbers categories from 0

This shows that the accuracy for each class individually varies. For our purposes here, there's no reason to think that one category's accuracy is more important than another, so examples will take the overall multiclass precision as a good, single measure of the accuracy of predictions.

Although 70% accuracy sounds decent, it's not immediately clear whether it is outstanding or poor. How well would a simplistic approach do, to establish a baseline? Just as a broken clock is correct twice a day, randomly guessing a classification for each example would also occasionally produce the correct answer.

We could construct such a "classifier" by picking a class at random in proportion to its prevalence in the training set. Each classification would be correct in proportion to its prevalence in the CV set. For example, a class that makes up 20% of the training set and 10% of the CV set will contribute 20% of 10%, or 2%, to the overall accuracy. That 10% will be correctly "classified" 20% of the time through guessing. We can evaluate the accuracy by summing these products of probabilities:

```
import org.apache.spark.rdd._

def classProbabilities(data: RDD[LabeledPoint]): Array[Double] = {
  val countsByCategory = data.map(_.label).countByValue()  ❶
  val counts = countsByCategory.toArray.sortBy(_._1).map(_._2)  ❷
  counts.map(_.toDouble / counts.sum)
```

```
}

val trainPriorProbabilities = classProbabilities(trainData)
val cvPriorProbabilities = classProbabilities(cvData)
trainPriorProbabilities.zip(cvPriorProbabilities).map { ❸
  case (trainProb, cvProb) => trainProb * cvProb
}.sum

...
0.37737764750734776
```

❶   Count (category,count) in data

❷   Order counts by category and extract counts

❸   Pair probability in training, CV set and sum products

Random guessing achieves 37% accuracy then, which makes 70% seem like a good result after all. But this result was achieved with default arguments to Decision Tree.trainClassifier(). We can do even better by exploring what these arguments —hyperparameters—mean for the tree-building process.

Decision Tree Hyperparameters

In Chapter 3, the ALS algorithm exposed several hyperparameters whose values we had to choose by building models with various combinations of values, and then assessing the quality of each result using some metric. The process is the same here, although the metric is now multiclass accuracy instead of AUC, and the hyperparameters controlling how the tree's decisions are chosen are maximum depth, maximum bins, and impurity measure.

Maximum depth simply limits the number of levels in the decision tree. It is the maximum number of chained decisions that the classifier will make to classify an example. It is useful to limit this to avoid overfitting the training data, as illustrated previously in the pet store example.

The decision tree algorithm is responsible for coming up with potential decision rules to try at each level, like the weight >= 100 or weight >= 500 decisions in the pet store example. Decisions are always of the same form: for numeric features, decisions are of the form feature >= value, and for categorical features they are of the form feature in (value1, value2, …). So, the set of decision rules to try is really a set of values to plug in to the decision rule. These are referred to as "bins" in the Spark MLlib implementation. A larger number of bins requires more processing time but may lead to finding a more optimal decision rule.

What makes a decision rule good? Intuitively, a good rule would meaningfully distinguish examples by target category value. For example, a rule that divides the Covtype data set into examples with only categories 1–3 on the one hand, and 4–7 on the other, would be excellent because it clearly separates some categories from the others. A rule that resulted in about the same mix of all categories as are found in the whole data set doesn't seem helpful. Following either branch of such a decision leads to about the same distribution of possible target values, and so doesn't really make progress toward a confident classification.

Put another way, good rules divide the training data's target values into relatively homogeneous, or "pure," subsets. Picking a best rule means minimizing the impurity of the two subsets it induces. There are two commonly used measures of impurity: Gini impurity (*http://en.wikipedia.org/wiki/Decision_tree_learning#Gini_impurity*) and entropy (*http://en.wikipedia.org/wiki/Entropy_(information_theory)*).

Gini impurity is directly related to the accuracy of the random-guess classifier. Within a subset, it is the probability that a randomly chosen classification of a randomly chosen example (both according to the distribution of classes in the subset) is *incorrect*. This is the sum of products of proportions of classes, but with themselves, and subtracted from 1. If a subset has N classes and p_i is the proportion of examples of class i, then its Gini impurity is given in the Gini impurity equation:

$$I_G(p) = 1 - \sum_{i=1}^{N} p_i^2$$

If the subset contains only one class, this value is 0 because it is completely "pure." When there are N classes in the subset, this value is larger than 0 and is largest when the classes occur the same number of times—maximally impure.

Entropy is another measure of impurity, borrowed from information theory. Its nature is more difficult to explain, but it captures how much uncertainty the collection of target values in the subset contains. A subset containing one class only is completely certain, and has 0 entropy. Hence low entropy, like low Gini impurity, is a good thing. Entropy is defined in the entropy equation:

$$I_E(p) = \sum_{i=1}^{N} p_i \log\left(\frac{1}{p}\right) = -\sum_{i=1}^{N} p_i \log\left(p_i\right)$$

Interestingly, uncertainty has units. Because the logarithm is the natural log (base e), the units are *nats*, the base-e counterpart to more familiar *bits* (which we can obtain by using log base 2 instead). It really is measuring information, and so it's also common to talk about the *information gain* of a decision rule when using entropy with decision trees.

One or the other measure may be a better metric for picking decision rules in a given data set. The default in Spark's implementation is Gini impurity.

Some decision tree implementations will impose a minimum information gain, or decrease in impurity, for candidate decision rules. Rules that do not improve the subsets impurity enough are rejected. Like a lower maximum depth, this can help the model resist overfitting, because decisions that barely help divide the training input may in fact not helpfully divide future data at all. However, rules like minimum information gain are not implemented in Spark MLlib yet.

Tuning Decision Trees

It's not obvious from looking at the data which impurity measure leads to better accuracy, or what maximum depth or number of bins is enough without being excessive. Fortunately, as in Chapter 3, it's simple to let Spark try a number of combinations of these values and report the results:

```
val evaluations =
  for (impurity <- Array("gini", "entropy");
       depth    <- Array(1, 20);
       bins     <- Array(10, 300)) ❶
    yield {
      val model = DecisionTree.trainClassifier(
        trainData, 7, Map[Int,Int](), impurity, depth, bins)
      val predictionsAndLabels = cvData.map(example =>
        (model.predict(example.features), example.label)
      )
      val accuracy =
        new MulticlassMetrics(predictionsAndLabels).precision
      ((impurity, depth, bins), accuracy)
    }

evaluations.sortBy(_._2).reverse.foreach(println) ❷

...
((entropy,20,300),0.9125545571245186)
((gini,20,300),0.9042533162173727)
((gini,20,10),0.8854428754813863)
((entropy,20,10),0.8848951647411211)
((gini,1,300),0.6358065896448438)
((gini,1,10),0.6355669661959777)
((entropy,1,300),0.4861446298673513)
((entropy,1,10),0.4861446298673513)
```

❶ Again, read as a triply nested for loop

❷ Sort by second value (accuracy), descending, and print

Clearly, maximum depth 1 is too small and produces inferior results. More bins helps a little. The two impurity measures seem comparable, for reasonable settings of maximum depth. This process could be continued to explore these hyperparameters. More bins should never hurt, but will slow down the building process and increase memory usage. Both impurity measures should be tried in all cases. More depth will help up to a point.

So far, the code samples here have ignored the 10% of data held out as the test set. If the purpose of the CV set was to evaluate *parameters* fit to the *training* set, then the purpose of the test set is to evaluate *hyperparameters* that were "fit" to the CV set. That is, the test set ensures an unbiased estimate of the accuracy of the final, chosen model and its hyperparameters.

The preceding test suggests that entropy-based impurity, maximum depth 20, and 300 bins are the best-known hyperparameter settings so far, and achieves about 91.2% accuracy. However, there's an element of randomness in how these models are built. By chance, this model and evaluation could have turned out unusually well. The top model and evaluation result could have benefited from a bit of luck, and so, its accuracy estimate is likely to be slightly optimistic. Put another way, hyperparameters can overfit too.

To really assess how well this best model is likely to perform on future examples, we need to evaluate it on examples that were not used to train it, certainly. But we also need to avoid examples in the CV set that were used to evaluate it. That is why a third subset, the test set, was held out. As a final step, we can use the hyperparameters to build a model on the training and CV sets together, and evaluate as before:

```
val model = DecisionTree.trainClassifier(
  trainData.union(cvData), 7, Map[Int,Int](), "entropy", 20, 300)
```

The result is about 91.6% accuracy, which is about the same, so the initial estimate appears to have been reliable.

This is an interesting point at which to revisit the issue of overfitting. As discussed previously, it's possible to build a decision tree so deep and elaborate that it fits the given training examples very well or perfectly, but fails to generalize to other examples because it has fit the idiosyncrasies and noise of the training data too closely. This is a problem common to most machine learning algorithms, not just decision trees.

When a decision tree has overfit, it will exhibit high accuracy when run on the same training data that it fit the model to, but low accuracy on other examples. Here, the final model's accuracy was about 91.6% on other, new examples. Accuracy can just as easily be evaluated over the same data that the model was trained on, `train Data.union(cvData)`. This gives an accuracy of about 95.3%.

The difference is not large, but suggests the decision tree has overfit the training data to some extent. A lower maximum depth might be a better choice.

Categorical Features Revisited

The code samples so far have included the argument `Map[Int,Int]()` without explanation. This parameter, like the 7, specifies the number of distinct values to expect for each categorical feature in the input. The keys in this `Map` are indices of features in the input `Vector`, and values are distinct value counts. At this time, the implementation requires this information in advance.

The empty `Map()` indicates that no features should be treated as categorical; all are numeric. All of the features are in fact numbers, but some represent categorical features, conceptually. As mentioned earlier, it would be an error to treat a categorical feature that had simply been mapped to distinct numbers as a numeric value, because the algorithm would be trying to learn from an ordering that has no meaning.

Thankfully, the categorical features here are one-hot encoded as several binary 0/1 values. Treating these individual features as numeric turns out to be fine, because any decision rule on the "numeric" features will choose thresholds between 0 and 1, and all are equivalent since all values are 0 or 1.

Of course, this encoding forces the decision tree algorithm to consider the values of the underlying categorical feature individually. It is not limited in this way when learning from a single categorical feature. With one 40-valued categorical feature, the decision tree can create decisions based on groups of categories in one decision, which may be more direct and optimal. On the other hand, having 40 numeric features represent one 40-valued categorical feature also increases memory usage and slows things down.

What about undoing the one-hot encoding? The following alternative parsing of the input turns the two categorical features from one-hot encoding to a series of distinct numeric values:

```
val data = rawData.map { line =>
  val values = line.split(',').map(_.toDouble)
  val wilderness = values.slice(10, 14).indexOf(1.0).toDouble ❶
  val soil = values.slice(14, 54).indexOf(1.0).toDouble ❷
  val featureVector =
    Vectors.dense(values.slice(0, 10) :+ wilderness :+ soil) ❸
  val label = values.last - 1
  LabeledPoint(label, featureVector)
}
```

❶ Which of 4 "wilderness" features is 1

❷ Similarly for following 40 "soil" features

❸ Add derived features back to first 10

We can repeat the same process of train/CV/test split and evaluation. This time, the count of distinct values for the two new categorical features is given, which causes these features to be treated as categorical, and not numeric. `DecisionTree` requires the number of bins to increase to at least 40, because the soil feature has 40 distinct values. Given previous results, deeper trees are built, up to the maximum of depth 30 that `DecisionTree` currently supports. Finally, both train and CV accuracy are reported:

```
val evaluations =
  for (impurity <- Array("gini", "entropy");
       depth    <- Array(10, 20, 30);
       bins     <- Array(40, 300))
    yield {
      val model = DecisionTree.trainClassifier(
        trainData, 7, Map(10 -> 4, 11 -> 40),
        impurity, depth, bins) ❶
      val trainAccuracy = getMetrics(model, trainData).precision
      val cvAccuracy = getMetrics(model, cvData).precision
      ((impurity, depth, bins), (trainAccuracy, cvAccuracy)) ❷
    }

...
((entropy,30,300),(0.9996922984231909,0.9438383977425239))
((entropy,30,40),(0.9994469978654548,0.938934581368939))
((gini,30,300),(0.9998622874061833,0.937127912178671))
((gini,30,40),(0.9995180059216415,0.9329467634811934))
((entropy,20,40),(0.9725865867933623,0.9280773598540899))
((gini,20,300),(0.9702347139020864,0.9249630062975326))
((entropy,20,300),(0.9643948392205467,0.9231391307340239))
((gini,20,40),(0.9679344832334917,0.9223820503114354))
((gini,10,300),(0.7953203539213661,0.7946763481193434))
((gini,10,40),(0.7880624698753701,0.7860215423792973))
((entropy,10,40),(0.78206336500723,0.7814790598437661))
((entropy,10,300),(0.7821903188046547,0.7802746137169208))
```

❶ Specify value count for categorical features 10, 11

❷ Return train and CV accuracy

If you run this on a cluster, you may notice that the tree-building process completes several times faster than before.

At depth 30, the training set is fit nearly perfectly; it is overfitting to some degree, but still providing the best accuracy on the cross-validation set. Entropy, and a larger number of bins, appear to help accuracy again. The accuracy on the test set is 94.5%. By treating categorical features as actual categorical features, the classifier improved its accuracy by almost 3%.

Random Decision Forests

If you have been following along with the code examples, you may have noticed that your results differ slightly from those presented in code listings in the book. That is because there is an element of randomness in building decision trees, and the randomness comes into play when you're deciding what data to use and what decision rules to explore.

The algorithm does not consider every possible decision rule at every level. To do so could take an incredible amount of time. For a categorical feature over N values, there are $2^N - 2$ possible decision rules (every subset except the empty set and entire set). For even moderately large N this would create billions of candidate decision rules.

Instead, decision trees use several heuristics to be smarter about which few rules to actually consider. The process of picking rules also involves some randomness; only a few features picked at random are looked at each time, and only values from a random subset of the training data. This trades a bit of accuracy for a lot of speed, but it also means that the decision tree algorithm won't build the same tree every time. This is a good thing.

It's good for the same reason that the "wisdom of the crowds" usually beats individual predictions.

To illustrate, take this quick quiz: How many black taxis operate in London?

Don't peek at the answer; guess first.

I guessed 10,000, which is well off the correct answer of about 19,000. Because I guessed low, you're a bit more likely to have guessed higher than I did, and so the average of our answers will tend to be more accurate. There's that regression to the mean again. The average guess from an informal poll of 13 people in the office was indeed closer: 11,170.

A key to this effect is that the guesses were independent and didn't influence one another. (You didn't peek, did you?) The exercise would be useless if we had all agreed on and used the same methodology to make a guess, because the guesses would have been the same answer—the same potentially quite wrong answer. It would even have been different and worse if I'd merely influenced you by stating my guess upfront.

It would be great to have not one tree, but many trees, each producing reasonable but different and independent estimations of the right target value. Their collective average prediction should fall close to the true answer, more than any individual tree's does. It's the *randomness* in the process of building that helps create this independence. This is the key to random decision *forests*.

Through `RandomForest`, Spark MLlib can build random decision forests, which are, as the name suggests, collections of independently built decision trees. The invocation is virtually the same:

```
val forest = RandomForest.trainClassifier(
    trainData, 7, Map(10 -> 4, 11 -> 40), 20,
    "auto", "entropy", 30, 300)
```

Two new parameters appear, compared to `DecisionTree.trainClassifier()`. First is a number of trees to build: here 20. This model-building process may take significantly longer than before, because 20 trees are being built instead of one.

Second is a strategy for choosing which features to evaluate at each level of the tree, which is here set to `"auto"`. The random decision forest implementation will not even consider every *feature* as the basis of a decision rule, but only a subset of all features. This parameter controls how it picks the subset. Checking only a few features is of course faster, and speed is helpful now that so many more trees are being constructed.

However, it also makes the individual trees' decisions more independent, and makes the forest as a whole less prone to overfitting. If a particular feature contains noisy data, or is deceptively predictive only in the *training* set, then most trees will not have considered this problem feature, most of the time. Most trees will not have fit the noise and will tend to "outvote" the ones that have in the forest.

In fact, when you're building a random decision forest, each tree will not even necessarily see all of the training data. They may be fed a randomly chosen subset of it instead, for similar reasons.

The prediction of a random decision forest is simply a weighted average of the trees' predictions. For a categorical target, this can be a majority vote, or the most probable value based on the average of probabilities produced by the trees. Random decision forests, like decision trees, also support regression, and the forest's prediction in this case is the average of the number predicted by each tree.

The accuracy from this `RandomForestModel` model is 96.3% off the bat—about 2% better already, although viewed another way, that's a 33% reduction in the error rate over the best decision tree built previously, from 5.5% down to 3.7%.

Random decision forests are appealing in the context of big data because trees are supposed to be built independently, and big-data technologies like Spark and MapReduce inherently need *data-parallel* problems, where parts of the overall solution can be computed independently on parts of the data. The fact that trees can, and should, train on only a subset of features or input data makes it trivial to parallelize building of the trees.

Although Spark MLlib does not yet support it directly, random decision forests can also evaluate their own accuracy along the way, because often trees are built on just a subset of all training data and can be internally cross-validated against the remaining data. This means that the forest can even know which of its trees appear to be the most accurate and weight accordingly.

This property also leads to a way to assess which features of the input are most helpful in predicting the target, and thus help with the problem of feature selection. This is also beyond the scope of this chapter, and MLlib, at the moment.

Making Predictions

Building a classifier, while interesting and a nuanced process, is not the end goal. The goal is to make predictions. This is the payoff, and it is comparatively quite easy. The training set consisted of `LabeledPoint` instances, each of which contained a `Vector` and a target value. These are an input and known output, respectively. When we're making predictions—especially about the future, says Mr. Bohr—the output is of course not known.

The results of the `DecisionTree` and `RandomForest` training shown so far are `DecisionTreeModel` and `RandomForestModel` objects, respectively. Both contain essentially one method, `predict()`. It accepts a `Vector`, just like the feature vector portion of `LabeledPoint`. So, we can classify a new example by converting it to a feature vector in the same way and predicting its target class:

```
val input = "2709,125,28,67,23,3224,253,207,61,6094,0,29"
val vector = Vectors.dense(input.split(',').map(_.toDouble))
forest.predict(vector) ❶
```

❶ Can also predict for a whole RDD at once

The result should be 4.0, which corresponds to class 5 (the original feature was 1-indexed) in the original Covtype data set. The predicted cover type for the land described in this example is "Aspen." Obviously.

Where to Go from Here

This chapter introduced two related and important types of machine learning, classification and regression, along with some foundational concepts in building and tuning models: features, vectors, training, and cross-validation. It demonstrated how to predict a type of forest cover from things like location and soil type, using the Covtype data set, with decision trees and forests implemented in Spark MLlib.

As with recommenders in Chapter 3, it could be useful to continue exploring the effect of hyperparameters on accuracy. Most decision tree hyperparameters trade time for accuracy: more bins and trees generally produce better accuracy, but hit a point of diminishing returns.

The classifier here turned out to be very accurate. It's unusual to achieve more than 95% accuracy. In general, you will achieve further improvements in accuracy by including more features, or transforming existing features into a more predictive form. This is a common, repeated step in iteratively improving a classifier model. For example, for this data set, the two features encoding horizontal and vertical distance to surface water features could produce a third feature: straight-line distance to surface water features. This might turn out to be more useful than either original feature. Or, if it were possible to collect more data, we might try adding new information like soil moisture in order to improve classification.

Of course, not all prediction problems in the real world are exactly like the Covtype data set. For example, some problems require predicting a continuous numeric value, not a categorical value. Much of the same analysis and code applies to this type of *regression* problem; the `trainRegressor()` method will be of use in this case instead of `trainClassifier()`.

Furthermore, decision trees and forests are not the only classification or regression algorithms, and not the only ones implemented in Spark MLlib. For classification, it includes implementations of:

- Naïve Bayes (*http://en.wikipedia.org/wiki/Naive_Bayes_classifier*)
- Support vector machines (*http://en.wikipedia.org/wiki/Support_vector_machine*) (SVMs)
- Logistic regression (*http://en.wikipedia.org/wiki/Logistic_regression*)

Yes, logistic regression is a classification technique. Underneath the hood, it classifies by predicting a continuous function of a class probability. This detail is not necessary to understand.

Each of these algorithms operates quite differently from decision trees and forests. However, many elements are the same: they accept an RDD of `LabeledPoint` as input, and have hyperparameters that you must select using training, cross-validation, and test subsets of the input data. The same general principles, with these other algorithms, can also be deployed to model classification and regression problems.

These have been examples of supervised learning. What happens when some, or all, of the target values are unknown? The following chapter will explore what can be done in this situation.

CHAPTER 5

Anomaly Detection in Network Traffic with K-means Clustering

Sean Owen

There are known knowns; there are things that we know that we know. We also know there are known unknowns; that is to say, we know there are some things we do not know. But there are also unknown unknowns, the ones we don't know we don't know.
—Donald Rumsfeld

Classification and regression are powerful, well-studied techniques in machine learning. Chapter 4 demonstrated a classifier as a predictor of unknown values. There was a catch: in order to predict unknown values for new data, we had to know that target value for many previously seen examples. Classifiers can only help if we, the data scientists, know what we are looking for already, and can provide plenty of examples where input produced a known output. These were collectively known as supervised learning (*http://en.wikipedia.org/wiki/Supervised_learning*) techniques, because their learning process receives the correct output value for each example in the input.

However, there are problems in which the correct output is unknown for some or all examples. Consider the problem of dividing up an ecommerce site's customers by their shopping habits and tastes. The input features are their purchases, clicks, demographic information, and more. The output should be groupings of customers. Perhaps one group will represent fashion-conscious buyers, another will turn out to correspond to price-sensitive bargain hunters, and so on.

If you were asked to determine this target label for each new customer, you would quickly run into a problem in applying a supervised learning technique like a classifier: you don't know *a priori* who should be considered fashion-conscious, for example. In fact, you're not even sure if "fashion-conscious" is a meaningful grouping of the site's customers to begin with!

Fortunately, unsupervised learning (*http://en.wikipedia.org/wiki/Unsupervised_learning*) techniques can help. These techniques do not learn to predict any target value, because none is available. They can, however, learn structure in data, and find groupings of similar inputs, or learn what types of input are likely to occur and what types are not. This chapter will introduce unsupervised learning using clustering implementations in MLlib.

Anomaly Detection

The problem of anomaly detection is, as its name implies, that of finding unusual things. If we already knew what "anomalous" meant for a data set, we could easily detect anomalies in the data with supervised learning. An algorithm would receive inputs labeled "normal" and "anomaly" and learn to distinguish the two. However, the nature of anomalies is that they are unknown unknowns. Put another way, an anomaly that has been observed and understood is no longer an anomaly.

Anomaly detection is often used to find fraud, detect network attacks, or discover problems in servers or other sensor-equipped machinery. In these cases, it's important to be able to find new types of anomalies that have never been seen before—new forms of fraud, new intrusions, new failure modes for servers.

Unsupervised learning techniques are useful in these cases, because they can learn what input data normally looks like, and therefore detect when new data is unlike past data. Such new data is not necessarily attacks or fraud; it is simply unusual, and therefore, worth further investigation.

K-means Clustering

Clustering is the best-known type of unsupervised learning. Clustering algorithms try to find natural groupings in data. Data points that are like one another, but unlike others, are likely to represent a meaningful grouping, and so clustering algorithms try to put such data into the same cluster.

K-means (*http://en.wikipedia.org/wiki/K-means_clustering*) clustering is maybe the most widely used clustering algorithm. It attempts to detect k clusters in a data set, where k is given by the data scientist. k is a hyperparameter of the model, and the right value will depend on the data set. In fact, choosing a good value for k will be a central plot point in this chapter.

What does "like" mean when the data set contains information like customer activity? Or transactions? K-means requires a notion of distance between data points. It is common to use simple Euclidean distance to measure distance between data points with K-means, and as it happens, this is the only distance function supported by Spark MLlib as of this writing. The Euclidean distance is defined for data points whose features are all numeric. "Like" points are those whose intervening distance is small.

To K-means, a cluster is simply a point: the center of all the points that make up the cluster. These are in fact just feature vectors containing all numeric features, and can be called vectors. It may be more intuitive to think of them as points here, because they are treated as points in a Euclidean space.

This center is called the cluster *centroid*, and is the arithmetic mean of the points—hence the name K-*means*. To start, the algorithm picks some data points as the initial cluster centroids. Then each data point is assigned to the nearest centroid. Then for each cluster, a new cluster centroid is computed as the mean of the data points just assigned to that cluster. This process is repeated.

Enough about K-means for now. Some more interesting details will emerge in the course of the use case to follow.

Network Intrusion

So-called cyber attacks are increasingly visible in the news. Some attacks attempt to flood a computer with network traffic to crowd out legitimate traffic. But in other cases, attacks attempt to exploit flaws in networking software to gain unauthorized access to a computer. While it's quite obvious when a computer is being bombarded with traffic, detecting an exploit can be like searching for a needle in an incredibly large haystack of network requests.

Some exploit behaviors follow known patterns. For example, accessing every port on a machine in rapid succession is not something any normal software program would need to do. However, it is a typical first step for an attacker, who is looking for services running on the computer that may be exploitable.

If you were to count the number of distinct ports accessed by a remote host in a short time, you would have a feature that probably predicts a port-scanning attack quite well. A handful is probably normal; hundreds indicates an attack. The same goes for detecting other types of attacks from other features of network connections—number of bytes sent and received, TCP errors, and so forth.

But what about those unknown unknowns? The biggest threat may be the one that has never yet been detected and classified. Part of detecting potential network intrusions is detecting anomalies. These are connections that aren't known to be attacks, but do not resemble connections that have been observed in the past.

Here, unsupervised learning techniques like K-means can be used to detect anomalous network connections. K-means can cluster connections based on statistics about each of them. The resulting clusters themselves aren't interesting per se, but they collectively define types of connections that are like past connections. Anything not close to a cluster could be anomalous. Clusters are interesting insofar as they define regions of normal connections; everything else outside is unusual and potentially anomalous.

KDD Cup 1999 Data Set

The KDD Cup (*http://www.sigkdd.org/kddcup/index.php*) was an annual data mining competition organized by a special interest group of the ACM. Each year, a machine learning problem was posed, along with a data set, and researchers were invited to submit a paper detailing their best solution to the problem. It was like Kaggle (*http://www.kaggle.com/*), before there was Kaggle. In 1999 (*http://bit.ly/1ALCqZN*), the topic was network intrusion, and the data set is still available (*http://bit.ly/1ALCuZN*). This chapter will walk through building a system to detect anomalous network traffic, using Spark, by learning from this data.

 Don't use this data set to build a real network intrusion system! The data did not necessarily reflect real network traffic at the time, and in any event it only reflects traffic patterns as of 15 years ago.

Fortunately, the organizers had already processed raw network packet data into summary information about individual network connections. The data set is about 708 MB and contains about 4.9M connections. This is large, if not massive, but will be large enough for our purposes here. For each connection, the data set contains information like the number of bytes sent, login attempts, TCP errors, and so on. Each connection is one line of CSV-formatted data, containing 38 features, like this:

```
0,tcp,http,SF,215,45076,
0,0,0,0,0,1,0,0,0,0,0,0,0,0,0,1,1,
0.00,0.00,0.00,0.00,1.00,0.00,0.00,0,0,0.00,
0.00,0.00,0.00,0.00,0.00,0.00,0.00,normal.
```

This connection, for example, was a TCP connection to an HTTP service—215 bytes were sent and 45,706 bytes were received. The user was logged in, and so on. Many features are counts, like num_file_creations in the 17th column.

Many features take on the value 0 or 1, indicating the presence or absence of a behavior, like su_attempted in the 15th column. They look like the one-hot encoded categorical features from Chapter 4, but are not grouped and related in the same way. Each is like a yes/no feature, and is therefore arguably a categorical feature. It is not always valid to translate categorical features to numbers and treat them as if they had an ordering. However, in the special case of a binary categorical feature, in most machine learning algorithms, it will happen to work well to map these to a numeric feature taking on values 0 and 1.

The rest are ratios like `dst_host_srv_rerror_rate` in the next-to-last column, and take on values from 0.0 to 1.0, inclusive.

Interestingly, a label is given in the last field. Most connections are labeled `normal.`, but some have been identified as examples of various types of network attacks. These would be useful in learning to distinguish a known attack from a normal connection, but the problem here is anomaly detection, and finding potentially new and unknown attacks. This label will be mostly set aside for our purposes here.

A First Take on Clustering

Unzip the *kddcup.data.gz* data file and copy it into HDFS. This example, like others, will assume the file is available at */user/ds/kddcup.data*. Open the `spark-shell`, and load the CSV data as an RDD of `String`:

```
val rawData = sc.textFile("hdfs:///user/ds/kddcup.data")
```

Begin by exploring the data set. What labels are present in the data, and how many are there of each? The following code counts by label into label-count tuples, sorts them descending by count, and prints the result:

```
rawData.map(_.split(',').last).countByValue().toSeq.
  sortBy(_._2).reverse.foreach(println)
```

A lot can be accomplished in a line in Spark and Scala! There are 23 distinct labels, and the most frequent are `smurf.` and `neptune.` attacks:

```
(smurf.,2807886)
(neptune.,1072017)
(normal.,972781)
(satan.,15892)
...
```

Note that the data contains nonnumeric features. For example, the second column may be `tcp`, `udp`, or `icmp`, but K-means clustering requires numeric features. The final label column is also nonnumeric. To begin, these will simply be ignored. The following Spark code splits the CSV lines into columns, removes the three categorical value columns starting from index 1, and removes the final column. The remaining values are converted to an array of numeric values (`Double` objects), and emitted with the final label column in a tuple:

```
import org.apache.spark.mllib.linalg._

val labelsAndData = rawData.map { line =>
  val buffer = line.split(',').toBuffer ❶
  buffer.remove(1, 3)
  val label = buffer.remove(buffer.length-1)
  val vector = Vectors.dense(buffer.map(_.toDouble).toArray)
  (label,vector)
```

```
    }
    val data = labelsAndData.values.cache()
```

❶   `toBuffer` creates `Buffer`, a *mutable* list

K-means will operate on just the feature vectors. So, the RDD `data` contains just the second element of each tuple, which in an RDD of tuples are accessed with `values`. Clustering the data with Spark MLlib is as simple as importing the `KMeans` implementation and running it. The following code clusters the data to create a `KMeansModel`, and then prints its centroids:

```
import org.apache.spark.mllib.clustering._

val kmeans = new KMeans()
val model = kmeans.run(data)

model.clusterCenters.foreach(println)
```

Two vectors will be printed, meaning K-means was fitting $k = 2$ clusters to the data. For a complex data set that is known to exhibit at least 23 distinct types of connections, this is almost certainly not enough to accurately model the distinct groupings within the data.

This is a good opportunity to use the given labels to get an intuitive sense of what went into these two clusters, by counting the labels within each cluster. The following code uses the model to assign each data point to a cluster, counts occurrences of cluster and label pairs, and prints them nicely:

```
val clusterLabelCount = labelsAndData.map { case (label,datum) =>
  val cluster = model.predict(datum)
  (cluster,label)
}.countByValue

clusterLabelCount.toSeq.sorted.foreach {
  case ((cluster,label),count) =>
    println(f"$cluster%1s$label%18s$count%8s")  ❶
}
```

❶   Format string interpolates and formats variables

The result shows that the clustering was not at all helpful. Only one data point ended up in cluster 1!

```
0              back.     2203
0   buffer_overflow.       30
0         ftp_write.        8
0      guess_passwd.       53
0              imap.       12
0           ipsweep.    12481
0              land.       21
```

```
0      loadmodule.          9
0         multihop.          7
0          neptune.    1072017
0             nmap.       2316
0           normal.     972781
0             perl.          3
0              phf.          4
0              pod.        264
0       portsweep.      10412
0          rootkit.         10
0            satan.      15892
0            smurf.    2807886
0              spy.          2
0         teardrop.        979
0      warezclient.       1020
0      warezmaster.         20
1       portsweep.          1
```

Choosing k

Two clusters are plainly insufficient. How many clusters are appropriate for this data set? It's clear that there are 23 distinct patterns in the data, so it seems that k could be at least 23, or likely, even more. Typically, many values of k are tried to find the best one. But what is "best"?

A clustering could be considered good if each data point were near to its closest centroid. So, we define a Euclidean distance function, and a function that returns the distance from a data point to its nearest cluster's centroid:

```
def distance(a: Vector, b: Vector) =
  math.sqrt(a.toArray.zip(b.toArray).
    map(p => p._1 - p._2).map(d => d * d).sum)

def distToCentroid(datum: Vector, model: KMeansModel) = {
  val cluster = model.predict(datum)
  val centroid = model.clusterCenters(cluster)
  distance(centroid, datum)
}
```

You can read off the definition of Euclidean distance here by unpacking the Scala function, in reverse: sum (sum) the squares (map(d => d * d)) of differences (map(p => p._1 - p._2)) in corresponding elements of two vectors (a.toArray.zip(b.toArray)), and take the square root (math.sqrt).

From this, it's possible to define a function that measures the average distance to centroid, for a model built with a given k:

```
import org.apache.spark.rdd._

def clusteringScore(data: RDD[Vector], k: Int) = {
```

```
    val kmeans = new KMeans()
    kmeans.setK(k)
    val model = kmeans.run(data)
    data.map(datum => distToCentroid(datum, model)).mean()
}
```

Now, this can be used to evaluate values of *k* from, say, 5 to 40:

```
(5 to 40 by 5).map(k => (k, clusteringScore(data, k))).
    foreach(println)
```

The (x to y by z) syntax is a Scala idiom for creating a collection of numbers between a start and end (inclusive), with a given difference between successive elements. This is a compact way to create the values "5, 10, 15, 20, 25, 30, 35, 40" for *k*, and then do something with each.

The printed result shows that the score decreases as *k* increases:

```
(5,1938.858341805931)
(10,1689.4950178959496)
(15,1381.315620528147)
(20,1318.256644582388)
(25,932.0599419255919)
(30,594.2334547238697)
(35,829.5361226176625)
(40,424.83023056838846)
```

> Again, your values will be somewhat different. The clustering depends on a randomly chosen initial set of centroids.

However, this much is obvious. As more clusters are added, it should always be possible to make data points closer to a nearest centroid. In fact, if *k* is chosen to equal the number of data points, the average distance will be 0, because every point will be its own cluster of one!

Worse, in the preceding results, the distance for *k* = 35 is higher than for *k* = 30. This shouldn't happen, because higher *k* always permits at least as good a clustering as a lower *k*. The problem is that K-means is not necessarily able to find the optimal clustering for a given *k*. Its iterative process can converge from a random starting point to a local minimum, which may be good but not optimal.

This is still true even when more intelligent methods are used to choose initial centroids. K-means++ and K-means|| are variants with selection algorithms that are more likely to choose diverse, separated centroids, and lead more reliably to a good clustering. Spark MLlib, in fact, implements K-means|| (*http://stanford.io/1ALCOaN*).

However, all still have an element of randomness in selection, and can't guarantee an optimal clustering.

The random starting set of clusters chosen for $k = 35$ perhaps led to a particularly suboptimal clustering, or, it may have stopped early before it reached its local optimum. We can improve this by running the clustering many times for a value of k, with a different random starting centroid set each time, and picking the best clustering. The algorithm exposes setRuns() to set the number of times the clustering is run for one k.

We can improve it by running the iteration longer. The algorithm has a threshold via setEpsilon() that controls the minimum amount of cluster centroid movement that is considered significant; lower values means the K-means algorithm will let the centroids continue to move longer.

Run the same test again, but try larger values, from 30 to 100. In the following example, the range from 30 to 100 is turned into a parallel collection in Scala. This causes the computation for each k to happen in parallel *in the Spark shell*. Spark will manage the computation of each at the same time. Of course, the computation of each k is also a distributed operation on the cluster. It's parallelism inside parallelism. This may increase overall throughput by fully exploiting a large cluster, although at some point, submitting a very large number of tasks simultaneously will become counterproductive:

```
...
kmeans.setRuns(10)
kmeans.setEpsilon(1.0e-6) ❶
...
(30 to 100 by 10).par.map(k => (k, clusteringScore(data, k))).
  toList.foreach(println)
```

❶ Decrease from default of 1.0e-4

This time, scores decrease consistently:

```
(30,862.9165758614838)
(40,801.679800071455)
(50,379.7481910409938)
(60,358.6387344388997)
(70,265.1383809649689)
(80,232.78912076732163)
(90,230.0085251067184)
(100,142.84374573413373)
```

We want to find a point past which increasing k stops reducing the score much, or an "elbow" in a graph of k versus score, which is generally decreasing but eventually flattens out. Here, it seems to be decreasing notably past 100. The right value of k may be past 100.

Visualization in R

At this point, it could be useful to look at a plot of the data points. Spark itself has no tools for visualization. However, data can be easily exported to HDFS, and then read into a statistical environment like R (*http://www.r-project.org/*). This brief section will demonstrate using R to visualize the data set.

While R provides libraries for plotting points in two or three dimensions, this data set is 38-dimensional. It will have to be projected down into at most three dimensions. Further, R itself is not suited to handle large data sets, and this data set is certainly large for R. It will have to be sampled to fit into memory in R.

To start, build a model with $k = 100$ and map each data point to a cluster number. Write the features as lines of CSV text to a file on HDFS:

```
val sample = data.map(datum =>
  model.predict(datum) + "," + datum.toArray.mkString(",") ❶
).sample(false, 0.05)

sample.saveAsTextFile("/user/ds/sample")
```

❶ mkString joins a collection to a string with a delimiter

sample() is used to select a small subset of all lines, so that it more comfortably fits in memory in R. Here, 5% of the lines are selected (without replacement).

The following R code reads CSV data from HDFS. This can also be accomplished with libraries like rhdfs (*https://github.com/RevolutionAnalytics/RHadoop/wiki*), which can take some setup and installation. Here it just uses a locally installed hdfs command from a Hadoop distribution, for simplicity. This requires HADOOP_CONF_DIR to be set to the location of Hadoop configuration, with configuration that defines the location of the HDFS cluster.

It creates a three-dimensional data set out of a 38-dimensional data set by choosing three random unit vectors and projecting the data onto these three vectors. This is a simplistic, rough-and-ready form of dimension reduction. Of course, there are more sophisticated dimension reduction algorithms, like Principal Component Analysis (*http://en.wikipedia.org/wiki/Principal_component_analysis*) or the Singular Value Decomposition (*http://en.wikipedia.org/wiki/Singular_value_decomposition*). These are available in R, but take much longer to run. For purposes of visualization in this example, a random projection achieves much the same result, faster.

The result is presented as an interactive 3D visualization. Note that this will require running R in an environment that supports the rgl library and graphics (for example, on Mac OS X, it requires X11 from Apple's Developer Tools to be installed):

```
install.packages("rgl") # First time only
library(rgl)
```

```
clusters_data <-
  read.csv(pipe("hadoop fs -cat /user/ds/sample/*")) ❶
clusters <- clusters_data[1]
data <- data.matrix(clusters_data[-c(1)])
rm(clusters_data)

random_projection <- matrix(data = rnorm(3*ncol(data)), ncol = 3)
random_projection_norm <-
  random_projection /
    sqrt(rowSums(random_projection*random_projection)) ❷

projected_data <- data.frame(data %*% random_projection_norm) ❸

num_clusters <- nrow(unique(clusters))
palette <- rainbow(num_clusters)
colors = sapply(clusters, function(c) palette[c])
plot3d(projected_data, col = colors, size = 10)
```

❶ Read cluster and data with `hdfs` command

❷ Create random unit vectors in 3D

❸ Project the data

The resulting visualization in Figure 5-1 shows data points shaded by cluster number in 3D space. Many points fall on top of one another, and the result is sparse and hard to interpret. However, the dominant feature of the visualization is its "L" shape. The points seem to vary along two distinct dimensions, and little in other dimensions.

This makes sense, because the data set has two features that are on a much larger scale than the others. Whereas most features have values between 0 and 1, the bytes-sent and bytes-received features vary from 0 to tens of thousands. The Euclidean distance between points is therefore almost completely determined by these two features. It's almost as if the other features don't exist! So, it's important to normalize away these differences in scale to put features on near-equal footing.

Feature Normalization

We can normalize each feature by converting it to a standard score (*http://en.wikipe dia.org/wiki/Standard_score*). This means subtracting the mean of the feature's values from each value, and dividing by the standard deviation, as shown in the standard score equation:

$$normalized_i = \frac{feature_i - \mu_i}{\sigma_i}$$

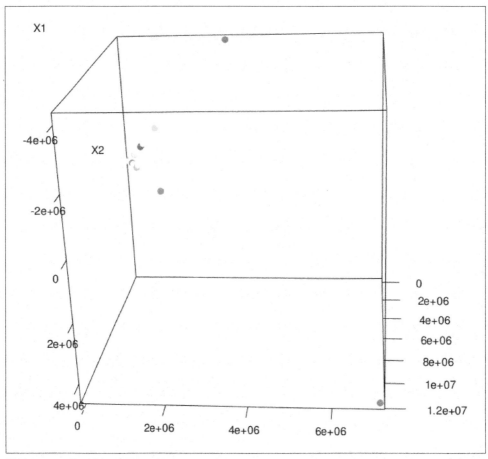

Figure 5-1. Random 3D projection

In fact, subtracting means has no effect on the clustering, because the subtraction effectively shifts all of the data points by the same amount in the same directions. This does not affect interpoint Euclidean distances. For consistency, however, the mean will be subtracted anyway.

Standard scores can be computed from the count, sum, and sum-of-squares of each feature. This can be done jointly, with `reduce` operations used to add entire arrays at once, and `aggregate` used to accumulate sums of squares from an array of zeros:

```
val dataAsArray = data.map(_.toArray)
val numCols = dataAsArray.first().length
val n = dataAsArray.count()
val sums = dataAsArray.reduce(
  (a,b) => a.zip(b).map(t => t._1 + t._2))
val sumSquares = dataAsArray.aggregate(
    new Array[Double](numCols)
```

```
    )(
      (a,b) => a.zip(b).map(t => t._1 + t._2 * t._2),
      (a,b) => a.zip(b).map(t => t._1 + t._2)
    )
val stdevs = sumSquares.zip(sums).map {
  case(sumSq,sum) => math.sqrt(n*sumSq - sum*sum)/n
}
val means = sums.map(_ / n)

def normalize(datum: Vector) = {
  val normalizedArray = (datum.toArray, means, stdevs).zipped.map(
    (value, mean, stdev) =>
      if (stdev <= 0) (value - mean) else (value - mean) / stdev
  )
  Vectors.dense(normalizedArray)
}
```

We can run the same test with normalized data, on a higher range of k:

```
val normalizedData = data.map(normalize).cache()
(60 to 120 by 10).par.map(k =>
  (k, clusteringScore(normalizedData, k))).toList.foreach(println)
```

This yields some evidence that $k = 100$ may be a reasonably good choice:

```
(60,0.0038662664156513646)
(70,0.003284024281015404)
(80,0.00308768458568131)
(90,0.0028326001931487516)
(100,0.002550914511356702)
(110,0.002516106387216959)
(120,0.0021317966227260106)
```

Another 3D visualization of the normalized data points reveals a richer structure, as expected. Some points are spaced in regular, discrete intervals in a direction; these are likely projections of discrete dimensions in the data, like counts. With 100 clusters, it's hard to make out which points come from which clusters. One large cluster seems to dominate, and many clusters correspond to small compact subregions (some of which are omitted from this zoomed detail of the entire 3D visualization). The result, shown in Figure 5-2, does not necessarily advance the analysis, but is an interesting sanity check.

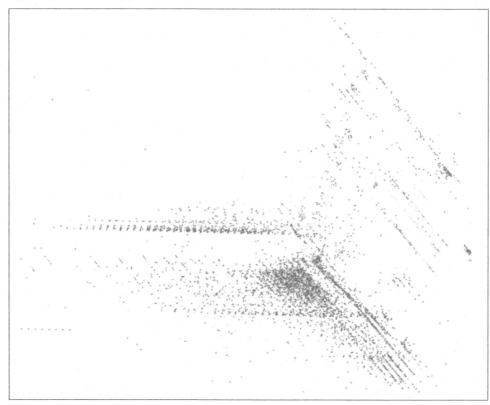

Figure 5-2. Random 3D projection of normalized data

Categorical Variables

Earlier, three categorical features were excluded, because nonnumeric features can't be used with the Euclidean distance function that K-means uses in MLlib. This is the reverse of the issue noted in Chapter 4, where numeric features were used to represent categorical values, but a categorical feature was desired.

The categorical features can translate into several binary indicator features using one-hot encoding, which can be viewed as numeric dimensions. For example, the second column contains the protocol type: `tcp`, `udp`, or `icmp`. This feature could be thought of as *three* features, perhaps `is_tcp`, `is_udp`, and `is_icmp`. The single feature value `tcp` might become `1,0,0`; udp might be `0,1,0`; and so on. The accompanying source code implements this transformation to replace these categorical values with a one-hot encoding; it is not reproduced here.

This new, larger data set can be normalized again, and clustered again, perhaps trying larger *k* as well. Because the individual clustering jobs are getting large, it may be best to remove the `.par` and return to computing one model at a time:

```
(80,0.038867919526032156)
(90,0.03633130732772693)
(100,0.025534431488492226)
(110,0.02349979741110366)
(120,0.01579211360618129)
(130,0.011155491535441237)
(140,0.010273258258627196)
(150,0.008779632525837223)
(160,0.009000858639068911)
```

These sample results suggest $k = 150$, although even with 10 runs each, at this size, $k = 160$ fails to produce a better clustering. There is still some uncertainty about these scores.

Using Labels with Entropy

Earlier, we used the given label for each data point to create a quick sanity check of the quality of the clustering. This notion can be formalized further and used as an alternative means of evaluating clustering quality, and therefore, of choosing k.

It stands to reason that a good clustering would create clusters that contain one or a few types of the known attacks, and little of anything else. You may recall from Chapter 4 that we have metrics for homogeneity: Gini impurity and entropy. Entropy will be used here for illustration.

A good clustering would have clusters whose collections of labels are homogeneous and so have low entropy. A weighted average of entropy can therefore be used as a cluster score:

```
def entropy(counts: Iterable[Int]) = {
  val values = counts.filter(_ > 0)
  val n: Double = values.sum
  values.map { v =>
    val p = v / n
    -p * math.log(p)
  }.sum
}

def clusteringScore(
    normalizedLabelsAndData: RDD[(String,Vector)],
    k: Int) = {
  ...

  val model = kmeans.run(normalizedLabelsAndData.values)

  val labelsAndClusters =
    normalizedLabelsAndData.mapValues(model.predict) ❶

  val clustersAndLabels = labelsAndClusters.map(_.swap) ❷
```

```
val labelsInCluster = clustersAndLabels.groupByKey().values ❸

val labelCounts = labelsInCluster.map(
  _.groupBy(l => l).map(_._2.size)) ❹

val n = normalizedLabelsAndData.count()

labelCounts.map(m => m.sum * entropy(m)).sum / n ❺
}
```

❶ Predict cluster for each datum

❷ Swap keys/values

❸ Extract collections of labels, per cluster

❹ Count labels in collections

❺ Average entropy weighted by cluster size

As before, this analysis can be used to obtain some idea of a suitable value of k. Entropy will not necessarily decrease as k increases, so it is possible to look for a local minimum value. Here again, results suggest $k = 150$ is a reasonable choice:

```
(80,1.0079370754411006)
(90,0.9637681417493124)
(100,0.9403615199645968)
(110,0.4731764778562114)
(120,0.370566369006883805)
(130,0.36584249542565717)
(140,0.10532529463749402)
(150,0.10380319762303959)
(160,0.14469129892579444)
```

Clustering in Action

Finally, with confidence, we can cluster the full normalized data set with $k = 150$. Again, we can print the labels for each cluster to get some sense of the resulting clustering. Clusters do seem to contain mostly one label:

```
0            back.        6
0         neptune.   821239
0          normal.      255
0       portsweep.      114
0           satan.       31
...
90        ftp_write.       1
90       loadmodule.       1
90          neptune.       1
90           normal.   41253
```

```
90      warezclient.    12
...
93          normal.      8
93        portsweep.   7365
93      warezclient.      1
```

Now, we can make an actual anomaly detector. Anomaly detection amounts to measuring a new data point's distance to its nearest centroid. If this distance exceeds some threshold, it is anomalous. This threshold might be chosen to be the distance of, say, the 100th-farthest data point from among known data:

```
val distances = normalizedData.map(
  datum => distToCentroid(datum, model)
)
val threshold = distances.top(100).last
```

The final step is to apply this threshold to all new data points as they arrive. For example, Spark Streaming can be used to apply this function to small batches of input data arriving from sources like Flume, Kafka, or files on HDFS. Data points exceeding the threshold might trigger an alert that sends an email or updates a database.

As an example, we will apply it to the original data set, to see some of the data points that are, we might believe, most anomalous within the input. To interpret the results, we keep the original line of input with the parsed feature vector:

```
val model = ...
val originalAndData = ...
val anomalies = originalAndData.filter { case (original, datum) =>
  val normalized = normalizeFunction(datum)
  distToCentroid(normalized, model) > threshold
}.keys
```

For fun, the winner is the following data point, which is the most anomalous in the data, according to this model:

```
0,tcp,http,S1,299,26280,
0,0,0,1,0,1,0,1,0,0,0,0,0,0,0,15,16,
0.07,0.06,0.00,0.00,1.00,0.00,0.12,231,255,1.00,
0.00,0.00,0.01,0.01,0.01,0.00,0.00,normal.
```

A network security expert would be more able to interpret why this is or is not actually a strange connection. It appears unusual at least because it is labeled normal., but involved more than 200 different connections to the same service in a short time, and ended in an unusual TCP state, S1.

Where to Go from Here

The KMeansModel is, by itself, the essence of an anomaly detection system. The preceding code demonstrated how to apply it to data to detect anomalies. This same code could be used within Spark Streaming (*https://spark.apache.org/streaming/*) to score new data as it arrives in near real time, and perhaps trigger an alert or review.

MLlib also includes a variation called `StreamingKMeans`, which can update a clustering incrementally as new data arrives in a `StreamingKMeansModel`. We could use this to continue to learn, approximately, how new data affects the clustering, and not just assess new data against existing clusters. It can be integrated with Spark Streaming as well.

This model is only a simplistic one. For example, Euclidean distance is used in this example because it is the only distance function supported by Spark MLlib at this time. In the future, it may be possible to use distance functions that can better account for the distributions of and correlations between features, such as the Mahalanobis distance (*http://en.wikipedia.org/wiki/Mahalanobis_distance*).

There are also more sophisticated cluster quality evaluation metrics (*http://en.wikipedia.org/wiki/Cluster_analysis#Internal_evaluation*) that could be applied, even without labels, to pick *k*, such as the Silhouette coefficient (*http://en.wikipedia.org/wiki/Silhouette_(clustering)*). These tend to evaluate not just closeness of points within one cluster, but closeness of points to other clusters.

Finally, different models could be applied too, instead of simple K-means clustering; for example, a Gaussian mixture model (*http://bit.ly/1GzKhLJ*) or DBSCAN (*http://bit.ly/1GzKCOG*) could capture more subtle relationships between data points and the cluster centers.

Implementations of these may become available in Spark MLlib or other Spark-based libraries in the future.

Of course, clustering isn't just for anomaly detection either. In fact, it's more usually associated with use cases where the actual clusters matter! For example, clustering can also be used to group customers according to their behaviors, preferences, and attributes. Each cluster, by itself, might represent a usefully distinguishable type of customer. This is a more data-driven way to segment customers rather than leaning on arbitrary, generic divisions like "age 20–34" and "female."

CHAPTER 6

Understanding Wikipedia with Latent Semantic Analysis

Sandy Ryza

Where are the Snowdens of yesteryear?
—Capt. Yossarian

Most of the work in data engineering consists of assembling data into some sort of queryable format. We can query structured data with formal languages. For example, when this structured data is tabular, we can use SQL. While it is by no means an easy task in practice, at a high level, the work of making tabular data accessible is often straightforward—pull data from a variety of data sources into a single table, perhaps cleansing or fusing intelligently along the way. Unstructured text data presents a whole different set of challenges. The process of preparing data into a format that humans can interact with is not so much "assembly," but rather "indexing" in the nice case or "coercion" when things get ugly. A standard search index permits fast queries for the set of documents that contains a given set of terms. Sometimes, however, we want to find documents that relate to the concepts surrounding a particular word whether or not the documents contain that exact string. Standard search indexes often fail to capture the latent structure in the text's subject matter.

Latent Semantic Analysis (LSA) is a technique in natural language processing and information retrieval that seeks to better understand a corpus of documents and the relationships between the words in those documents. It attempts to distill the corpus into a set of relevant *concepts*. Each concept captures a thread of variation in the data and often corresponds to a topic that the corpus discusses. Without yet delving into the mathematics, each concept consists of three attributes: a level of affinity for each document in the corpus, a level of affinity for each term in the corpus, and an importance score reflecting how useful the concept is in describing variance in the data set. For example, LSA might discover a concept with high affinity for the terms "Asimov" and "robot," and high affinity for the documents "Foundation series" and "Science Fiction." By selecting only the most important concepts, LSA can throw away some irrelevant noise and merge co-occurring strands to come up with a simpler representation of the data.

We can employ this concise representation in a variety of tasks. It can provide scores of similarity between terms and other terms, between documents and other documents, and between terms and documents. By encapsulating the patterns of variance in the corpus, it can base these scores on a deeper understanding than simply counting occurrences and co-occurrences of words. These similarity measures are ideal for tasks such as finding the set of documents relevant to query terms, grouping documents into topics, and finding related words.

LSA discovers this lower-dimensional representation using a linear algebra technique called *singular value decomposition* (SVD). SVD can be thought of as a more powerful version of the ALS factorization described in Chapter 3. It starts with a *term-document matrix* generated through counting word frequencies for each document. In this matrix, each document corresponds to a column, each term corresponds to a row, and each element represents the importance of a word to a document. SVD then factorizes this matrix into three matrices, one of which expresses concepts in regard to documents, one of which expresses concepts in regard to terms, and one of which contains the importance for each concept. The structure of these matrices is such that we can achieve a *low-rank approximation* of the original matrix by removing a set of their rows and columns corresponding to the least important concepts. That is, the matrices in this low-rank approximation can be multiplied to produce a matrix close to the original, with increasing loss of fidelity as each concept is removed.

In this chapter, we'll embark upon the modest task of enabling queries against the full extent of human knowledge, based on its latent semantic relationships. More specifically, we'll apply LSA to a corpus consisting of the full set of articles contained in Wikipedia, about 46 GB of raw text. We'll cover how to use Spark for preprocessing the data: reading it, cleansing it, and coercing it into a numerical form. We'll show how to compute the SVD and explain how to interpret and make use of it.

SVD has wide applications outside LSA. It appears in such diverse places as detecting climatological trends (Michael Mann's famous hockey-stick graph (*http://en.wikipe dia.org/wiki/Hockey_stick_controversy*)), face recognition, and image compression. Spark's implementation can perform the matrix factorization on enormous data sets, which opens up the technique to a whole new set of applications.

The Term-Document Matrix

Before performing any analysis, LSA requires transforming the raw text of the corpus into a term-document matrix. In this matrix, each row represents a term that occurs in the corpus, and each column represents a document. Loosely, the value at each position should correspond to the importance of the row's term to the column's document. A few weighting schemes have been proposed, but by far the most common is *term frequency* times *inverse document frequency*, commonly abbreviated as TF-IDF:

```
def termDocWeight(termFrequencyInDoc: Int, totalTermsInDoc: Int,
    termFreqInCorpus: Int, totalDocs: Int): Double = {
  val tf = termFrequencyInDoc.toDouble / totalTermsInDoc
  val docFreq = totalDocs.toDouble / termFreqInCorpus
  val idf = math.log(docFreq)
  tf * idf
}
```

TF-IDF captures two intuitions about the relevance of a term to a document. First, we would expect that the more often a term occurs in a document, the more important it is to that document. Second, not all terms are equal in a global sense. It is more meaningful to encounter a word that occurs rarely in the entire corpus than a word that appears in most of the documents, thus the metric uses the *inverse* of the word's appearance in documents in the full corpus.

The frequency of words in a corpus tends to be distributed exponentially. A common word will often appear ten times as often as a mildly common word, which in turn might appear ten or a hundred times as often as a rare word. Basing a metric on the raw inverse document frequency would give rare words enormous weight and practically ignore the impact of all other words. To capture this distribution, the scheme uses the *log* of the inverse document frequency. This mellows the differences in document frequencies by transforming the multiplicative gaps between them into additive gaps.

The model relies on a few assumptions. It treats each document as a "bag of words," meaning that it pays no attention to the ordering of words, sentence structure, or negations. By representing each term once, the model has difficulty dealing with polysemy, the use of the same word for multiple meanings. For example, the model can't distinguish between the use of *band* in "Radiohead is the best band ever" and "I broke a rubber band." If both sentences appear often in the corpus, it may come to associate *Radiohead* with *rubber*.

The corpus has 10 million documents. Counting obscure technical jargon, the English language contains about a million terms, some subset in the tens of thousands of which is likely useful for understanding the corpus. Because the corpus contains far more documents than terms, it makes the most sense to generate the term-document matrix as a row matrix, a collection of sparse vectors, each corresponding to a document.

Getting from the raw Wikipedia dump into this form requires a set of preprocessing steps. First, the input consists of a single enormous XML file with documents delimited by <page> tags. This needs to be broken up to feed to the next step, turning

Wiki-formatting into plain text. The plain text then is split into tokens, which are reduced from their different inflectional forms to a root term through a process called *lemmatization*. These tokens can then be used to compute term frequencies and document frequencies. A final step ties these frequencies together and builds the actual vector objects.

The first steps can be performed for each document fully in parallel (which in Spark means as a set of map functions), but computing the inverse document frequencies requires aggregation across all the documents. A number of useful general NLP and Wikipedia-specific extraction tools exist that can aid in these tasks.

Getting the Data

Wikipedia makes dumps of all its articles available. The full dump comes in a single large XML file. These can be downloaded from *http://dumps.wikimedia.org/enwiki* and then placed on HDFS. For example:

```
$ curl -s -L http://dumps.wikimedia.org/enwiki/20150304/\
$ enwiki-20150304-pages-articles-multistream.xml.bz2 \
$   | bzip2 -cd \
$   | hadoop fs -put - /user/ds/wikidump.xml
```

This will take a little while.

Parsing and Preparing the Data

Here's a snippet at the beginning of the dump:

```
<page>
  <title>Anarchism</title>
  <ns>0</ns>
  <id>12</id>
  <revision>
    <id>584215651</id>
    <parentid>584213644</parentid>
    <timestamp>2013-12-02T15:14:01Z</timestamp>
    <contributor>
      <username>AnomieBOT</username>
      <id>7611264</id>
    </contributor>
    <comment>Rescuing orphaned refs (&quot;autogenerated1&quot; from rev
    584155010; &quot;bbc&quot; from rev 584155010)</comment>
    <text xml:space="preserve">{{Redirect|Anarchist|the fictional character|
    Anarchist (comics)}}
{{Redirect|Anarchists}}
{{pp-move-indef}}
{{Anarchism sidebar}}

'''Anarchism''' is a [[political philosophy]] that advocates [[stateless society|
```

```
stateless societies]] often defined as [[self-governance|self-governed]] voluntary
institutions,&lt;ref&gt;&quot;ANARCHISM, a social philosophy that rejects
authoritarian government and maintains that voluntary institutions are best suited
to express man's natural social tendencies.&quot; George Woodcock.
&quot;Anarchism&quot; at The Encyclopedia of Philosophy&lt;/ref&gt;&lt;ref&gt;
&quot;In a society developed on these lines, the voluntary associations which
already now begin to cover all the fields of human activity would take a still
greater extension so as to substitute
...
```

Let's fire up the Spark shell. In this chapter, we rely on several libraries to make our lives easier. The GitHub repo contains a Maven project that can be used to build a JAR file that packages all these dependencies together:

```
$ cd lsa/
$ mvn package
$ spark-shell --jars target/ch06-lsa-1.0.0.jar
```

We've provided a class, XmlInputFormat, derived from the Apache Mahout project, that can split up the enormous Wikipedia dump into documents. To create an RDD with it:

```
import com.cloudera.datascience.common.XmlInputFormat
import org.apache.hadoop.conf.Configuration
import org.apache.hadoop.io._

val path = "hdfs:///user/ds/wikidump.xml"
@transient val conf = new Configuration()
conf.set(XmlInputFormat.START_TAG_KEY, "<page>")
conf.set(XmlInputFormat.END_TAG_KEY, "</page>")
val kvs = sc.newAPIHadoopFile(path, classOf[XmlInputFormat],
  classOf[LongWritable], classOf[Text], conf)
val rawXmls = kvs.map(p => p._2.toString)
```

Turning the Wiki XML into the plain text of article contents could require a chapter of its own, but, luckily, the Cloud9 project provides APIs that handle this entirely:

```
import edu.umd.cloud9.collection.wikipedia.language._
import edu.umd.cloud9.collection.wikipedia._

def wikiXmlToPlainText(xml: String): Option[(String, String)] = {
  val page = new EnglishWikipediaPage()
  WikipediaPage.readPage(page, xml)
  if (page.isEmpty) None
  else Some((page.getTitle, page.getContent))
}

val plainText = rawXmls.flatMap(wikiXmlToPlainText)
```

Lemmatization

With the plain text in hand, next we need to turn it into a bag of terms. This step requires care for a couple of reasons. First, common words like *the* and *is* take up space but at best offer no useful information to the model. Filtering out a list of *stop words* can both save space and improve fidelity. Second, terms with the same meaning can often take slightly different forms. For example, *monkey* and *monkeys* do not deserve to be separate terms. Nor do *nationalize* and *nationalization*. Combining these different inflectional forms into single terms is called *stemming* or *lemmatization*. Stemming refers to heuristics-based techniques for chopping off characters at the ends of words, while lemmatization refers to more principled approaches. For example, the former might truncate *drew* to *dr*, while the latter might more correctly output *draw*. The Stanford Core NLP project provides an excellent lemmatizer with a Java API that Scala can take advantage of. The following snippet takes the RDD of plain-text documents and both lemmatizes it and filters out stop words. Note that this code relies on a file of stopwords called *stopwords.txt*, which is available in the accompanying source code repo at *https://github.com/sryza/aas/blob/master/ch06-lsa/src/main/resources/stopwords.txt* and should be downloaded into the current working directory first:

```scala
import scala.collection.JavaConversions._
import edu.stanford.nlp.pipeline._
import edu.stanford.nlp.ling.CoreAnnotations._

def createNLPPipeline(): StanfordCoreNLP = {
  val props = new Properties()
  props.put("annotators", "tokenize, ssplit, pos, lemma")
  new StanfordCoreNLP(props)
}

def isOnlyLetters(str: String): Boolean = {
  str.forall(c => Character.isLetter(c))
}

def plainTextToLemmas(text: String, stopWords: Set[String],
    pipeline: StanfordCoreNLP): Seq[String] = {
  val doc = new Annotation(text)
  pipeline.annotate(doc)

  val lemmas = new ArrayBuffer[String]()
  val sentences = doc.get(classOf[SentencesAnnotation])
  for (sentence <- sentences;
      token <- sentence.get(classOf[TokensAnnotation])) {
    val lemma = token.get(classOf[LemmaAnnotation])
    if (lemma.length > 2 && !stopWords.contains(lemma)
        && isOnlyLetters(lemma)) { ❶
      lemmas += lemma.toLowerCase
    }
```

```
    }
    lemmas
  }

  val stopWords = sc.broadcast(
    scala.io.Source.fromFile("stopwords.txt").getLines().toSet).value

  val lemmatized: RDD[Seq[String]] = plainText.mapPartitions(it => {
    val pipeline = createNLPPipeline()
    it.map { case(title, contents) =>
      plainTextToLemmas(contents, stopWords, pipeline)
    }
  }) ❷
```

❶ Specify some minimal requirements on lemmas to weed out garbage.

❷ Use mapPartitions so that we only initialize the NLP pipeline object once per partition instead of once per document.

Computing the TF-IDFs

At this point, lemmatized refers to an RDD of arrays of terms, each corresponding to a document. The next step is to compute the frequencies for each term within each document and for each term within the entire corpus. The following code builds up a map of terms to occurrence counts for each document:

```
import scala.collection.mutable.HashMap

val docTermFreqs = lemmatized.map(terms => {
  val termFreqs = terms.foldLeft(new HashMap[String, Int]()) {
    (map, term) => {
      map += term -> (map.getOrElse(term, 0) + 1)
      map
    }
  }
  termFreqs
})
```

The resulting RDD will be used at least twice after this point: to calculate the inverse document frequencies and to calculate the final term-document matrix. So caching it in memory is a good idea:

```
docTermFreqs.cache()
```

It is worth considering a couple of approaches for calculating the document frequencies (i.e., for each term, the number of documents in which it appears within the entire corpus). The first uses the aggregate action to build a local map of terms to frequencies at each partition and then merge all these maps at the driver. aggregate accepts two functions: a function for merging a record into the per-partition result object and a function for merging two of these result objects together. In this case, each record is a map of terms to frequencies within a document, and the result object is a map of terms to frequencies within the set of documents. When the records being aggregated and the result object have the same type (e.g., in a sum), reduce is useful, but when the types differ, as they do here, aggregate is a more powerful alternative:

```
val zero = new HashMap[String, Int]()
def merge(dfs: HashMap[String, Int], tfs: HashMap[String, Int])
  : HashMap[String, Int] = {
  tfs.keySet.foreach { term =>
    dfs += term -> (dfs.getOrElse(term, 0) + 1)
  }
  dfs
}
def comb(dfs1: HashMap[String, Int], dfs2: HashMap[String, Int])
  : HashMap[String, Int] = {
  for ((term, count) <- dfs2) {
    dfs1 += term -> (dfs1.getOrElse(term, 0) + count)
  }
  dfs1
}
docTermFreqs.aggregate(zero)(merge, comb)
```

Running this on the entire corpus spits out:

```
java.lang.OutOfMemoryError: Java heap space
```

What is going on? It appears that the full set of terms from all the documents cannot fit into memory and is overwhelming the driver. Just how many terms are there?

```
docTermFreqs.flatMap(_.keySet).distinct().count()
...
res0: Long = 9014592
```

Many of these terms are garbage or appear only once in the corpus. Filtering out less frequent terms can both improve performance and remove noise. A reasonable choice is to leave out all but the top N most frequent words, where N is somewhere in the tens of thousands. The following code computes the document frequencies in a distributed fashion. This resembles the classic word count job widely used to showcase a simple MapReduce program. A key-value pair with the term and the number 1 is emitted for each unique occurrence of a term in a document, and a reduceByKey sums these numbers across the data set for each term:

```
val docFreqs = docTermFreqs.flatMap(_.keySet).map((_, 1)).
  reduceByKey(_ + _)
```

The top action returns the N records with the highest values to the driver. A custom Ordering is used to allow it to operate on term-count pairs:

```
val numTerms = 50000
val ordering = Ordering.by[(String, Int), Int](_._2)
val topDocFreqs = docFreqs.top(numTerms)(ordering)
```

With the document frequencies in hand, we can compute the inverse document frequencies. Calculating these on the driver instead of in executors each time a term is referenced saves some redundant floating-point math:

```
val numDocs = docTermFreqs.count()
val idfs = docFreqs.map{
  case (term, count) => (term, math.log(numDocs.toDouble / count))
}.collectAsMap()
```

The term frequencies and inverse document frequencies constitute the numbers needed to compute the TF-IDF vectors. However, there remains one final hitch: the data currently resides in maps keyed by strings, but feeding these into MLlib requires transforming them into vectors keyed by integers. To generate the latter from the former, assign a unique ID to each term:

```
val idTerms = idfs.keys.zipWithIndex.toMap
val termIds = idTerms.map(_.swap)
```

Because the term ID map is fairly large and we'll use it in a few different places, let's broadcast it along with the IDFs:

```
val bIdfs = sc.broadcast(idfs).value
val bIdTerms = sc.broadcast(idTerms).value
```

Finally, we tie it all together by creating a TF-IDF-weighted vector for each document. Note that we use sparse vectors because each document will only contain a small subset of the full set of terms. We can construct MLlib's sparse vectors by giving a size and a list of index-value pairs:

```
import org.apache.spark.mllib.linalg.Vectors

val vecs = docTermFreqs.map(termFreqs => {
  val docTotalTerms = termFreqs.values.sum
  val termScores = termFreqs.filter {
    case (term, freq) => bIdTerms.contains(term)
  }.map{
    case (term, freq) => (bIdTerms(term),
      bIdfs(term) * termFreqs(term) / docTotalTerms)
  }.toSeq
  Vectors.sparse(bIdTerms.size, termScores)
})
```

Singular Value Decomposition

With the term-document matrix M in hand, the analysis can proceed to the factorization and dimensionality reduction. MLlib contains an implementation of the singular value decomposition (SVD) that can handle enormous matrices. The singular value decomposition takes an $m \times n$ matrix and returns three matrices that approximately equal it when multiplied together:

$$M \approx U\, S\, V^T$$

- U is an $m \times k$ matrix whose columns form an orthonormal basis for the document space.
- S is a $k \times k$ diagonal matrix, each of whose entries correspond to the strength of one of the concepts.
- V^T is a $k \times n$ matrix whose columns form an orthonormal basis for the term space.

In the LSA case, m is the number of documents and n is the number of terms. The decomposition is parameterized with a number k, less than or equal to n, that indicates how many concepts to keep around. When $k = n$, the product of the factor matrices reconstitutes the original matrix exactly. When $k < n$, the multiplication results in a low-rank approximation of the original matrix. k is typically chosen to be much smaller than n. SVD ensures that the approximation will be the closest possible to the original matrix (as defined by the L2 Norm—that is, the sum of squares—of the difference), given the constraint that it needs to be expressible in only k concepts.

To find the singular value decomposition of a matrix, simply wrap an RDD of row vectors in a `RowMatrix` and call `computeSVD`:

```
import org.apache.spark.mllib.linalg.distributed.RowMatrix

vecs.cache()
val mat = new RowMatrix(vecs)
val k = 1000
val svd = mat.computeSVD(k, computeU=true)
```

The RDD should be cached in memory beforehand because the computation requires multiple passes over the data. The computation requires $O(nk)$ storage on the driver, $O(n)$ storage for each task, and $O(k)$ passes over the data.

As a reminder, a vector in *term space* means a vector with a weight on every term, a vector in *document space* means a vector with a weight on every document, and a vector in *concept space* means a vector with a weight on every concept. Each term, document, or concept defines an *axis* in its respective space, and the weight ascribed to the term, document, or concept means a length along that axis. Every term or document vector can be mapped to a corresponding vector in concept space. Every concept vector has possibly many term and document vectors that map to it, including a canonical term and document vector that it maps to when transformed in the reverse direction.

V is an $n \times k$ matrix where each row corresponds to a term and each column corresponds to a concept. It defines a mapping between term space (the space where each point is an n-dimensional vector holding a weight for each term) and concept space (the space where each point is a k-dimensional vector holding a weight for each concept).

Similarly, U is an $m \times k$ matrix where each row corresponds to a document and each column corresponds to a concept. It defines a mapping between document space and concept space.

S is a $k \times k$ diagonal matrix that holds the singular values. Each diagonal element in S corresponds to a single concept (and thus a column in V and a column in U). The magnitude of each of these singular values corresponds to the importance of that concept: its power in explaining the variance in the data. An (inefficient) implementation of SVD could find the rank-k decomposition by starting with the rank-n decomposition and throwing away the $n - k$ smallest singular values until there are k left (along with their corresponding columns in U and V). A key insight of LSA is that only a small number of concepts are important to representing that data. The entries in the S matrix directly indicate the importance of each concept. They also happen to be the square roots of the eigenvalues of $M\,M^T$.

Finding Important Concepts

So SVD outputs a bunch of numbers. How can we inspect these to verify they actually relate to anything useful? The V matrix represents concepts through the terms that are important to them. As discussed earlier, V contains a column for every concept and a row for every term. The value at each position can be interpreted as the relevance of that term to that concept. This means that the most relevant terms to each of the top concepts can be found with something like this:

```scala
import scala.collection.mutable.ArrayBuffer

val v = svd.V
val topTerms = new ArrayBuffer[Seq[(String, Double)]]()
val arr = v.toArray
for (i <- 0 until numConcepts) {
  val offs = i * v.numRows
  val termWeights = arr.slice(offs, offs + v.numRows).zipWithIndex
  val sorted = termWeights.sortBy(-_._1)
  topTerms += sorted.take(numTerms).map{
    case (score, id) => (termIds(id), score)
  }
}
topTerms
```

Note that V is a matrix in memory locally in the driver process, and the computation occurs in a nondistributed manner. We can find the terms relevant to each of the top concepts in a similar manner using U, but the code looks a little bit different because U is stored as a distributed matrix:

```
def topDocsInTopConcepts(
    svd: SingularValueDecomposition[RowMatrix, Matrix],
    numConcepts: Int, numDocs: Int, docIds: Map[Long, String])
  : Seq[Seq[(String, Double)]] = {
  val u  = svd.U
  val topDocs = new ArrayBuffer[Seq[(String, Double)]]()
  for (i <- 0 until numConcepts) {
    val docWeights = u.rows.map(_.toArray(i)).zipWithUniqueId()
    topDocs += docWeights.top(numDocs).map{
      case (score, id) => (docIds(id), score) ❶
    }
  }
  topDocs
}
```

❶ While it's not difficult, for continuity, we've elided how we create the doc ID mapping. Refer to the repo for this.

Let's inspect the first few concepts:

```
val topConceptTerms = topTermsInTopConcepts(svd, 4, 10, termIds)
val topConceptDocs = topDocsInTopConcepts(svd, 4, 10, docIds)
for ((terms, docs) <- topConceptTerms.zip(topConceptDocs)) {
  println("Concept terms: " + terms.map(_._1).mkString(", "))
  println("Concept docs: " + docs.map(_._1).mkString(", "))
  println()
}
```

```
Concept terms: summary, licensing, fur, logo, album, cover, rationale,
  gif, use, fair
Concept docs: File:Gladys-in-grammarland-cover-1897.png,
  File:Gladys-in-grammarland-cover-2010.png, File:1942ukrpoljudeakt4.jpg,
  File:Σακελλαρίδης.jpg, File:Baghdad-texas.jpg, File:Realistic.jpeg,
  File:DuplicateBoy.jpg, File:Garbo-the-spy.jpg, File:Joysagar.jpg,
  File:RizalHighSchoollogo.jpg

Concept terms: disambiguation, william, james, john, iran, australis,
  township, charles, robert, river
Concept docs: G. australis (disambiguation), F. australis (disambiguation),
  U. australis (disambiguation), L. maritima (disambiguation),
  G. maritima (disambiguation), F. japonica (disambiguation),
  P. japonica (disambiguation), Velo (disambiguation),
  Silencio (disambiguation), TVT (disambiguation)

Concept terms: licensing, disambiguation, australis, maritima, rawal,
  upington, tallulah, chf, satyanarayana, valérie
Concept docs: File:Rethymno.jpg, File:Ladycarolinelamb.jpg,
  File:KeyAirlines.jpg, File:NavyCivValor.gif, File:Vitushka.gif,
  File:DavidViscott.jpg, File:Bigbrother13cast.jpg, File:Rawal Lake1.JPG,
  File:Upington location.jpg, File:CHF SG Viewofaltar01.JPG

Concept terms: licensing, summarysource, summaryauthor, wikipedia,
  summarypicture, summaryfrom, summaryself, rawal, chf, upington
```

```
Concept docs: File:Rethymno.jpg, File:Wristlock4.jpg, File:Meseanlol.jpg,
  File:Sarles.gif, File:SuzlonWinMills.JPG, File:Rawal Lake1.JPG,
  File:CHF SG Viewofaltar01.JPG, File:Upington location.jpg,
  File:Driftwood-cover.jpg, File:Tallulah gorge2.jpg

Concept terms: establishment, norway, country, england, spain, florida,
  chile, colorado, australia, russia
Concept docs: Category:1794 establishments in Norway,
  Category:1838 establishments in Norway,
  Category:1849 establishments in Norway,
  Category:1908 establishments in Norway,
  Category:1966 establishments in Norway,
  Category:1926 establishments in Norway,
  Category:1957 establishments in Norway,
  Template:EstcatCountry1stMillennium,
  Category:2012 establishments in Chile,
  Category:1893 establishments in Chile
```

The documents in the first concept appear to all be image files, and the terms appear to be related to image attributes and licensing. The second concept appears to be disambiguation pages. It seems that perhaps this dump is not restricted to the raw Wikipedia articles and is cluttered by administrative pages as well as discussion pages. Inspecting the output of intermediate stages is useful for catching this kind of issue early. Luckily, it appears that Cloud9 provides some functionality for filtering these out. An updated version of the `wikiXmlToPlainText` method looks like the following:

```
def wikiXmlToPlainText(xml: String): Option[(String, String)] = {
  ...
  if (page.isEmpty || !page.isArticle || page.isRedirect ||
      page.getTitle.contains("(disambiguation)")) {
    None
  } else {
    Some((page.getTitle, page.getContent))
  }
}
```

Rerunning the pipeline on the filtered set of documents yields a much more reasonable result:

```
Concept terms: disambiguation, highway, school, airport, high, refer,
  number, squadron, list, may, division, regiment, wisconsin, channel,
  county
Concept docs: Tri-State Highway (disambiguation),
  Ocean-to-Ocean Highway (disambiguation), Highway 61 (disambiguation),
  Tri-County Airport (disambiguation), Tri-Cities Airport (disambiguation),
  Mid-Continent Airport (disambiguation), 99 Squadron (disambiguation),
  95th Squadron (disambiguation), 94 Squadron (disambiguation),
  92 Squadron (disambiguation)

Concept terms: disambiguation, nihilistic, recklessness, sullen, annealing,
  negativity, initialization, recapitulation, streetwise, pde, pounce,
  revisionism, hyperspace, sidestep, bandwagon
```

Concept docs: Nihilistic (disambiguation), Recklessness (disambiguation),
    Manjack (disambiguation), Wajid (disambiguation), Kopitar (disambiguation),
    Rocourt (disambiguation), QRG (disambiguation),
    Maimaicheng (disambiguation), Varen (disambiguation), Gvr (disambiguation)

Concept terms: department, commune, communes, insee, france, see, also,
    southwestern, oise, marne, moselle, manche, eure, aisne, isère
Concept docs: Communes in France, Saint-Mard, Meurthe-et-Moselle,
    Saint-Firmin, Meurthe-et-Moselle, Saint-Clément, Meurthe-et-Moselle,
    Saint-Sardos, Lot-et-Garonne, Saint-Urcisse, Lot-et-Garonne, Saint-Sernin,
    Lot-et-Garonne, Saint-Robert, Lot-et-Garonne, Saint-Léon, Lot-et-Garonne,
    Saint-Astier, Lot-et-Garonne

Concept terms: genus, species, moth, family, lepidoptera, beetle, bulbophyllum,
    snail, database, natural, find, geometridae, reference, museum, noctuidae
Concept docs: Chelonia (genus), Palea (genus), Argiope (genus), Sphingini,
    Cribrilinidae, Tahla (genus), Gigartinales, Parapodia (genus),
    Alpina (moth), Arycanda (moth)

Concept terms: province, district, municipality, census, rural, iran,
    romanize, population, infobox, azerbaijan, village, town, central,
    settlement, kerman
Concept docs: New York State Senate elections, 2012,
    New York State Senate elections, 2008,
    New York State Senate elections, 2010,
    Alabama State House of Representatives elections, 2010,
    Albergaria-a-Velha, Municipalities of Italy, Municipality of Malmö,
    Delhi Municipality, Shanghai Municipality, Göteborg Municipality

Concept terms: genus, species, district, moth, family, province, iran, rural,
    romanize, census, village, population, lepidoptera, beetle, bulbophyllum
Concept docs: Chelonia (genus), Palea (genus), Argiope (genus), Sphingini,
    Tahla (genus), Cribrilinidae, Gigartinales, Alpina (moth), Arycanda (moth),
    Arauco (moth)

Concept terms: protein, football, league, encode, gene, play, team, bear,
    season, player, club, reading, human, footballer, cup
Concept docs: Protein FAM186B, ARL6IP1, HIP1R, SGIP1, MTMR3,
    Gem-associated protein 6, Gem-associated protein 7, C2orf30, OS9 (gene),
    RP2 (gene)

The first two concepts remain ambiguous, but the rest appear to correspond to meaningful categories. The third appears to be composed of locales in France, the fourth and sixth of animal and bug taxonomies. The fifth concerns elections, municipalities, and government. The articles in the seventh concern proteins, while some of the terms also reference football, perhaps with a crossover of fitness of performance-enhancing drugs? While unexpected words appear in each, all the concepts exhibit some thematic coherence.

Querying and Scoring with the Low-Dimensional Representation

How relevant is a term to a document? How relevant are two terms to each other? Which documents most closely match a set of query terms? The original term-document matrix provides a shallow way to answer these questions. We can achieve a relevance score between two terms by computing the *cosine similarity* between their two column vectors in the matrix. Cosine similarity measures the angle between two vectors. Vectors that point in the same direction in the high-dimensional document space are thought to be relevant to each other. It is computed as the dot product of the vectors divided by the product of their lengths. Cosine similarity sees wide use as a similarity metric between vectors of term and document weights in natural language and information retrieval applications. Likewise, for two documents, a relevance score can be computed as the cosine similarity between their two row vectors. A relevance score between a term and a document can simply be the element in the matrix at the intersection of both.

However, these scores come from shallow knowledge about the relationships between these entities, relying on simple frequency counts. LSA provides the ability to base these scores on a deeper understanding of the corpus. For example, if the term *artillery* appears nowhere in a document on the *Normandy landings* article, but it mentions *howitzer* frequently, the LSA representation may be able to recover the relation between *artillery* and the article based on the co-occurrence of *artillery* and *howitzer* in other documents.

The LSA representation also offers benefits from an efficiency standpoint. It packs the important information into a lower-dimensional representation that can be operated on instead of the original term-document matrix. Consider the task of finding the set of terms most relevant to a particular term. The naive approach requires computing the dot product between that term's column vector and every other column vector in the term-document matrix. This involves a number of multiplications proportional to the number of terms times the number of documents. LSA can achieve the same by looking up its concept-space representation and mapping it back into term space, requiring a number of multiplications only proportional to the number of terms times k. The low-rank approximation encodes the relevant patterns in the data so the full corpus need not be queried.

Term-Term Relevance

LSA understands the relation between two terms as the cosine similarity between their two columns in the reconstructed low-rank matrix; that is, the matrix that would be produced if the three approximate factors were multiplied back together.

One of the ideas behind LSA is that this matrix offers a more useful representation of the data. It offers this in a few ways:

- Accounting for synonymy by condensing related terms.
- Accounting for polysemy by placing less weight on terms that have multiple meanings.
- Throwing out noise.

However, we need not actually calculate the contents of this matrix to discover the cosine similarity. Some linear algebra manipulation reveals that the cosine similarity between two columns in the reconstructed matrix is exactly equal to the cosine similarity between the corresponding columns in $S\ V^T$. Consider the task of finding the set of terms most relevant to a particular term. Finding the cosine similarity between a term and all other terms is equivalent to normalizing each row in $V\ S$ to length 1 and then multiplying the row corresponding to that term by it. Each element in the resulting vector will contain a similarity between a term and the query term.

For the sake of brevity, the implementations of the methods that compute $V\ S$ and normalize its rows are omitted, but they can be found in the repository:

```
import breeze.linalg.{DenseVector => BDenseVector}
import breeze.linalg.{DenseMatrix => BDenseMatrix}

def topTermsForTerm(
    normalizedVS: BDenseMatrix[Double],
    termId: Int): Seq[(Double, Int)] = {
  val rowVec = new BDenseVector[Double](
    row(normalizedVS, termId).toArray) ❶

  val termScores = (normalizedVS * rowVec).toArray.zipWithIndex ❷

  termScores.sortBy(-_._1).take(10) ❸
}

val VS = multiplyByDiagonalMatrix(svd.V, svd.s)

val normalizedVS = rowsNormalized(VS)

def printRelevantTerms(term: String) {
  val id = idTerms(term)
  printIdWeights(topTermsForTerm(normalizedVS, id, termIds)
}
```

❶ Look up the row in VS corresponding to the given term ID

❷ Compute scores against every term

❸ Find the terms with the highest scores

Here are the highest-scored terms for a few example terms:

```
printRelevantTerms("algorithm")

(algorithm,1.000000000000002), (heuristic,0.8773199836391916),
(compute,0.8561015487853708), (constraint,0.8370707630657652),
(optimization,0.8331940333186296), (complexity,0.823738607119692),
(algorithmic,0.8227315888559854), (iterative,0.822364922633442),
(recursive,0.8176921180556759), (minimization,0.8160188481409465)

printRelevantTerms("radiohead")

(radiohead,0.9999999999999993), (lyrically,0.8837403315233519),
(catchy,0.8780717902060333), (riff,0.861326571452104),
(lyricsthe,0.8460798060853993), (lyric,0.8434937575368959),
(upbeat,0.8410212279939793), (song,0.8280655506697948),
(musically,0.8239497926624353), (anthemic,0.8207874883055177)

printRelevantTerms("tarantino")

(tarantino,1.0), (soderbergh,0.780999345687437),
(buscemi,0.7386998898933894), (screenplay,0.7347041267543623),
(spielberg,0.7342534745182226), (dicaprio,0.7279146798149239),
(filmmaking,0.7261103750076819), (lumet,0.7259812377657624),
(directorial,0.7195131565316943), (biopic,0.7164037755577743)
```

Document-Document Relevance

The same goes for computing relevance scores between documents. To find the similarity between two documents, compute the cosine similarity between $u_1^T S$ and $u_2^T S$, where u_i is the row in U corresponding to document i. To find the similarity between a document and all other documents, compute normalized($U S$) u_i.

In this case, the implementation is slightly different because U is backed by an RDD, not a local matrix:

```
import org.apache.spark.mllib.linalg.Matrices

def topDocsForDoc(normalizedUS: RowMatrix, docId: Long)
  : Seq[(Double, Long)] = {
  val docRowArr = row(normalizedUS, docId) ❶
  val docRowVec = Matrices.dense(docRowArr.length, 1, docRowArr)

  val docScores = normalizedUS.multiply(docRowVec) ❷

  val allDocWeights = docScores.rows.map(_.toArray(0)).
    zipWithUniqueId() ❸

  allDocWeights.filter(!_._1.isNaN).top(10) ❹
}
val US = multiplyByDiagonalMatrix(svd.U, svd.s)

val normalizedUS = rowsNormalized(US)
```

```
def printRelevantDocs(doc: String) {
  val id = idDocs(doc)
  printIdWeights(topDocsForDoc(normalizedUS, id, docIds)
}
```

❶ Look up the row in US corresponding to the given doc ID.

❷ Compute scores against every doc.

❸ Find the docs with the highest scores.

❹ Docs can end up with NaN score if their row in U is all zeros. Filter these out.

Here are the most similar documents for a few example documents:

```
printRelevantDocs("Romania")

(Romania,0.9999999999999994), (Roma in Romania,0.9229332158078395),
(Kingdom of Romania,0.9176138537751187),
(Anti-Romanian discrimination,0.9131983116426412),
(Timeline of Romanian history,0.9124093989500675),
(Romania and the euro,0.9123191881625798),
(History of Romania,0.9095848558045102),
(Romania-United States relations,0.9016913779787574),
(Wiesel Commission,0.9016106300096606),
(List of Romania-related topics,0.8981305676612493)

printRelevantDocs("Brad Pitt")

(Brad Pitt,0.9999999999999984), (Aaron Eckhart,0.8935447577397551),
(Leonardo DiCaprio,0.8930359829082504), (Winona Ryder,0.8903497762653693),
(Ryan Phillippe,0.8847178312465214), (Claudette Colbert,0.8812403821804665),
(Clint Eastwood,0.8785765085978459), (Reese Witherspoon,0.876540742663427),
(Meryl Streep in the 2000s,0.8751593996242115),
(Kate Winslet,0.873124888198288)

printRelevantDocs("Radiohead")

(Radiohead,1.0000000000000016), (Fightstar,0.9461712602479349),
(R.E.M.,0.9456251852095919), (Incubus (band),0.9434650141836163),
(Audioslave,0.9411291455765148), (Tonic (band),0.9374518874425788),
(Depeche Mode,0.9370085419199352), (Megadeth,0.9355302294384438),
(Alice in Chains,0.9347862053793862), (Blur (band),0.9347436350811016)
```

Term-Document Relevance

What about computing a relevance score between a term and a document? This is equivalent to finding the element corresponding to that term and document in the reduced-rank approximation of the term-document matrix. This is equal to $u_d^T S v_t$, where u_d is the row in U corresponding to the document and v_t is the row in V corresponding to the term. Some simple linear algebra manipulation reveals that comput-

---

ing a similarity between a term and *every* document is equivalent to $U\,S\,v_t$. Each element in the resulting vector will contain a similarity between a document and the query term. In the other direction, the similarity between a document and every term comes from $u_d^T\,S\,V$:

```scala
def topDocsForTerm(US: RowMatrix, V: Matrix, termId: Int)
  : Seq[(Double, Long)] = {
  val rowArr = row(V, termId).toArray
  val rowVec = Matrices.dense(termRowArr.length, 1, termRowArr)

  val docScores = US.multiply(termRowVec) ❶

  val allDocWeights = docScores.rows.map(_.toArray(0)).
    zipWithUniqueId() ❷
  allDocWeights.top(10)
}

def printRelevantDocs(term: String) {
  val id = idTerms(term)
  printIdWeights(topDocsForTerm(normalizedUS, svd.V, id, docIds)
}
```

❶ Compute scores against every doc

❷ Find the docs with the highest scores

```scala
printRelevantDocs("fir")
```

```
(Silver tree,0.006292909647173194),
(See the forest for the trees,0.004785047583508223),
(Eucalyptus tree,0.004592837783089319),
(Sequoia tree,0.004497446632469554),
(Willow tree,0.004442871594515006),
(Coniferous tree,0.004429936059594164),
(Tulip Tree,0.004420469113273123),
(National tree,0.004381572286629475),
(Cottonwood tree,0.004374705020233878),
(Juniper Tree,0.004370895085141889)
```

```scala
printRelevantDocs("graph")
```

```
(K-factor (graph theory),0.07074443599385992),
(Mesh Graph,0.05843133228896666), (Mesh graph,0.05843133228896666),
(Grid Graph,0.05762071784234877), (Grid graph,0.05762071784234877),
(Graph factor,0.056799669054782564), (Graph (economics),0.05603848473056094),
(Skin graph,0.05512936759365371), (Edgeless graph,0.05507918292342141),
(Traversable graph,0.05507918292342141)
```

Multiple-Term Queries

Lastly, what about servicing queries with multiple terms? Finding documents relevant to a single term involved selecting the row corresponding to that term from *V*. This is equivalent to multiplying *V* by a term vector with a single nonzero entry. To move to multiple terms, instead compute the concept-space vector by simply multiplying *V* by a term vector with nonzero entries for multiply terms. To maintain the weighting scheme used for the original term-document matrix, set the value for each term in the query to its inverse document frequency. In one sense, querying in this way is like adding a new document to the corpus with just a few terms, finding its representation as a new row of the low-rank term-document matrix approximation, and then discovering the cosine similarity between it and the other entries in this matrix:

```
import breeze.linalg.{SparseVector => BSparseVector}

def termsToQueryVector(
    terms: Seq[String],
    idTerms: Map[String, Int],
    idfs: Map[String, Double]): BSparseVector[Double] = {
  val indices = terms.map(idTerms(_)).toArray
  val values = terms.map(idfs(_)).toArray
  new BSparseVector[Double](indices, values, idTerms.size)
}

def topDocsForTermQuery(
    US: RowMatrix,
    V: Matrix,
    query: BSparseVector[Double]): Seq[(Double, Long)] = {
  val breezeV = new BDenseMatrix[Double](V.numRows, V.numCols,
    V.toArray)
  val termRowArr = (breezeV.t * query).toArray

  val termRowVec = Matrices.dense(termRowArr.length, 1, termRowArr)

  val docScores = US.multiply(termRowVec) ❶

  val allDocWeights = docScores.rows.map(_.toArray(0)).
    zipWithUniqueId() ❷
  allDocWeights.top(10)
}

def printRelevantDocs(terms: Seq[String]) {
  val queryVec = termsToQueryVector(terms, idTerms, idfs)
  printIdWeights(topDocsForTermQuery(US, svd.V, queryVec), docIds)
}
```

❶ Compute scores against every doc

❷ Find the docs with the highest scores

```
printRelevantDocs(Seq("factorization", "decomposition"))

(K-factor (graph theory),0.04335677416674133),
(Matrix Algebra,0.038074479507460755),
(Matrix algebra,0.038074479507460755),
```

```
(Zero Theorem,0.03758005783639301),
(Birkhoff-von Neumann Theorem,0.03594539874814679),
(Enumeration theorem,0.03498444607374629),
(Pythagoras' theorem,0.03489110483887526),
(Thales theorem,0.03481592682203685),
(Cpt theorem,0.03478175099368145),
(Fuss' theorem,0.034739350150484904)
```

Where to Go from Here

The singular value decomposition and its sister technique, principal component analysis, have a wide variety of applications outside of text analysis. A common method of recognizing human faces known as *eigenfaces* relies on it to understand the patterns of variation in human appearance. In climate research, it is used to find global temperature trends from disparate noisy data sources like tree rings. Michael Mann's famous "hockey stick" graph (*http://en.wikipedia.org/wiki/Hockey_stick_controversy*), depicting the rise of temperatures throughout the 20th century, in fact depicts a *concept*. Singular value decomposition and PCA are also useful in visualization of high-dimensional data sets. When a data set is reduced down to its first two or three concepts, it can be plotted on a graph that humans can view.

A variety of other methods exist for understanding large corpuses of text. For example, a technique known as Latent Dirichlet Allocation (*http://en.wikipedia.org/wiki/Latent_Dirichlet_allocation*) (LDA) is useful in many similar applications. As a *topic model*, it infers a set of topics from a corpus and assigns each document a level of participation in each topic.

CHAPTER 7

Analyzing Co-occurrence Networks with GraphX

Josh Wills

It's a small world. It keeps recrossing itself.
—David Mitchell

Data scientists come in all shapes and sizes and from a remarkably diverse set of academic backgrounds. Although many have some training in disciplines like computer science, mathematics, and physics, other successful data scientists have studied neuroscience, sociology, and political science. Although these fields study different things (e.g., brains, people, political institutions) and have not traditionally required students to learn how to program, they all share two important characteristics that have made them fertile training ground for data scientists.

First, all of these fields are interested in understanding *relationships* between entities, whether between neurons, individuals, or countries, and how these relationships affect the observed behavior of the entities. Second, the explosion of digital data over the past decade gave researchers access to vast quantities of information about these relationships, and required that they develop new skills in order to acquire and manage these data sets.

As these researchers began to collaborate with each other and with computer scientists, they also discovered that many of the techniques that they were using to analyze relationships could be applied to problems across domains, and the field of *network science* was born. Network science applies tools from *graph theory*, the mathematical discipline that studies the properties of pairwise relationships (called *edges*) between a set of entities (called *vertices*). Graph theory is also widely used in computer science to study everything from data structures to computer architecture to the design of networks like the Internet.

Graph theory and network science have had a significant impact in the business world as well. Almost every major Internet company derives a significant fraction of its value by its ability to build and analyze an important network of relationships better than any of its competitors: the recommendation algorithms that are used at Amazon and Netflix rely on the networks of consumer-item purchases (Amazon) and user-movie ratings (Netflix) that each company creates and controls. Facebook and LinkedIn built graphs of relationships between people that they analyze in order to organize content feeds, promote advertisements, and broker new connections. And perhaps most famously of all, Google used the PageRank algorithm that the founders developed to create a fundamentally better way to search the World Wide Web.

The computational and analytical needs of these network-centric companies helped drive the creation of distributed processing frameworks like MapReduce as well as the hiring of data scientists who were capable of using these new tools to analyze and create value from the ever-expanding volume of data. One of the earliest use cases for MapReduce was to create a scalable and reliable way to solve the equation at the heart of PageRank. Over time, as the graphs became larger and data scientists needed to analyze them faster, new graph-parallel processing frameworks, like Pregel at Google, Giraph at Yahoo!, and GraphLab at Carnegie Mellon, were developed. These frameworks supported fault-tolerant, in-memory, iterative, and graph-centric processing, and were capable of performing certain types of graph computations orders of magnitude faster than the equivalent data-parallel MapReduce jobs.

In this chapter, we're going to introduce a Spark library called GraphX, which extends Spark to support many of the graph-parallel processing tasks that Pregel, Giraph, and GraphLab support. Although it cannot handle every graph computation as quickly as the custom graph frameworks do, the fact that it is a Spark library means that it is relatively easy to bring GraphX into your normal data analysis workflow whenever you want to analyze a network-centric data set. With it, you can combine graph-parallel programming with the familiar Spark abstractions that you are used to working with.

The MEDLINE Citation Index: A Network Analysis

MEDLINE (Medical Literature Analysis and Retrieval System Online) is a database of academic papers that have been published in journals covering the life sciences and medicine. It is managed and released by the United States National Library of Medicine (NLM), a division of the National Institute of Health (NIH). Its citation index, which tracks the publication of articles across thousands of journals, can trace its history back to 1879, and it has been available online to medical schools since 1971 and to the general public via the World Wide Web since 1996. The main database contains more than 20 million articles going back to the early 1950s and is updated five days a week.

Due to the volume of citations and the frequency of updates, the research community developed an extensive set of semantic tags called MeSH (Medical Subject Headings) that are applied to all of the citations in the index. These tags provide a meaningful framework that can be used to explore relationships between documents to facilitate literature reviews, and they have also been used as the basis for building data products: in 2001, PubGene demonstrated one of the first production applications of biomedical text mining by launching a search engine that allowed users to explore the graph of MeSH terms that connect related documents together.

In this chapter, we're going to use Scala, Spark, and GraphX to acquire, transform, and then analyze the network of MeSH terms on a recently published subset of citation data from MEDLINE. The network analysis we'll be performing was inspired by the paper "Large-Scale Structure of a Network of Co-Occurring MeSH Terms: Statistical Analysis of Macroscopic Properties," by Kastrin et al. (2014), although we'll be using a different subset of the citation data and performing the analysis with GraphX instead of the R packages and C++ code that was used in that paper.

Our goal will be to get a feel for the shape and properties of the citation graph. We'll attack this from a few different angles to get a full view of the data set. First, we'll get our feet wet by looking at the major topics and their co-occurrences, a simpler analysis that doesn't require using GraphX. Then, we'll look for *connected components*— can one follow a path of citations from any topic to any other topic, or is the data actually a set of separate smaller graphs? We'll move on to look at the *degree distribution* of the graph, which gives a sense of how the relevance of topics can vary, and find the topics that are connected to the most other topics. Last, we'll compute a couple of slightly more advanced graph statistics: the *clustering coefficient* and the *average path length*. Among other uses, these allow us to understand how similar the citation graph is to other common real-world graphs like the World Wide Web and Facebook's social network.

Getting the Data

We can retrieve a sample of the citation index data from the NIH's FTP server:

```
$ mkdir medline_data
$ cd medline_data
$ wget ftp://ftp.nlm.nih.gov/nlmdata/sample/medline/*.gz
```

Let's uncompress the citation data and examine it before we load it into HDFS:

```
$ gunzip *.gz
$ ls -ltr
...
total 843232
-rw-r--r-- 1 spark spark 162130087 Dec 17  2013 medsamp2014h.xml
-rw-r--r-- 1 spark spark 146357238 Dec 17  2013 medsamp2014g.xml
-rw-r--r-- 1 spark spark 132427298 Dec 17  2013 medsamp2014f.xml
```

```
-rw-r--r-- 1 spark spark 102401546 Dec 17  2013 medsamp2014e.xml
-rw-r--r-- 1 spark spark 102715615 Dec 17  2013 medsamp2014d.xml
-rw-r--r-- 1 spark spark  89355057 Dec 17  2013 medsamp2014c.xml
-rw-r--r-- 1 spark spark  69209079 Dec 17  2013 medsamp2014b.xml
-rw-r--r-- 1 spark spark  58856903 Dec 17  2013 medsamp2014a.xml
```

The sample files contain about 600 MB of XML-formatted data, uncompressed. Each entry in the sample files is a `MedlineCitation` record, which contains information about the publication of an article in a biomedical journal, including the journal name, issue, publication date, the names of the authors, the abstract, and the set of MeSH keywords that are associated with the article. In addition, each of the MeSH keywords has an attribute to indicate whether or not the concept the keyword refers to was a major topic of the article. Let's take a look at the first citation record in *medsamp2014a.xml*:

```
<MedlineCitation Owner="PIP" Status="MEDLINE">
<PMID Version="1">12255379</PMID>
<DateCreated>
  <Year>1980</Year>
  <Month>01</Month>
  <Day>03</Day>
</DateCreated>
...
<MeshHeadingList>
...
  <MeshHeading>
    <DescriptorName MajorTopicYN="N">Intelligence</DescriptorName>
  </MeshHeading>
  <MeshHeading>
    <DescriptorName MajorTopicYN="Y">Maternal-Fetal Exchange</DescriptorName>
  </MeshHeading>
...
</MeshHeadingList>
...
</MedlineCitation>
```

In our latent semantic analysis of Wikipedia articles, we were primarily interested in the unstructured article text that was contained in each of the XML records. But for our co-occurrence analysis, we're going to want to extract the values contained within the `DescriptorName` tags by parsing the structure of the XML directly. Fortunately, Scala comes with an excellent library called *scala-xml* for parsing and querying XML documents directly that we can use to help us out.

Let's get started by loading the citation data into HDFS:

```
$ hadoop fs -mkdir medline
$ hadoop fs -put *.xml medline
```

Now we can start up an instance of the Spark shell. The chapter relies on the code described in Chapter 6 for parsing XML-formatted data. To compile this code into a

JAR so that we can make use of it, go into the *common/* directory in the Git repo and build it with Maven:

```
$ cd common/
$ mvn package
$ spark-shell --jars target/common-1.0.0.jar
```

Let's write a function to read the XML-formatted MEDLINE data into the shell:

```
import com.cloudera.datascience.common.XmlInputFormat
import org.apache.spark.SparkContext
import org.apache.hadoop.io.{Text, LongWritable}
import org.apache.hadoop.conf.Configuration

def loadMedline(sc: SparkContext, path: String) = {
  @transient val conf = new Configuration()
  conf.set(XmlInputFormat.START_TAG_KEY, "<MedlineCitation ")
  conf.set(XmlInputFormat.END_TAG_KEY, "</MedlineCitation>")
  val in = sc.newAPIHadoopFile(path, classOf[XmlInputFormat],
      classOf[LongWritable], classOf[Text], conf)
  in.map(line => line._2.toString)
}
val medline_raw = loadMedline(sc, "medline")
```

We are setting the value of the START_TAG_KEY configuration parameter to be the prefix of the MedlineCitation start tag, because the values of the tag's attributes may change from record to record. The XmlInputFormat will include these varying attributes in the record values that are returned.

Parsing XML Documents with Scala's XML Library

Scala has an interesting history with XML. Since version 1.2, Scala has treated XML as a first-class data type. This means that the following code is syntactically valid:

```
import scala.xml._

val cit = <MedlineCitation>data</MedlineCitation>
```

This support for XML literals has always been somewhat unusual among major programming languages, especially as other serialization formats such as JSON have come into widespread use. In 2012, Martin Odersky published the following note to the Scala language mailing list:

> [XML literals] Seemed a great idea at the time, now it sticks out like a sore thumb. I believe with the new string interpolation scheme we will be able to put all of XML processing in the libraries, which should be a big win.

As of Scala 2.11, the scala.xml package is no longer a part of the core Scala libraries. After you upgrade, you will need to explicitly include the scala-xml dependency to use the Scala XML libraries in your projects.

With that caveat in mind, Scala's support for parsing and querying XML documents is truly excellent, and we will be availing ourselves of it to help extract the information we want from the MEDLINE citations. Let's get started by pulling the unparsed first citation record into our Spark shell:

```
val raw_xml = medline_raw.take(1)(0)
val elem = XML.loadString(raw_xml)
```

The `elem` variable is an instance of the `scala.xml.Elem` class, which is how Scala represents an individual node in an XML document. The class contains a number of built-in functions for retrieving information about the node and its contents, such as:

```
elem.label
elem.attributes
```

It also contains a small set of operators for finding the children of a given XML node; the first one, for retrieving a node's direct children by name, is called \:

```
elem \ "MeshHeadingList"
...
NodeSeq(<MeshHeadingList>
<MeshHeading>
<DescriptorName MajorTopicYN="N">Behavior</DescriptorName>
</MeshHeading>
...
```

The \ operator only works on *direct* children of the node; if we execute `elem \ "Mesh Heading"`, the result is an empty `NodeSeq`. To extract nondirect children of a given node, we need to use the \\ operator:

```
elem \\ "MeshHeading"
...
NodeSeq(<MeshHeading>
<DescriptorName MajorTopicYN="N">Behavior</DescriptorName>
</MeshHeading>,
...
```

We can also use the \\ operator to get at the `DescriptorName` entries directly, and then retrieve the MeSH tags within each node by calling the `text` function on each element of the `NodeSeq`:

```
(elem \\ "DescriptorName").map(_.text)
...
List(Behavior, Congenital Abnormalities, ...
```

Finally, note that each of the `DescriptorName` entries has an attribute called `MajorTo picYN` that indicates whether or not this MeSH tag was a major topic of the cited article. We can look up the value of attributes of XML tags using the \ and \\ operators if we preface the attribute name with an "@" symbol. We can use this to create a filter that only returns the names of the major MeSH tags for each article:

```
def majorTopics(elem: Elem): Seq[String] = {
  val dn = elem \\ "DescriptorName"
  val mt = dn.filter(n => (n \ "@MajorTopicYN").text == "Y")
  mt.map(n => n.text)
}
majorTopics(elem)
```

Now that we have our XML parsing code working locally, let's apply it to parse the MeSH codes for each citation record in our RDD and cache the result:

```
val mxml: RDD[Elem] = medline_raw.map(XML.loadString)
val medline: RDD[Seq[String]] = mxml.map(majorTopics).cache()
medline.take(1)(0)
```

Analyzing the MeSH Major Topics and Their Co-occurrences

Now that we've extracted the MeSH tags we want from the MEDLINE citation records, let's get a feel for the overall distribution of tags in our data set by calculating some basic summary statistics, such as the number of records and a histogram of the frequencies of various major MeSH topics:

```
medline.count()
val topics: RDD[String] = medline.flatMap(mesh => mesh)
val topicCounts = topics.countByValue()
topicCounts.size
val tcSeq = topicCounts.toSeq
tcSeq.sortBy(_._2).reverse.take(10).foreach(println)
...
(Research,5591)
(Child,2235)
(Infant,1388)
(Toxicology,1251)
(Pharmacology,1242)
(Rats,1067)
(Adolescent,1025)
(Surgical Procedures, Operative,1011)
(Pregnancy,996)
(Pathology,967)
```

The most frequently occurring major topics are, unsurprisingly, some of the most general ones, like the uber-generic "Research," or the slightly less generic "Toxicology," "Pharmacology," and "Pathology." The frequent topic list also includes references to various patient populations, like "Child," "Infant," "Rats," or (the even more odious) "Adolescent." Fortunately, there are more than 13,000 different major topics in our data set, and given that the most frequently occurring major topic only occurs in a small fraction of all the documents (5,591/240,000 ~ 2.3%), we would expect that the overall distribution of the number of documents containing a topic has a relatively long tail. We can verify this by creating a frequency count of the values of the topicCounts map:

```
val valueDist = topicCounts.groupBy(_._2).mapValues(_.size)
valueDist.toSeq.sorted.take(10).foreach(println)
...
(1,2599)
(2,1398)
(3,935)
(4,761)
(5,592)
(6,461)
(7,413)
(8,394)
(9,345)
(10,297)
```

Of course, our primary interest is in co-occurring MeSH topics. Each entry in the medline data set is a list of strings that are the names of topics that are mentioned in each citation record. To get the co-occurrences, we need to generate all of the two-element subsets of this list of strings. Fortunately, Scala's collections library has a built-in method called combinations to make generating these sublists extremely easy. combinations returns an Iterator, meaning that the combinations need not all be held in memory at the same time:

```
val list = List(1, 2, 3)
val combs = list.combinations(2)
combs.foreach(println)
```

When using this function to generate sublists that we are going to aggregate with Spark, we need to be careful that all of the lists are sorted in the same way. This is because the lists returned from the combinations function depend on the order of the input elements, and lists with the same elements in a different order are not equal to one another:

```
val combs = list.reverse.combinations(2)
combs.foreach(println)
List(3, 2) == List(2, 3)
```

Therefore, when we generate the two-element sublists for each citation record, we'll ensure that the list of topics is sorted before we call combinations:

```
val topicPairs = medline.flatMap(t => t.sorted.combinations(2))
val cooccurs = topicPairs.map(p => (p, 1)).reduceByKey(_+_)
cooccurs.cache()
cooccurs.count()
```

Because there are 13,034 topics in our data, there are potentially 13,034*13033/2 = 84,936,061 unordered co-occurrence pairs. However, the count of co-occurrences reveals that only 259,920 pairs actually appear in the data set, a tiny fraction of the possible pairs. If we look at the most frequently appearing co-occurrence pairs in the data, we see this:

```
val ord = Ordering.by[(Seq[String], Int), Int](_._2)
cooccurs.top(10)(ord).foreach(println)
...
(List(Child, Infant),1097)
(List(Rats, Research),995)
(List(Pharmacology, Research),895)
(List(Rabbits, Research),581)
(List(Adolescent, Child),544)
(List(Mice, Research),505)
(List(Dogs, Research),469)
(List(Research, Toxicology),438)
(List(Biography as Topic, History),435)
(List(Metabolism, Research),414)
```

As we might have suspected from the counts of the most frequently occurring major topics, the most frequently occurring co-occurrence pairs are also relatively uninteresting. Most of the top pairs, like ("Child," "Infant") and ("Rats," "Research"), are simply the product of two of the most frequently occurring individual topics. There's nothing surprising or informative about the fact that these pairs exist in the data.

Constructing a Co-occurrence Network with GraphX

As we saw in the preceding section, when we're studying co-occurrence networks, our standard tools for summarizing data don't provide us much insight. The overall summary statistics we can calculate, like raw counts, don't give us a feel for the overall structure of the relationships in the network, and the co-occurrence pairs that we can see at the extremes of the distribution are usually the ones that we care about least.

What we really want to do is analyze the co-occurrence network *as a network*: by thinking of the topics as vertices in a graph, and the existence of a citation record that features both topics as an edge between those two vertices. Then, we could compute network-centric statistics that would help us understand the overall structure of the network and identify interesting local outlier vertices that are worthy of further investigation.

We can also use co-occurrence networks to identify meaningful interactions between entities that are worthy of further investigation. Figure 7-1 shows part of a co-occurrence graph for combinations of cancer drugs that were associated with adverse events in the patients who were taking them. We can use the information in these graphs to help us design clinical trials to study these interactions.

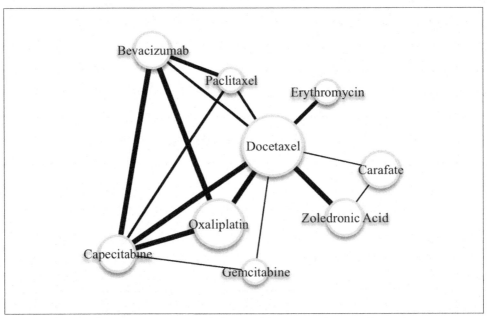

Figure 7-1. Partial co-occurrence graph for combinations of cancer drugs that were asso-ciated with adverse events in patients

In the same way that MLlib provides a set of patterns and algorithms for creating machine learning models in Spark, GraphX is a Spark library that is designed to help us analyze various kinds of networks using the language and tools of graph theory. Because GraphX builds on top of Spark, it inherits all of Spark's scalability properties, which means that it is capable of carrying out analyses on extremely large graphs that are distributed across multiple machines. GraphX also integrates well with the rest of the Spark platform, and as we will see, makes it easy for data scientists to move from writing data-parallel ETL routines against RDDs, to executing graph-parallel algorithms against a graph, to analyzing and summarizing the output of the graph computation in a data-parallel fashion again. It is the seamless way that GraphX allows us to introduce graph-style processing into our analytic workflow that makes it so powerful.

GraphX is based on two specialized RDD implementations that are optimized for graphs. The VertexRDD[VD] is a specialized implementation of RDD[(VertexId, VD)], where the VertexID type is an instance of Long and is required for every vertex, while the VD can be any other type of data that is associated with the vertex, and is called the *vertex attribute*. The EdgeRDD[ED] is a specialized implementation of RDD[Edge[ED]], where Edge is a case class that contains two VertexId values and an *edge attribute* of type ED. Both the VertexRDD and the EdgeRDD have internal indices within each partition of the data that is designed to facilitate fast joins and attribute updates. Given both a `VertexRDD` and an associated `EdgeRDD`, we can create an instance of the `Graph` class, which contains a number of methods for efficiently performing graph computations.

The first requirement in creating a graph is to have a `Long` value that can be used as an identifier for each vertex in the graph. This is a bit of a problem for us in constructing our co-occurrence network, because all of our topics are identified as strings. We need a way to come up with a unique 64-bit value that can be associated with each topic string, and ideally, we'd like to do it in a distributed fashion so that it can be done quickly across all of our data.

One option we could use would be to use the built-in `hashCode` method that will generate a 32-bit integer for any given Scala object. For our problem, which only has 13,000 vertices in the graph, the hash code trick will probably work. But for graphs that have millions or tens of millions of vertices, the probability of a hash code collision might be unacceptably high. For this reason, we're going to use the `Hashing` library from Google's Guava Library to create a unique 64-bit identifier for each topic using the MD5 hashing algorithm:

```
import com.google.common.hash.Hashing

def hashId(str: String) = {
  Hashing.md5().hashString(str).asLong()
}
```

We can apply this hashing function to our MEDLINE data to generate an `RDD[(Long, String)]` that will be the basis for the set of vertices in our co-occurrence graph. We can also do a simple verification check to ensure that the hash value was unique for each topic:

```
val vertices = topics.map(topic => (hashId(topic), topic))
val uniqueHashes = vertices.map(_._1).countByValue()
val uniqueTopics = vertices.map(_._2).countByValue()
uniqueHashes.size == uniqueTopics.size
```

We will generate the edges for the graph from the co-occurrence counts that we created in the previous section, using the hashing function to map each topic name to its corresponding vertex ID. A good habit to get into when you are generating edges is to ensure that the left side `VertexId` (which GraphX refers to as the `src`) is *less* than the right side `VertexId` (which GraphX refers to as the `dst`). Although most of the algorithms in the GraphX library do not assume anything about the relationship between `src` and `dst`, there are a few that do, so it's a good idea to implement this pattern early so that you don't have to think about it later on:

```
import org.apache.spark.graphx._

val edges = cooccurs.map(p => {
  val (topics, cnt) = p
```

```
    val ids = topics.map(hashId).sorted
    Edge(ids(0), ids(1), cnt)
})
```

Now that we have both the vertices and the edges, we can create our `Graph` instance, and mark it as cached so we can keep it around for subsequent processing:

```
val topicGraph = Graph(vertices, edges)
topicGraph.cache()
```

The `vertices` and `edges` arguments that we used to construct the `Graph` instance were regular RDDs—we didn't even deduplicate the entries in the `vertices` so that there was only a single instance of each topic. Fortunately, the Graph API does this for us, converting the RDDs we passed in to a `VertexRDD` and an `EdgeRDD`, so that the vertex counts are now unique:

```
vertices.count()
...
280823

topicGraph.vertices.count()
...
13034
```

Note that if there are duplicate entries in the `EdgeRDD` for a given pair of vertices, the Graph API will not deduplicate them: GraphX allows us to create *multigraphs*, which can have multiple edges with different values between the same pair of vertices. This can be useful in applications where the vertices in the graph represent rich objects, like people or businesses, that may have many different kinds of relationships between them (e.g., friends, family members, customers, partners, etc.). It also allows us to treat the edges as either directed or undirected, depending on the context.

Understanding the Structure of Networks

When we explore the contents of a table, there are a number of summary statistics about the columns that we want to calculate right away so that we can get a feel for the structure of the data and explore any problem areas. The same principle applies when we are investigating a new graph, although the summary statistics we are interested in are slightly different. The `Graph` class provides built-in methods for calculating a number of these statistics, and in combination with the regular Spark RDD APIs, makes it easy for us to quickly get a feel for the structure of a graph to guide our exploration.

Connected Components

One of the most basic things we want to know about a graph is whether or not it is *connected*. In a connected graph, it is possible for any vertex to reach any other vertex

---

by following a *path*, which is simply a sequence of edges that lead from one vertex to another. If the graph isn't connected, it may be divided into a smaller set of connected subgraphs that we can investigate individually.

Connectedness is a fundamental graph property, and so it shouldn't be surprising that GraphX includes a built-in method for identifying the connected components in a graph. You'll note that as soon as you call the connectedComponents method on the graph, a number of Spark jobs will be launched, and then you'll finally see the result of the computation:

```
val connectedComponentGraph: Graph[VertexId, Int] =
    topicGraph.connectedComponents()
```

Look at the type of the object returned by the connectedComponents method: it's another instance of the Graph class, but the type of the vertex attribute is a VertexId that is used as a unique identifier for the component that each vertex belongs to. To get a count of the number of connected components and their size, we can use the trusty countByValue method against the VertexId values for each vertex in the Ver texRDD. We'll write a function to find a list of all the connected components, sorted by their sizes:

```
def sortedConnectedComponents(
    connectedComponents: Graph[VertexId, _])
  : Seq[(VertexId, Long)] = {
  val componentCounts = connectedComponents.vertices.map(_._2).
    countByValue
  componentCounts.toSeq.sortBy(_._2).reverse
}
```

Let's look at how many connected components there are, and then a little closer at the 10 largest:

```
val componentCounts = sortedConnectedComponents(
  connectedComponentGraph)
componentCounts.size
...
1039

componentCounts.take(10).foreach(println)
...
(-9222594773437155629,11915)
(-6468702387578666337,4)
(-7038642868304457401,3)
(-7926343550108072887,3)
(-5914927920861094734,3)
(-4899133687675445365,3)
(-9022462685920786023,3)
(-7462290111155674971,3)
(-5504525564549659185,3)
(-7557628715678213859,3)
```

The largest component includes more than 90% of the vertices, while the second largest contains only 4%—a vanishingly small fraction of the graph. It's worthwhile to take a look at the topics for some of these smaller components, if only to understand why they were not connected to the largest component. To see the names of the topics associated with these smaller components, we'll need to join the VertexRDD for the connected components graph with the vertices from our original concept graph. VertexRDD provides an innerJoin transformation that can take advantage of the way GraphX lays out data for much better performance than Spark's regular join transformation. The innerJoin method requires that we provide a function on the VertexID and the data contained inside of each of the two VertexRDDs that returns a value that will be used as the new data type for the resulting VertexRDD. In this case, we want to understand the names of the concepts for each connected component, so we'll return a tuple that contains both values:

```
val nameCID = topicGraph.vertices.
  innerJoin(connectedComponentGraph.vertices) {
    (topicId, name, componentId) => (name, componentId)
}
```

Let's take a look at the topic names for the largest connected component that wasn't a part of the giant component:

```
val c1 = nameCID.filter(x => x._2._2 == componentCounts(1)._1)
c1.collect().foreach(x => println(x._2._1))
...
Reverse Transcriptase Inhibitors
Zidovudine
Anti-HIV Agents
Nevirapine
```

If we look up the terms [Zidovudine] and [Nevirapine] in Google, we find the Wikipedia entry for Nevirapine, which indicates that the two drugs are used in conjunction for the treatment of HIV-1, the most severe form of HIV.

It's surprising that this subgraph was not connected to any other topics about HIV or AIDS in the overall subgraph. If we take a look at the distribution of topics that mention HIV in the overall data, we see this:

```
val hiv = topics.filter(_.contains("HIV")).countByValue()
hiv.foreach(println)
...
(HIV Seronegativity,10)
(HIV Long Terminal Repeat,2)
(HIV Long-Term Survivors,1)
(HIV Integrase Inhibitors,1)
(HIV Infections,104)
(HIV-2,2)
(HIV Seroprevalence,6)
(Anti-HIV Agents,1)
```

```
(HIV-1,72)
(HIV,16)
(HIV Seropositivity,41)
```

It feels like this distinct subcomponent in the graph is an artifact of the data—likely a result of a parsimonious labeling of the major topics for an individual citation in the index that excluded other major topics, like HIV-1, that would have tied this paper into the giant component of the graph. The lesson here is that the topic co-occurrence network is tending toward being fully connected as we add more citations to it over time, and there do not appear to be structural reasons that we would expect it to become disconnected into distinct subgraphs.

Under the covers, the connectedComponents method is performing a series of iterative computations on our graph in order to identify the component that each vertex belongs to, taking advantage of the fact that the VertexId is a unique numeric identifier for each vertex. During each phase of the computation, each vertex broadcasts the smallest VertexID value that it has seen to each of its neighbors. During the first iteration, this will simply be the vertex's own ID, but this will generally be updated in subsequent iterations. Each vertex keeps track of the smallest VertexID it has seen, and when none of these smallest IDs changes during an iteration, the connected component computation is complete, with each vertex assigned to the component that is represented by the smallest VertexID value for a vertex that was a part of that component. These kinds of iterative computations on graphs are common, and later in this chapter, we will see how we can use this iterative pattern to compute other graph metrics that illuminate the structure of the graph.

Degree Distribution

A connected graph can be structured in many different ways. For example, there might be a single vertex that is connected to all of the other vertices, but none of those other vertices connect to each other. If we eliminated that single central vertex, the graph would shatter into individual vertices. We might also have a situation in which every vertex in the graph was connected to exactly two other vertices, so that the entire connected component formed a giant loop.

Figure 7-2 illustrates how connected graphs may have radically different degree distributions.

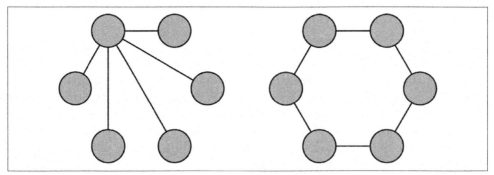

Figure 7-2. Degree distributions in connected graphs

To gain additional insight into how the graph is structured, it's helpful to look at the *degree* of each vertex, which is simply the number of edges that a particular vertex belongs to. In a graph without loops (i.e., an edge that connects a vertex to itself), the sum of the degrees of the vertices will be equal to twice the number of edges, because each edge will contain two distinct vertices.

In GraphX, we can get the degree of each vertex by calling the `degrees` method on the `Graph` object. This method returns a `VertexRDD` of integers that is the degree at each vertex. Let's get the degree distribution and some basic summary statistics on it for our concept network:

```
val degrees: VertexRDD[Int] = topicGraph.degrees.cache()
degrees.map(_._2).stats()
...
(count: 12065, mean: 43.09,
 stdev: 97.63, max: 3753.0, min: 1.0)
```

There are a few interesting bits of information in the degree distribution. First, note that the number of entries in the `degrees` RDD is less than the number of vertices in the graph: while the graph contains 13,034 vertices, the `degrees` RDD only has 12,065 entries. Some vertices have no edges that touch them. This is probably caused by citations in the MEDLINE data that only had a single major topic, which means that they would not have had any other topics to co-occur with in our data. We can confirm that this is the case by revisiting the original `medline` RDD:

```
val sing = medline.filter(x => x.size == 1)
sing.count()
...
48611

val singTopic = sing.flatMap(topic => topic).distinct()
singTopic.count()
...
8084
```

There are 8,084 distinct topics that occur as singletons inside of 48,611 MEDLINE documents. Let's remove the instances of those topics that already occur in the topic Pairs RDD:

```
val topic2 = topicPairs.flatMap(p => p)
singTopic.subtract(topic2).count()
...
969
```

This leaves 969 topics that only occur as singletons inside of MEDLINE documents, and 13,034 – 969 is 12,065, the number of entries in the degrees RDD.

Next, note that although the mean is relatively small, indicating that the average vertex in the graph is only connected to a small fraction of the other nodes, the maximum value indicates that there is at least one highly connected node in the graph that is connected to almost a third of the other nodes in the graph.

Let's take a closer look at the concepts for these high-degree vertices by joining the degrees VertexRDD to the vertices in the concept graph using GraphX's innerJoin method and an associated function for combining the name of a concept and the degree of the vertex into a tuple. Remember, the innerJoin method only returns vertices that are present in *both* of the VertexRDDs, so the concepts that do not have any co-occurring concepts will be filtered out. We'll write a function that we can reuse later to find the names of the topics with the highest degrees:

```
def topNamesAndDegrees(degrees: VertexRDD[Int],
    topicGraph: Graph[String, Int]): Array[(String, Int)] = {
  val namesAndDegrees = degrees.innerJoin(topicGraph.vertices) {
    (topicId, degree, name) => (name, degree)
  }
  val ord = Ordering.by[(String, Int), Int](_._2)
  namesAndDegrees.map(_._2).top(10)(ord)
}
```

When we print the top 10 elements of the namesAndDegrees VertexRDD ordered by the value of the degree, we get this:

```
topNamesAndDegrees(degrees, topicGraph).foreach(println)
...
(Research,3753)
(Child,2364)
(Toxicology,2019)
(Pharmacology,1891)
(Adolescent,1884)
(Pathology,1781)
(Rats,1573)
(Infant,1568)
(Geriatrics,1546)
(Pregnancy,1431)
```

Unsurprisingly, most of the high-degree vertices refer to the same generic concepts that we've been seeing throughout this analysis. In the next section, we'll use some new functionality of the GraphX API and a bit of old-fashioned statistics to filter out some of the less interesting co-occurrence pairs from the graph.

Filtering Out Noisy Edges

In the current co-occurrence graph, the edges are weighted based on the count of how often a pair of concepts appears in the same paper. The problem with this simple weighting scheme is that it doesn't distinguish concept pairs that occur together because they have a meaningful semantic relationship from concept pairs that occur together because they happen to both occur frequently for any type of document. We need to use a new edge weighting scheme that takes into account how "interesting" or "surprising" a particular pair of concepts is for a document given the overall prevalence of those concepts in the data. We will use Pearson's *chi-squared test* to calculate this "interestingness" in a principled way—that is, to test whether the occurrence of a particular concept is independent from the occurrence of another concept.

For any pair of concepts A and B, we can create a 2×2 contingency table that contains the counts of how those concepts co-occur in MEDLINE documents:

	Yes B	No B	A Total
Yes A	YY	YN	YA
No A	NY	NN	NA
B Total	YB	NB	T

In this table, the entries YY, YN, NY, and NN represent the raw counts of presence/absence for concepts A and B. The entries YA and NA are the row sums for concept A, and YB and NB are the column sums for concept B, and the value T is the total number of documents.

For the chi-squared test, we think of YY, YN, NY, and NN as sampled from an unknown distribution. We can compute a *chi-squared statistic* from these values with:

$$\chi^2 = T\frac{(|YY*NN - YN*NY| - T/2)^2}{YA*NA*YB*NB}$$

Note that this formulation of the chi-squared statistic includes a term "- T / 2". This is Yates's continuity correction (*http://en.wikipedia.org/wiki/Yates%27s_correction_for_continuity*) and it is not included in some formulations.

If our samples are in fact independent, we would expect the value of this statistic to be drawn from a *chi-squared distribution* with the appropriate degrees of freedom. Where r and c are the cardinalities of the two random variables being compared, the degrees of freedom is calculated as $(r - 1)(c - 1) = 1$. A large chi-squared statistic indicates that the variables are less likely to be independent, and thus we find the pair of concepts more interesting. More specifically, the CDF of the one-degree chi-squared distribution yields a *p*-value that is the level of confidence with which we can reject the null hypothesis that the variables are independent.

In this section, we'll compute the value of the chi-squared statistic for each pair of concepts in our co-occurrence graph using GraphX.

Processing EdgeTriplets

The easiest part of the chi-squared statistic to count is T, the total number of documents under consideration. We can get this easily by simply counting the number of entries in the medline RDD:

```
val T = medline.count()
```

It's also relatively easy for us to get the counts of how many documents feature each concept; we already did this analysis to create the map of topicCounts earlier in this chapter, but now we'll get the counts as an RDD on the cluster:

```
val topicCountsRdd = topics.map(x => (hashId(x), 1)).reduceByKey(_+_)
```

Once we have this VertexRDD of counts, we can create a new graph using it as the vertex set, along with the existing edges RDD:

```
val topicCountGraph = Graph(topicCountsRdd, topicGraph.edges)
```

Now we have all of the information we need to compute the chi-squared statistic for each edge in the topicCountGraph. To do the calculation, we need to combine data that is stored at both the vertices (i.e., the counts of how often each concept appears in a document) as well as the edges (the count of how often each pair of concepts occurs in the same document). GraphX supports this kind of computation via a data structure called an EdgeTriplet[VD, ED], which has information about the attributes of both the vertices and the edges contained within a single object, as well as the IDs of both of the vertices. Given a EdgeTriplet over our topicCountGraph, we can calculate the chi-squared statistic as follows:

```
def chiSq(YY: Int, YB: Int, YA: Int, T: Long): Double = {
  val NB = T - YB
  val NA = T - YA
  val YN = YA - YY
  val NY = YB - YY
  val NN = T - NY - YN - YY
  val inner = math.abs(YY * NN - YN * NY) - T / 2.0
```

```
    T * math.pow(inner, 2) / (YA * NA * YB * NB)
  }
```

We can then apply this method to transform the value of the graph edges via the `map` `Triplets` operator, which returns a new graph whose edge attributes will be the value of the chi-squared statistic for each co-occurrence pair, and then get an idea of the distribution of the values for this statistic across the edges:

```
val chiSquaredGraph = topicCountGraph.mapTriplets(triplet => {
  chiSq(triplet.attr, triplet.srcAttr, triplet.dstAttr, T)
})
chiSquaredGraph.edges.map(x => x.attr).stats()
...
(count: 259920, mean: 546.97,
  stdev: 3428.85, max: 222305.79, min: 0.0)
```

Having calculated the chi-squared statistic value, we want to use it to filter out edges that don't appear to have any meaningful relationship between the co-occurring concepts. As we can see from the distribution of the edge values, there is an enormous range of values for the chi-squared statistic across the data, which should make us feel comfortable experimenting with an aggressive filtering criterion to eliminate noisy edges. For a 2×2 contingency table in which there is no relationship between the variables, we expect that the value of the chi-squared metric will follow the chi-squared distribution with one degree of freedom. The 99.999th percentile of the chi-squared distribution with one degree of freedom is approximately 19.5, so let's try this value as a cutoff to eliminate edges from the graph, leaving us with only those edges where we are *extremely* confident that they represent an interesting co-occurrence relationship. We'll perform this filtering on the graph with the `subgraph` method, which takes a boolean function of an `EdgeTriplet` to determine which edges to include in the subgraph:

```
val interesting = chiSquaredGraph.subgraph(
  triplet => triplet.attr > 19.5)
interesting.edges.count
...
170664
```

Our extremely strict filtering rule removed about one third of the edges in the original co-occurrence graph. It isn't a bad thing that the rule didn't remove more of the edges, because we expect that most of the co-occurring concepts in the graph are actually semantically related to one another, and so they would co-occur more often than they would simply by chance. In the next section, we'll analyze the connectedness and overall degree distribution of the subgraph, to see if there was any major impact to the structure of the graph when we removed these noisy edges.

Analyzing the Filtered Graph

We'll start by rerunning the connected component algorithm on the subgraph and checking the component counts and sizes, using the function we wrote earlier for the original graph:

```
val interestingComponentCounts = sortedConnectedComponents(
  interesting.connectedComponents())
interestingComponentCounts.size
...
1042

interestingComponentCounts.take(10).foreach(println)
...
(-9222594773437155629,11912)
(-6468702387578666337,4)
(-7038642868304457401,3)
(-7926343550108072887,3)
(-5914927920861094734,3)
(-4899133687675445365,3)
(-9022462685920786023,3)
(-7462290111155674971,3)
(-5504525564549659185,3)
(-7557628715678213859,3)
```

Filtering out a third of the edges in the graph led to a small change in the connectedness of the graph: three additional islands exist in the filtered graph (1,042 versus 1,039 in the original), and the size of the largest connected component has fallen by three vertices (11,912 versus 11,915). This indicates that three weakly connected concepts have been pruned from the largest component into individual islands. Even so, the largest connected component is still roughly the same size as before; pruning a third of the edges in the graph did not cause the largest component to break up into a number of large pieces. This indicates that the connected structure of the graph is reasonably robust to filtering out the noisy edges. When we look at the degree distribution for the filtered graph, we see a similar story:

```
val interestingDegrees = interesting.degrees.cache()
interestingDegrees.map(_._2).stats()
...
(count: 12062, mean: 28.30,
 stdev: 44.84, max: 1603.0, min: 1.0)
```

The mean degree for the original graph was about 43, and the mean degree for the filtered graph has fallen a bit, to about 28. More interesting, however, is the precipitous drop in the size of the largest degree vertex, which has fallen from 3,753 in the original graph to 1,603 in the filtered graph. If we look at the association between concept and degree in the filtered graph, we see this:

```
topNamesAndDegrees(interestingDegrees, topicGraph).foreach(println)
...
```

```
(Research,1603)
(Pharmacology,873)
(Toxicology,814)
(Rats,716)
(Pathology,704)
(Child,617)
(Metabolism,587)
(Rabbits,560)
(Mice,526)
(Adolescent,510)
```

Our chi-squared filtering criterion appears to have the desired effect: it's eliminating edges in our graph related to generic concepts, while preserving the edges in the rest of the graph that represent meaningful and interesting semantic relationships between concepts. We can continue to experiment with different chi-squared filtering criteria to see how they impact the connectedness and degree distribution in the graph; it would be interesting to find out what value of the chi-squared distribution would cause the large connected component in the graph to break up into smaller pieces, or if the largest component would simply continue to "melt," like a giant iceberg slowly losing tiny pieces over time.

Small-World Networks

The connectedness and degree distribution of a graph can give us a basic idea of its overall structure, and GraphX makes it easy to calculate and analyze these properties. In this section, we'll go a bit deeper into the GraphX APIs and show how we can use them to calculate some more advanced properties of a graph that do not have built-in support in GraphX.

With the rise of computer networks like the World Wide Web and social networks like Facebook and Twitter, data scientists now have rich data sets that describe the structure and formation of real-world networks versus the idealized networks that mathematicians and graph theorists have traditionally studied. One of the first papers to describe the properties of these real-world networks, and how they differed from the idealized models, was published in 1998 by Duncan Watts and Steven Strogatz and was titled "Collective dynamics of 'small-world' networks" (*http://research.yahoo.com/files/w_s_NATURE_0.pdf*). It was a seminal paper that outlined the first mathematical model for how to generate graphs that exhibited the two "small-world" properties that we see in real-world graphs:

• Most of the nodes in the network have a small degree and belong to a relatively dense cluster of other nodes; that is, a high fraction of a node's neighbors are also connected to each other.

- Despite the small degree and dense clustering of most nodes in the graph, it is possible to reach any node in the network from any other network relatively quickly by traversing a small number of edges.

For each of these properties, Watts and Strogatz defined a metric that could be used to rank graphs based on how strongly they expressed these properties. In this section, we will use GraphX to compute these metrics for our concept network, and compare the values that we get to the values we would get for an idealized random graph to test whether our concept network exhibits the small-world property.

Cliques and Clustering Coefficients

A graph is *complete* if every vertex is connected to every other vertex by an edge. In a given graph, there may be many subsets of vertices that are complete, and we call these complete subgraphs *cliques*. The presence of many large cliques in a graph indicates that the graph has the kind of locally dense structure that we see in real small-world networks.

Unfortunately, finding cliques in a given graph turns out to be very difficult to do. The problem of detecting whether or not a given graph has a clique of a given size is NP-complete, which means that finding cliques in even small graphs can be very computationally intensive.

Computer scientists have developed a number of simple metrics that give us a good feel for the local density of a graph without the computational costs of finding all of the cliques of a given size. One of these metrics is the *triangle count* at a vertex. A *triangle* is a complete graph on three vertices, and the triangle count at a vertex *V* is simply the number of triangles that contain *V*. The triangle count is a measure of how many neighbors of *V* are also connected to each other. Watts and Strogatz defined a new metric, called the *local clustering coefficient*, that is the ratio of the actual triangle count at a vertex to the number of possible triangles at that vertex based on how many neighbors it has. For an undirected graph, the local clustering coefficient *C* for a vertex that has *k* neighbors and *t* triangles is:

$$C = \frac{2t}{k(k-1)}$$

Let's use GraphX to compute the local clustering coefficients for each node in the filtered concept network. GraphX has a built-in method called `triangleCount` that returns a `Graph` whose `VertexRDD` contains the number of triangles at each vertex:

```
val triCountGraph = graph.triangleCount()
triCountGraph.vertices.map(x => x._2).stats()
...
```

```
(count: 13034, mean: 163.05,
   stdev: 616.56, max: 38602.0, min: 0.0)
```

To compute the local clustering coefficient, we'll need to normalize these triangle counts by the total number of possible triangles at each vertex, which we can compute from the degrees RDD:

```
val maxTrisGraph = graph.degrees.mapValues(d => d * (d - 1) / 2.0)
```

Now we'll join the `VertexRDD` of triangle counts from `triCountGraph` to the `VertexRDD` of normalization terms we calculated and compute the ratio of the two, being careful to avoid dividing by zero for any vertices that only have a single edge:

```
val clusterCoefGraph = triCountGraph.vertices.
  innerJoin(maxTrisGraph) { (vertexId, triCount, maxTris) => {
    if (maxTris == 0) 0 else triCount / maxTris
  }
}
```

Computing the average value of the local clustering coefficient for all of the vertices in the graph gives us the *network average clustering coefficient*:

```
clusterCoefGraph.map(_._2).sum() / graph.vertices.count()
...
0.2784084744308219
```

Computing Average Path Length with Pregel

The second property of small-world networks is that the length of the shortest path between any two randomly chosen nodes tends to be small. In this section, we'll compute the average path length for nodes contained in the large connected component of our filtered graph.

Computing the path length between vertices in a graph is an iterative process that is similar to the iterative process we use to find the connected components. At each phase of the process, each vertex will maintain a collection of the vertices that it knows about and how far away each vertex is. Each vertex will then query its neighbors about the contents of their lists, and it will update its own list with any new vertices that are contained in its neighbors' lists that were not contained in its own list. This process of querying neighbors and updating lists will continue across the entire graph until none of the vertices are able to add any new information to their lists.

This iterative, vertex-centric method of parallel programming on large, distributed graphs is based on a paper that Google published in 2009 called "Pregel: a system for large-scale graph processing" (*http://dl.acm.org/citation.cfm?id=1807184*). Pregel is based on a model of distributed computation that predates MapReduce called "bulk-synchronous parallel," or BSP. BSP programs divide parallel processing stages into two phases: *computation* and *communication*. During the computation phase, each vertex in the graph examines its own internal state and decides to send zero or more *messages* to other vertices in the graph. During the communication phase, the Pregel framework handles routing the messages that resulted from the previous communication phase to the appropriate vertices, which then process those messages, update their internal state, and potentially generate new messages during the next computation phase. The sequence of computation and communication steps continues until all of the vertices in the graph vote to halt, at which point the computation is finished.

BSP was one of the first parallel programming frameworks that was both fairly general-purpose as well as fault-tolerant: it was possible to design BSP systems in such a way that the state of the system at any computation phase could be captured and stored so that if a particular machine failed, the state of that machine could be replicated on another machine, the overall computation could be rolled back to the earlier state before the failure occurred, and then the computation could continue.

Since Google published its paper on Pregel, a number of open source projects have been developed that replicate aspects of the BSP programming model on top of HDFS, such as Apache Giraph and Apache Hama. These systems have proven very useful for specialized problems that fit nicely into the BSP computational model, such as large-scale PageRank computations, but they are not widely deployed as part of the analysis toolkit for regular data scientists because it is relatively difficult to integrate them into a standard data-parallel workflow. GraphX solves this problem by allowing data scientists to easily bring graphs into a data-parallel workflow when it is convenient for representing data and implementing algorithms, and it provides a built-in `pregel` operator for expressing BSP computations on top of graphs. In this section, we'll demonstrate how to use this operator to implement the iterative, graph-parallel computations we need to compute the average path length for a graph:

1. Figure out what state we need to keep track of at each vertex.
2. Write a function that takes the current state into account, and evaluates each pair of linked vertices to determine which messages to send at the next phase.
3. Write a function that merges the messages from all of the different vertices together before we pass the output of the function to the vertex for updating.

There are three major decisions we need to make in order to implement a distributed algorithm using `pregel`. First, we need to decide what data structure we're going to use to represent the state of each vertex, and what data structure we're going to use to represent the messages that are passed between vertices. For the average path length problem, we want each vertex to have a lookup table that contains the IDs of the vertices it currently knows about and how far away from those vertices it is. We'll store this information inside of a `Map[VertexId, Int]` that we maintain for each vertex. Similarly, the messages that are passed to each vertex should be a lookup table of vertex IDs and distances that are based on information that the vertex receives from its neighbors, and we can use a `Map[VertexId, Int]` to represent this information as well.

Once we know the data structures that we'll use for representing the state of the vertices and the content of the messages, we need to write two functions. The first one, which we'll call `mergeMaps`, is used to merge the information from the new messages into the state of the vertex. In this case, both the state and the message are of type `Map[VertexId, Int]`, so we need to merge the contents of these two maps while retaining the smallest value associated with any `VertexId` entries that occur in both maps:

```
def mergeMaps(m1: Map[VertexId, Int], m2: Map[VertexId, Int])
  : Map[VertexId, Int] = {
  def minThatExists(k: VertexId): Int = {
    math.min(
      m1.getOrElse(k, Int.MaxValue),
      m2.getOrElse(k, Int.MaxValue))
  }

  (m1.keySet ++ m2.keySet).map {
    k => (k, minThatExists(k))
  }.toMap
}
```

The vertex update function also includes the `VertexId` value as an argument, so we'll define a trivial `update` function that takes the `VertexId` along with the `Map[VertexId, Int]` arguments, but delegates all of the actual work to `mergeMaps`:

```
def update(
    id: VertexId,
    state: Map[VertexId, Int],
    msg: Map[VertexId, Int]) = {
  mergeMaps(state, msg)
}
```

Because the messages that we'll be passing during the algorithm are also of type `Map[VertexId, Int]`, and we want to merge them and keep the minimal value of each key they possess, we will be able to use the `mergeMaps` function for the reduce phase of the Pregel run as well.

The final step is usually the most involved: we need to write the code that constructs the message that will be sent to each vertex based on the information it receives from its neighbors at each iteration. The basic idea here is that each vertex should increment the value of each key in its current `Map[VertexId, Int]` by one, combine the incremented map values with the values from its neighbor using the `mergeMaps` method, and send the result of the `mergeMaps` function to the neighboring vertex if it differs from the neighbor's internal `Map[VertexId, Int]`. The code for performing this sequence of operations looks like this:

```
def checkIncrement(
    a: Map[VertexId, Int],
    b: Map[VertexId, Int],
    bid: VertexId) = {
  val aplus = a.map { case (v, d) => v -> (d + 1) }
  if (b != mergeMaps(aplus, b)) {
    Iterator((bid, aplus))
  } else {
    Iterator.empty
  }
}
```

With the checkIncrement function in hand, we can define the iterate function that we will use for performing the message updates at each Pregel iteration for both the src and dst vertices inside of an EdgeTriplet:

```
def iterate(e: EdgeTriplet[Map[VertexId, Int], _]) = {
  checkIncrement(e.srcAttr, e.dstAttr, e.dstId) ++
  checkIncrement(e.dstAttr, e.srcAttr, e.srcId)
}
```

During each iteration, we need to determine the path lengths that need to be communicated to each of the vertices based on the path lengths that they already know about, and then we need to return an Iterator that contains a tuple of (VertexId, Map[VertexId, Int]), where the first VertexId indicates where the message should be routed, and the Map[VertexId, Int] is the message itself.

If any vertex does not receive any messages during an iteration, the pregel operator assumes that this vertex is finished computing, and it will be excluded from subsequent processing. As soon as no more messages are sent to any vertex from the iterate method, the algorithm is complete.

 The implementation of the pregel operator in GraphX has a limitation compared to BSP systems like Giraph: GraphX can only send messages between vertices that are connected by an edge, whereas Giraph can send messages between *any* two vertices in a graph.

Now that our functions are completed, let's prepare the data for the BSP run. Given a large enough cluster and plenty of memory, we could compute the path lengths between every pair of vertices using a Pregel-style algorithm with GraphX. However, this isn't necessary for us to get an idea of the general distribution of path lengths in the graph; instead, we can randomly sample a small subset of the vertices and then compute the path lengths for each vertex to just that subset. Using the RDD sample method, let's select 2% of the VertexId values for our sample without replacement, using the value 1729L as the seed for the random number generator:

```
val fraction = 0.02
val replacement = false
val sample = interesting.vertices.map(v => v._1).
  sample(replacement, fraction, 1729L)
val ids = sample.collect().toSet
```

Now, we'll create a new `Graph` object whose vertex `Map[VertexId, Int]` values are only nonempty if the vertex is a member of the sampled IDs:

```
val mapGraph = interesting.mapVertices((id, _) => {
  if (ids.contains(id)) {
    Map(id -> 0)
  } else {
    Map[VertexId, Int]()
  }
})
```

Finally, to kick off the run, we need an initial message to send to the vertices. For this algorithm, that initial message is an empty `Map[VertexId, Int]`. We can then call the `pregel` method, followed by the `update`, `iterate`, and `mergeMaps` functions to execute during each iteration:

```
val start = Map[VertexId, Int]()
val res = mapGraph.pregel(start)(update, iterate, mergeMaps)
```

This should run for a few minutes; the number of iterations of the algorithm will be one plus the length of the longest path in our sample. Once it completes, we can `flat Map` the vertices to extract the tuples of (`VertexId`, `VertexId`, `Int`) values that represent the unique path lengths that were computed:

```
val paths = res.vertices.flatMap { case (id, m) =>
  m.map { case (k, v) =>
    if (id < k) {
      (id, k, v)
    } else {
      (k, id, v)
    }
  }
}.distinct()
paths.cache()
```

We can now compute summary statistics for the nonzero path lengths and compute the histogram of path lengths in our sample:

```
paths.map(_._3).filter(_ > 0).stats()
...
(count: 2701516, mean: 3.57,
 stdev: 0.84, max: 8.0, min: 1.0)

val hist = paths.map(_._3).countByValue()
hist.toSeq.sorted.foreach(println)
...
(0,248)
```

```
(1,5653)
(2,213584)
(3,1091273)
(4,1061114)
(5,298679)
(6,29655)
(7,1520)
(8,38)
```

The average path length of our sample was 3.57, while the clustering coefficient that we calculated in the last section was 0.274. Table 7-1 shows the values of these statistics for three different small-world networks as well as for random graphs that were generated on the same number of vertices and edges as each of the real-world networks, and is taken from a paper titled "Multiscale visualization of small world networks" (*http://dl.acm.org/citation.cfm?id=1947385*) by Auber et al. (2003).

Table 7-1. Example small-world networks

Graph	Avg path length (APL)	Clustering coefficient (CC)	Random APL	Random CC
IMDB	3.20	0.967	2.67	0.024
Mac OS 9	3.28	0.388	3.32	0.018
.edu sites	4.06	0.156	4.048	0.001

The IMDB graph was built from actors who had appeared in the same movies, the Mac OS 9 network referred to header files that were co-included in the same source files in the OS 9 operating system source code, and .edu sites refers to sites in the *.edu* top-level domain that linked to one another and are drawn from a paper by Adamic (1999) (*http://bit.ly/1wuHgfB*). Our analysis shows that the network of MeSH tags in the MEDLINE citation index fits naturally into the same range of average path length and clustering coefficient values that we see in other well-known small-world networks, with a much higher clustering coefficient value than we would expect given the relatively low average path length.

Where to Go from Here

At first, small-world networks were a curiosity; it was interesting that so many different types of real-world networks, from sociology and political science to neuroscience and cell biology, had such similar and peculiar structural properties. More recently, however, it seems that deviances from small-world structure in these networks can be indicative of the potential for functional problems. Dr. Jeffrey Petrella at Duke University gathered research (*http://bit.ly/1wuHi7f*) that indicates that the network of neurons in the brain exhibits a small-world structure, and that deviance from this structure occurs in patients who have been diagnosed with Alzheimer's disease, schizophrenia, depression, and attention deficit disorders. In general, real-world graphs should exhibit the small-world property; if they do not, that may be evidence of a problem, such as fraudulent activity in a small-world graph of transactions or trust relationships between businesses.

CHAPTER 8

Geospatial and Temporal Data Analysis on the New York City Taxi Trip Data

Josh Wills

Nothing puzzles me more than time and space;
and yet nothing troubles me less, as I never think about them.
—Charles Lamb

New York is widely known for its yellow taxis, and hailing one is just as much a part of the experience of visiting New York as eating a hot dog from a street vendor or riding the elevator to the top of the Empire State Building.

Residents of New York have all kinds of tips based on their anecdotal experiences about the best times and places to catch a cab, especially during rush hour and when it's raining. But there is one time of day when everyone will recommend that you simply take the subway instead: during the shift change that happens from 4 to 5 PM every day. During this time, yellow taxis have to return to their dispatch centers (often in Queens) so that one driver can quit for the day and the next one can start, and drivers who are late to return have to pay fines.

In March of 2014, the New York City Taxi and Limousine Commission shared an infographic on its Twitter account, @nyctaxi (*https://twitter.com/nyctaxi*), that showed the number of taxis on the road and the fraction of those taxis that was occupied at any given time. Sure enough, there was a noticeable dip of taxis on the road from 4 to 6 PM, and two-thirds of the taxis that were driving were occupied.

This tweet caught the eye of self-described urbanist, mapmaker, and data junkie Chris Whong, who sent a tweet to the @nyctaxi account to find out if the data it used in its infographic was publicly available. The taxi commission replied that he could have the data if he filed a Freedom of Information Law (FOIL) request and provided the commission with hard drives that they could copy the data on to. After filling out one

PDF form, buying two new 500 GB hard drives, and waiting two business days, Chris had access to all of the data on taxi rides from January 1st through December 31st 2013. Even better, he posted all of the fare data online, where it has been used as the basis for a number of beautiful visualizations of transportation in New York City.

One statistic that is important to understanding the economics of taxis is *utilization*: the fraction of time that a cab is on the road and is occupied by one or more passengers. One factor that impacts utilization is the passenger's destination: a cab that drops off passengers near Union Square at midday is much more likely to find its next fare in just a minute or two, whereas a cab that drops someone off at 2 AM on Staten Island may have to drive all the way back to Manhattan before it find its next fare. We'd like to quantify these effects and find out the average time it takes for a cab to find its next fare as a function of the borough in which it dropped its passengers off—Manhattan, Brooklyn, Queens, the Bronx, Staten Island, or none of the above (e.g., if it dropped the passenger off somewhere outside of the city, like Newark International Airport).

To carry out this analysis, we need to deal with two types that data that come up all the time: temporal data, such as dates and times, and geospatial information, like points of longitude and latitude and spatial boundaries. In this chapter, we're going to demonstrate how to use Scala and Spark to work with these data types.

Getting the Data

For this analysis, we're only going to consider the fare data from January 2013, which will be about 2.5 GB of data after we uncompress it. You can access the data for each month of 2013 at *http://www.andresmh.com/nyctaxitrips/*, and if you have a sufficiently large Spark cluster at your disposal, you can re-create the following analysis against all of the data for the year. For now, let's create a working directory on our client machine and take a look at the structure of the fare data:

```
$ mkdir taxidata
$ cd taxidata
$ wget https://nyctaxitrips.blob.core.windows.net/data/trip_data_1.csv.zip
$ unzip trip_data_1.csv.zip
$ head -n 10 trip_data_1.csv
```

Each row of the file after the header represents a single taxi ride in CSV format. For each ride, we have some attributes of the cab (a hashed version of the medallion number) as well as the driver (a hashed version of the *hack license*, which is what licenses to drive taxis are called), some temporal information about when the trip started and ended, and the longitude/latitude coordinates for where the passenger(s) were picked up and where they were dropped off.

Working with Temporal and Geospatial Data in Spark

One of the great features of the Java platform is the sheer volume of code that has been developed for it over the years: for any kind of data type or algorithm you might need to use, it's likely that someone else has written a Java library that you can use to solve your problem, and there's also a good chance that an open source version of that library exists that you can download and use without having to purchase a license.

Of course, just because a library exists and is freely available doesn't mean that you necessarily want to rely on it to solve your problem; open source projects have a lot of variation in terms of their quality, their state of development in terms of bug fixes and new features, and their ease-of-use in terms of API design and the presence of useful documentation and tutorials.

Our decision-making process is a bit different than that of a developer choosing a library for an application; we want something that will be pleasant to use for interactive data analysis and that is easy to use in a distributed application. In particular, we want to be sure that the main data types that we will be working with in our RDDs implement the `Serializable` interface and/or can be easily serialized using libraries like Kryo.

Additionally, we would like the libraries we use for interactive data analysis to have as few external dependencies as possible. Tools like Maven and SBT can help application developers deal with complex dependencies when building applications, but for interactive data analysis, we would much rather simply grab a JAR file with all of the code we need, load it into the Spark shell, and start our analysis. Additionally, bringing in libraries with lots of dependencies can cause version conflicts with other libraries that Spark itself depends on, which can cause difficult-to-diagnose error conditions that developers refer to as *JAR hell*.

Finally, we would like our libraries to have relatively simple and rich APIs that do not make extensive use of Java-oriented design patterns like abstract factories and visitors. Although these patterns can be very useful for application developers, they tend to add a lot of complexity to our code that is unrelated to our analysis. Even better, many Java libraries have Scala wrappers that take advantage of Scala's power to reduce the amount of boilerplate code required to use them.

Temporal Data with JodaTime and NScalaTime

For temporal data, there is of course the Java `Date` class and the `Calendar` class. But as anyone who has ever used these libraries knows, they're difficult to work with and can require massive amounts of boilerplate for simple operations. For many years now, JodaTime has been the Java library of choice for working with temporal data.

There is a wrapper library named NScalaTime that provides some additional syntactic sugar for working with JodaTime from Scala. We can get access to all its functionality with a single import:

```
import com.github.nscala_time.time.Imports._
```

JodaTime and NScalaTime revolve around the `DateTime` class. `DateTime` objects are immutable, like Java `Strings` (and unlike the `Calendar`/`Date` objects in the regular Java APIs), and provide a number of methods that we can use to perform calculations on temporal data. In the following example, `dt1` represents 9 AM on September 4th, 2014, and `dt2` represents 3 PM on October 31st, 2014:

```
val dt1 = new DateTime(2014, 9, 4, 9, 0)
dt1: org.joda.time.DateTime = 2014-09-04T09:00:00.000-07:00

dt1.dayOfYear.get
res60: Int = 247

val dt2 = new DateTime(2014, 10, 31, 15, 0)
dt2: org.joda.time.DateTime = 2014-10-31T15:00:00.000-07:00

dt1 < dt2
res61: Boolean = true

val dt3 = dt1 + 60.days
dt3: org.joda.time.DateTime = 2014-11-03T09:00:00.000-08:00

dt3 > dt2
res62: Boolean = true
```

For data analysis problems, we usually need to convert some string representation of a date into a `DateTime` object on which we can do calculations. A simple way to accomplish this is with Java's `SimpleDateFormat`, which is useful for parsing dates in different formats. The following parses dates in the format used by the taxi data set:

```
import java.text.SimpleDateFormat

val format = new SimpleDateFormat("yyyy-MM-dd HH:mm:ss")
val date = format.parse("2014-10-12 10:30:44")
val datetime = new DateTime(date)
```

Once we have parsed our `DateTime` objects, we often want to do a kind of temporal arithmetic on them to find out how many seconds or hours or days separate them. In JodaTime, we represent the concept of a span of time by the `Duration` class, which we can create from two `DateTime` instances like this:

```
val d = new Duration(dt1, dt2)
d.getMillis
d.getStandardHours
d.getStandardDays
```

JodaTime handles all of the tedious details of different time zones and quirks of the calendar like Daylight Saving Time when it performs these duration calculations so that you don't have to worry about them.

Geospatial Data with the Esri Geometry API and Spray

Working with temporal data on the JVM is easy: just use JodaTime, maybe with a wrapper like NScalaTime if it makes your analysis easier to understand. For geospatial data, the answer isn't nearly so simple; there are many different libraries and tools that have different functions, states of development, and maturity levels, so there is not a dominant Java library for all geospatial use cases.

First problem: what kind of geospatial data do you have? There are two major kinds, vector and raster, and there are different tools for working with the different kinds of data. In our case, we have latitude and longitude for our taxi trip records, and vector data stored in the GeoJSON format that represents the boundaries of the different boroughs of New York. So we need a library that can parse GeoJSON data and can handle spatial relationships, like detecting whether a given longitude/latitude pair is contained inside of a polygon that represents the boundaries of a particular borough.

Unfortunately, there isn't an open source library that fits our needs exactly. There is a GeoJSON parser library that can convert GeoJSON into Java objects, but there isn't an associated geospatial library that can analyze spatial relationships on the generated objects. There is the GeoTools project, but it has a long list of components and dependencies—exactly the kind of thing we try to avoid when choosing a library to work with from the Spark shell. Finally, there is the Esri Geometry API for Java, which has few dependencies and can analyze spatial relationships, but can only parse a subset of the GeoJSON standard, so it won't be able to parse the GeoJSON data we downloaded without us doing some preliminary data munging.

For a data analyst, this lack of tooling might be an insurmountable problem. But we are data scientists: if our tools don't allow us to solve a problem, we build new tools. In this case, we will add Scala functionality for parsing *all* of the GeoJSON data, including the bits that aren't handled by the Esri Geometry API, by leveraging one of the many Scala projects that support parsing JSON data. The code that we will be discussing in the next few sections is available in the book's Git repo, but has also been made available as a standalone library on GitHub (*http://github.com/jwills/geojson*), where it can be used for any kind of geospatial analysis project in Scala.

Exploring the Esri Geometry API

The core data type of the Esri library is the `Geometry` object. A `Geometry` describes a shape, accompanied by a geolocation where that shape resides. The library contains a set of spatial operations that allows analyzing geometries and their relationships.

These operations can do things like tell us the area of a geometry, tell us whether two geometries overlap, or compute the geometry formed by the union of two geometries.

In our case, we'll have geometry objects representing dropoff points for cab rides (longitude and latitude), and geometry objects that represent the boundaries of a borough in NYC. The spatial relationship we're interested in is containment: is a given point in space located inside one of the polygons associated with a borough of Manhattan?

The Esri API provides a convenience class called `GeometryEngine` that contains static methods for performing all of the spatial relationship operations, including a `contains` operation. The `contains` method takes three arguments: two `Geometry` objects, and one instance of the `SpatialReference` class, which represents the coordinate system used to perform the geospatial calculations. For maximum precision, we need to analyze spatial relationships relative to a coordinate plane that maps each point on the misshapen spheroid that is planet Earth into a two-dimensional coordinate system. Geospatial engineers have a standard set of well-known identifiers (referred to as WKIDs) that can be used to reference the most commonly used coordinate systems. For our purposes, we will be using WKID 4326, which is the standard coordinate system used by GPS.

As Scala developers, we're always on the lookout for ways to reduce the amount of typing we need to do as part of our interactive data analysis in the Spark shell, where we don't have access to development environments like Eclipse and IntelliJ that can automatically complete long method names for us and provide some syntactic sugar to make it easier to read certain kinds of operations. Following the naming convention we saw in the NScalaTime library, which defined wrapper classes like `RichDateTime` and `RichDuration`, we'll define our own `RichGeometry` class that extends the Esri `Geometry` object with some useful helper methods:

```
import com.esri.core.geometry.Geometry
import com.esri.core.geometry.GeometryEngine
import com.esri.core.geometry.SpatialReference

class RichGeometry(val geometry: Geometry,
    val spatialReference: SpatialReference =
      SpatialReference.create(4326)) {
  def area2D() = geometry.calculateArea2D()

  def contains(other: Geometry): Boolean = {
    GeometryEngine.contains(geometry, other, spatialReference)
  }

  def distance(other: Geometry): Double = {
    GeometryEngine.distance(geometry, other, spatialReference)
  }
}
```

We'll also declare a companion object for `RichGeometry` that provides support for implicitly converting instances of the `Geometry` class into `RichGeometry` instances:

```
object RichGeometry {
  implicit def wrapRichGeo(g: Geometry) = {
    new RichGeometry(g)
  }
}
```

Remember, to be able to take advantage of this conversion, we need to import the implicit function definition into the Scala environment, like this:

```
import RichGeometry._
```

Intro to GeoJSON

The data we'll use for the boundaries of boroughs in New York City comes written in a format called *GeoJSON*. The core object in GeoJSON is called a *feature*, which is made up of a *geometry* instance and a set of key-value pairs called *properties*. A geometry is a shape like a point, line, or polygon. A set of features is called a FeatureCollection. Let's pull down the GeoJSON data for the NYC borough maps and take a look at its structure.

In the *taxidata* directory on your client machine, download the data and rename the file to something a bit shorter:

```
$ wget https://nycdatastables.s3.amazonaws.com/2013-08-19T18:15:35.172Z/
  nyc-borough-boundaries-polygon.geojson
$ mv nyc-borough-boundaries-polygon.geojson nyc-boroughs.geojson
```

Open the file and look at a feature record; note the properties and the geometry objects—in this case, a polygon representing the boundaries of the borough, and the properties containing the name of the borough and other related information.

The Esri Geometry API will help us parse the `geometry` JSON inside of each feature, but won't help us with parsing the `id` or the `properties` fields, which can be arbitrary JSON objects. To parse these objects, we're going to need to use a Scala JSON library, of which there are many that we can choose from.

Spray, an open source toolkit for building web services with Scala, provides a JSON library that is up to the task. *spray-json* allows us to convert any Scala object to a corresponding `JsValue` by calling an implicit `toJson` method, and it also allows us to convert any `String` that contains JSON to a parsed intermediate form by calling `par seJson`, and then convert it to a Scala type `T` by calling `convertTo[T]` on the intermediate type. Spray comes with built-in conversion implementations for the common Scala primitive types as well as tuples and the collection types, and it also has a formatting library that allows us to declare the rules for converting custom types like our `RichGeometry` class to and from JSON.

First, we'll need to create a case class for representing GeoJSON features. According to the specification, a feature is a JSON object that is required to have one field named "geometry" that corresponds to a GeoJSON geometry type, and one field named "properties" that is a JSON object with any number of key-value pairs of any type. A feature may also have an optional "id" field that may be any JSON identifier. Our `Feature` case class will define corresponding Scala fields for each of the JSON fields, and will add some convenience methods for looking up values from the map of properties:

```
import spray.json.JsValue

case class Feature(
    val id: Option[JsValue],
    val properties: Map[String, JsValue],
    val geometry: RichGeometry) {
  def apply(property: String) = properties(property)
  def get(property: String) = properties.get(property)
}
```

We're representing the `geometry` field in `Feature` using an instance of our `RichGeometry` class, which we'll create with the help of the GeoJSON geometry parsing functions from the Esri Geometry API.

We'll also need a case class that corresponds to the GeoJson FeatureCollection. To make the `FeatureCollection` class a bit easier to use, we will have it extend the `IndexedSeq[Feature]` trait by implementing the appropriate `apply` and `length` methods, so that we can call the standard Scala Collections API methods like `map`, `filter`, and `sortBy` directly on the `FeatureCollection` instance itself, without having to access the underlying `Array[Feature]` value that it wraps:

```
case class FeatureCollection(features: Array[Feature])
    extends IndexedSeq[Feature] {
  def apply(index: Int) = features(index)
  def length = features.length
}
```

After we have defined the case classes for representing the GeoJSON data, we need to define the formats that tell Spray how to convert between our domain objects (`RichGeometry`, `Feature`, and `FeatureCollection`) and a corresponding `JsValue` instance. To do this, we need to create Scala singleton objects that extend the `RootJsonFormat[T]` trait, which defines abstract `read(jsv: JsValue): T` and `write(t: T): JsValue` methods. For the `RichGeometry` class, we can delegate most of the parsing and formatting logic to the Esri Geometry API, particularly the `geometryToGeoJson` and `geometryFromGeoJson` methods on the `GeometryEngine` class, but for our case classes, we need to write the formatting code ourselves. Here's the formatting code for the `Feature` case class, including some special logic to handle the optional `id` field:

```
implicit object FeatureJsonFormat extends
    RootJsonFormat[Feature] {
  def write(f: Feature) = {
    val buf = scala.collection.mutable.ArrayBuffer(
      "type" -> JsString("Feature"),
      "properties" -> JsObject(f.properties),
      "geometry" -> f.geometry.toJson)
    f.id.foreach(v => { buf += "id" -> v})
    JsObject(buf.toMap)
  }

  def read(value: JsValue) = {
    val jso = value.asJsObject
    val id = jso.fields.get("id")
    val properties = jso.fields("properties").asJsObject.fields
    val geometry = jso.fields("geometry").convertTo[RichGeometry]
    Feature(id, properties, geometry)
  }
}
```

The `FeatureJsonFormat` object uses the `implicit` keyword so that the Spray library can look it up when the `convertTo[Feature]` method is called on an instance of `JsValue`. You can see the rest of the `RootJsonFormat` implementations in the source code for the GeoJSON library on GitHub.

Preparing the New York City Taxi Trip Data

With the GeoJSON and JodaTime libraries in hand, it's time to begin analyzing the NYC taxi trip data interactively using Spark. Let's create a *taxidata* directory in HDFS and copy the trip data we have been looking at into the cluster:

```
$ hadoop fs -mkdir taxidata
$ hadoop fs -put trip_data_1.csv taxidata/
```

Now start the Spark shell, using the `--jars` argument to make the libraries we need available in the REPL:

```
$ mvn package
$ spark-shell --jars target/ch08-geotime-1.0.0.jar
```

Once the Spark shell has loaded, we can create an RDD from the taxi data and examine the first few lines, just as we have in other chapters:

```
val taxiRaw = sc.textFile("taxidata")
val taxiHead = taxiRaw.take(10)
taxiHead.foreach(println)
```

Let's begin by defining a case class that contains the information about each taxi trip that we want to use in our analysis. We'll define a case class called `Trip` that uses the `DateTime` class from the JodaTime API to represent pickup and dropoff times, and the `Point` class from the Esri Geometry API to represent the longitude and latitude of the pickup and dropoff locations. Note that the code listings below are only illustrative extracts from the complete code that you will need to execute to follow along with this chapter. Please refer to the accompanying Chapter 8 source code repository, in particular *GeoJson.scala*.

```
import com.esri.core.geometry.Point
import com.github.nscala_time.time.Imports._

case class Trip(
  pickupTime: DateTime,
  dropoffTime: DateTime,
  pickupLoc: Point,
  dropoffLoc: Point)
```

To parse the data from the `taxiRaw` RDD into instances of our case class, we will need to create some helper objects and functions. First, we'll process the pickup and dropoff times using an instance of our `SimpleDateFormat` with an appropriate formatting string:

```
val formatter = new SimpleDateFormat(
  "yyyy-MM-dd HH:mm:ss")
```

Next, we will parse the longitude and latitude of the pickup and dropoff locations using the `Point` class and the implicit `toDouble` method Scala provides for strings:

```
def point(longitude: String, latitude: String): Point = {
  new Point(longitude.toDouble, latitude.toDouble)
}
```

With these methods in hand, we can define a `parse` function that extracts a tuple containing the driver's hack license and an instance of the `Trip` class from each line of the `taxiraw` RDD:

```
def parse(line: String): (String, Trip) = {
  val fields = line.split(',')
  val license = fields(1)
  val pickupTime = new DateTime(formatter.parse(fields(5)))
  val dropoffTime = new DateTime(formatter.parse(fields(6)))
  val pickupLoc = point(fields(10), fields(11))
  val dropoffLoc = point(fields(12), fields(13))

  val trip = Trip(pickupTime, dropoffTime, pickupLoc, dropoffLoc)
  (license, trip)
}
```

We can test the `parse` function on several of the records from the `taxiHead` array to verify that it can correctly handle a sample of the data.

Handling Invalid Records at Scale

Anyone who has been working with large-scale, real-world data sets knows that they invariably contain at least a few records that do not conform to the expectations of the person who wrote the code to handle them. Many MapReduce jobs and Spark pipelines have failed because of invalid records that caused the parsing logic to throw an exception.

Typically, we handle these exceptions one at a time by checking the logs for the individual tasks, figuring out which line of code threw the exception, and then figuring out how to tweak the code to ignore or correct the invalid records. This is a tedious process, and it often feels like we're playing whack-a-mole: just as we get one exception fixed, we discover another one on a record that came later within the partition.

One strategy that experienced data scientists deploy when working with a new data set is to add a try-catch block to their parsing code so that any invalid records can be written out to the logs without causing the entire job to fail. If there are only a handful of invalid records in the entire data set, we might be okay with ignoring them and continuing with our analysis. With Spark, we can do even better: we can adapt our parsing code so that we can interactively analyze the invalid records in our data just as easily as we would perform any other kind of analysis.

For any individual record in an RDD, there are two possible outcomes for our parsing code: it will either parse the record successfully and return meaningful output, or it will fail and throw an exception, in which case we want to capture both the value of the invalid record and the exception that was thrown. Whenever an operation has two mutually exclusive outcomes, we can use Scala's Either[L, R] type to represent the return type of the operation. For us, the "left" outcome is the successfully parsed record and the "right" outcome is a tuple of the exception we hit and the input record that caused it.

The safe function takes an argument named f of type S => T and returns a new S => Either[T, (S, Exception)] that will return either the result of calling f or, if an exception is thrown, a tuple containing the invalid input value and the exception itself:

```scala
def safe[S, T](f: S => T): S => Either[T, (S, Exception)] = {
  new Function[S, Either[T, (S, Exception)]] with Serializable {
    def apply(s: S): Either[T, (S, Exception)] = {
      try {
        Left(f(s))
      } catch {
        case e: Exception => Right((s, e))
      }
    }
  }
}
```

We can now create a safe wrapper function called `safeParse` by passing our `parse` function (of type `String => Trip`) to the `safe` function, and then applying `safeParse` to the `taxiRaw` RDD:

```
val safeParse = safe(parse)
val taxiParsed = taxiRaw.map(safeParse)
taxiParsed.cache()
```

If we want to determine how many of the input lines were parsed successfully, we can use the `isLeft` method on `Either[L, R]` in combination with the `countByValue` action:

```
taxiParsed.map(_.isLeft).
countByValue().
foreach(println)
...
(false,87)
(true,14776529)
```

This looks like good news—only a small fraction of the input records threw exceptions. We would like to examine these records in the client to see which exception was thrown and determine if our parsing code can be improved to correctly handle them. One way to get the invalid records is to use a combination of the `filter` and `map` methods:

```
val taxiBad = taxiParsed.
  filter(_.isRight).
  map(_.right.get)
```

Alternatively, we can do both the filtering and the mapping in a single call using the `collect` method on the RDD class that takes a *partial function* as an argument. A partial function is a function that has an `isDefinedAt` method, which determines whether or not it is defined for a particular input. We can create partial functions in Scala either by extending the `PartialFunction[S, T]` trait or by the following special `case` syntax:

```
val taxiBad = taxiParsed.collect({
  case t if t.isRight => t.right.get
})
```

The `if` block determines the values for which the partial function is defined, and the expression after the `=>` gives the value the partial function returns. Be careful to distinguish between the `collect` transformation that applies a partial function to an RDD and the `collect()` action that takes no arguments and returns the contents of the RDD to the client:

```
taxiBad.collect().foreach(println)
```

Note that most of the bad records throw `ArrayIndexOutOfBoundsExceptions` because they are missing the fields that we are trying to extract in the `parse` function we wrote earlier. Because there are relatively few of these bad records (only 87 or so), we will drop them from consideration and continue our analysis, focusing on the records in the data that parsed correctly:

```
val taxiGood = taxiParsed.collect({
  case t if t.isLeft => t.left.get
})
taxiGood.cache()
```

Even though the records in the taxiGood RDD parsed correctly, they may still have data quality problems that we want to uncover and handle. To find the remaining data quality problems, we can start to think of conditions that we would expect to be true for any correctly recorded trip.

Given the temporal nature of our trip data, one reasonable invariant that we can expect is that the dropoff time for any trip will be sometime after the pickup time. We might also expect that trips will not take more than a few hours to complete, although it's certainly possible that long trips, trips that take place during rush hour, or trips that are delayed by accidents could go on for several hours. We're not exactly sure what the cutoff should be for a trip that takes a "reasonable" amount of time.

Let's define a helper function named hours that uses the JodaTime Duration class to compute the number of hours a taxi ride took. We can then use it to compute the histogram of the number of hours the trips in the taxiGood RDD took from start to finish:

```
import org.joda.time.Duration

def hours(trip: Trip): Long = {
  val d = new Duration(
    trip.pickupTime,
    trip.dropoffTime)
  d.getStandardHours
}

taxiGood.values.map(hours).
  countByValue().
  toList.
  sorted.
  foreach(println)
...
(-8,1)
(0,14752245)
(1,22933)
(2,842)
(3,197)
(4,86)
(5,55)
(6,42)
(7,33)
```

```
(8,17)
(9,9)
...
```

Everything looks fine here, except for one trip that took a negative eight hours to complete! Perhaps the DeLorean from *Back to the Future* is moonlighting as an NYC taxi? Let's examine this record:

```
taxiGood.values.
  filter(trip => hours(trip) == -8).
  collect().
  foreach(println)
```

This reveals the one odd record—a trip that began around 6 PM on January 25th and finished just before 10 AM the same day. It isn't obvious what exactly went wrong with the recording of this trip, but because it only seemed to happen for a single record, it should be okay to exclude it from our analysis for now.

Looking at the remainder of the trips that went on for a nonnegative number of hours, it appears that the vast majority of taxi rides last for no longer than three hours. We'll apply a filter to the `taxiGood` RDD so that we can focus on the distribution of these "typical" rides and ignore the outliers for now:

```
val taxiClean = taxiGood.filter {
  case (lic, trip) => {
    val hrs = hours(trip)
    0 <= hrs && hrs < 3
  }
}
```

Geospatial Analysis

Let's start examining the geospatial aspects of the taxi data. For each trip, we have a longitude/latitude pair representing where the passenger(s) were picked up and another one for where they were dropped off. We would like to be able to determine which borough each of these longitude/latitude pairs belongs to, and identify any trips that did not start or end in any of the five boroughs. For example, if a taxi took passengers from Manhattan to Newark International Airport, that would be a valid ride that would be interesting to analyze, even though it would not end within one of the five boroughs. However, if it looks as if a taxi took a passenger to the South Pole, we can be reasonably confident that the record is invalid and should be excluded from our analysis.

To perform our borough analysis, we'll need to load the GeoJSON data we downloaded earlier and stored in the *nyc-boroughs.geojson* file. The `Source` class in the `scala.io` package makes it easy to read the contents of a text file or URL into the client as a single `String`:

```
val geojson = scala.io.Source.
  fromFile("nyc-boroughs.geojson").
  mkString
```

Now we need to import the GeoJSON parsing tools we reviewed earlier in the chapter using Spray and Esri into the Spark shell so that we can parse the geojson string into an instance of our FeatureCollection case class:

```
import com.cloudera.datascience.geotime._
import GeoJsonProtocol._
import spray.json._

val features = geojson.parseJson.convertTo[FeatureCollection]
```

We can create a sample point to test out the functionality of the Esri Geometry API and verify that it can correctly identify which borough a particular point belongs to:

```
val p = new Point(-73.994499, 40.75066)
val borough = features.find(f => f.geometry.contains(p))
```

Before we use the features on the taxi trip data, we should take a moment to think about how to organize this geospatial data for maximum efficiency. One option would be to research data structures that are optimized for geospatial lookups, such as quad trees, and then find or write our own implementation. But let's see if we can come up with a quick heuristic that will allow us to bypass that bit of work.

The find method will iterate through the FeatureCollection until it finds a feature whose geometry contains the given Point of longitude/latitude. Most taxi rides in New York begin and end in Manhattan, so if the geospatial features that represent Manhattan are earlier in the sequence, most of the find calls will return relatively quickly. We can use the fact that the boroughCode property of each feature can be used as a sorting key, with the code for Manhattan equal to 1 and the code for Staten Island equal to 5. Within the features for each borough, we want the features associated with the largest polygons to come before the smaller polygons, because most trips will be to and from the "major" region of each borough. Sorting the features by the combination of the borough code and the area2D() of each feature's geometry should do the trick:

```
val areaSortedFeatures = features.sortBy(f => {
  val borough = f("boroughCode").convertTo[Int]
  (borough, -f.geometry.area2D())
})
```

Note that we're sorting based on the negation of the area2D() value, because we want the largest polygons to come first and Scala sorts in ascending order by default.

Now we can broadcast the sorted features in the areaSortedFeatures sequence to the cluster and write a function that uses these features to find out in which of the five boroughs (if any) a particular trip ended:

```
val bFeatures = sc.broadcast(areaSortedFeatures)

def borough(trip: Trip): Option[String] = {
  val feature: Option[Feature] = bFeatures.value.find(f => {
    f.geometry.contains(trip.dropoffLoc)
  })
  feature.map(f => {
    f("borough").convertTo[String]
  })
}
```

If none of the features contain the `dropoff_loc` for the trip, the value of `optf` will be None, and the result of calling `map` on a `None` value is still `None`. We can apply this function to the trips in the `taxiClean` RDD to create a histogram of trips by borough:

```
taxiClean.values.
  map(borough).
  countByValue().
  foreach(println)
...
(Some(Queens),672135)
(Some(Manhattan),12978954)
(Some(Bronx),67421)
(Some(Staten Island),3338)
(Some(Brooklyn),715235)
(None,338937)
```

As we expected, the vast majority of trips end in the borough of Manhattan, while relatively few trips end in Staten Island. One surprising observation is the number of trips that end outside of any borough; the number of `None` records is substantially larger than the number of taxi rides that end in the Bronx. Let's grab some examples of this kind of trip from the data:

```
taxiClean.values.
  filter(t => borough(t).isEmpty).
  take(10).foreach(println)
```

When we print out these records, we see that a substantial fraction of them start and end at the point `(0.0, 0.0)`, indicating that the trip location is missing for these records. We should filter these events out of our data set, because they won't help us with our analysis:

```
def hasZero(trip: Trip): Boolean = {
  val zero = new Point(0.0, 0.0)
  (zero.equals(trip.pickupLoc) || zero.equals(trip.dropoffLoc))
}

val taxiDone = taxiClean.filter {
  case (lic, trip) => !hasZero(trip)
}.cache()
```

When we rerun our borough analysis on the `taxiDone` RDD, we see this:

```
taxiDone.values.
  map(borough).
  countByValue().
  foreach(println)
...
(Some(Queens),670996)
(Some(Manhattan),12973001)
(Some(Bronx),67333)
(Some(Staten Island),3333)
(Some(Brooklyn),714775)
(None,65353)
```

Our zero point filter removed a small number of observations from the output boroughs, but it removed a large fraction of the None entries, leaving a much more reasonable number of observations that had dropoffs outside the city.

Sessionization in Spark

Our goal, from many pages ago, was to investigate the relationship between the borough in which a driver drops his passenger off and the amount of time it takes to acquire another fare. At this point, the taxiDone RDD contains all of the individual trips for each taxi driver in individual records that are distributed across different partitions of the data. To compute the length of time between the end of one ride and the start of the next one, we need to aggregate all of the trips from a shift by a single driver into a single record, and then sort the trips within that shift by time. The sort step allows us to compare the dropoff time of one trip to the pickup time of the next trip. This kind of analysis, in which we want to analyze a single entity as it executes a series of events over time, is called *sessionization*, and is commonly performed over web logs to analyze the behavior of the users of a website.

Sessionization can be a very powerful technique for uncovering insights in data and for building new data products that can be used to help people make better decisions. For example, Google's spell-correction engine is built on top of the sessions of user activity that Google builds each day from the logged records of every event (searches, clicks, maps visits, etc.) occurring on its web properties. To identify likely spell-correction candidates, Google processes those sessions looking for situations where a user typed in a query, didn't click anything, typed in a slightly different query a few seconds later, and then clicked a result and didn't come back to Google. Then it counts how often this pattern occurs for any pair of queries. If it occurs frequently enough (e.g., if every time we see the query "untied stats," it's followed a few seconds later by the query "united states"), then we assume that the second query is a spell correction of the first.

This analysis takes advantage of the patterns of human behavior that are represented in the event logs to build a spell-correction engine from data that is more powerful than any engine that could be created from a dictionary. The engine can be used to perform spell correction in any language, and can correct words that might not be included in any dictionary (e.g., the name of a new startup), and can even correct queries like "untied stats" where none of the words are misspelled! Google uses similar techniques to show recommended and related searches, as well as to decide which queries should return a OneBox result that gives the answer to a query on the search page itself, without requiring that the user click through to a different page. There are OneBoxes for weather, scores from sports games, addresses, and lots of other kinds of queries.

So far, information about the set of events that occurs to each entity is spread out across the RDD's partitions, so, for analysis, we need to place these relevant events next to each other and in chronological order. In the next section, we'll show how to efficiently construct and analyze sessions using some advanced functionality that was introduced in Spark 1.2.

Building Sessions: Secondary Sorts in Spark

The naive way to create sessions in Spark is to perform a `groupBy` on the identifier we want to create sessions for and then sort the events post-shuffle by a timestamp identifier. If we only have a small number of events for each entity, this approach will work reasonably well. However, because this approach requires all the events for any particular entity to be in memory at the same time, it will not scale as the number of events for each entity gets larger and larger. We need a way of building sessions that does not require all of the events for a particular entity to be held in memory at the same time for sorting.

In MapReduce, we can build sessions by performing a *secondary sort*, where we create a composite key made up of an identifier and a timestamp value, sort all of the records on the composite key, and then use a custom partitioner and grouping function to ensure that all of the records for the same identifier appear in the same output partition. Fortunately, Spark can also support this same secondary sort pattern by making use of its `repartitionAndSortWithinPartitions` transformation.

In the repo, we've provided an implementation of a `groupByKeyAndSortValues` transformation that does exactly this. Because the workings of this functionality are mostly orthogonal to the concepts this chapter is covering, we're omitting the gory details here. Work is progressing on Spark JIRA SPARK-3655 to add a transformation like this to core Spark.

The transformation accepts four parameters:

- The RDD of key-value pairs that we want to operate on.
- A function that accepts a value and extracts the secondary key to sort on.

- An optional splitting function that can break up sorted runs with the same key into multiple groups. In our case, we'll use this to break up multiple shifts from the same driver.

- The number of partitions in the output RDD.

Our secondary key in this case is the pickup time for the trip:

```
def secondaryKeyFunc(trip: Trip) = trip.pickupTime.getMillis
```

We need to decide what criteria we should use to determine when one shift ends and another one begins. Like some of the other choices we've made in this chapter (e.g., filtering out trips that go on for longer than three hours), this is a somewhat arbitrary choice, and we need to be conscious of how this choice may impact the results of our subsequent analysis. It's a good idea, especially in the early stages of a sessionization analysis, to try many different split criteria and see how the results of our analysis change. Once we settle on a reasonable window of time to distinguish between different shifts, the important thing is to make a choice—even though it is somewhat arbitrary—and to stick with that choice for the long haul. Our primary interest as data scientists is how things change over time, and keeping our definitions for data and metrics constant allows us to make valid comparisons over long periods.

Let's start out by choosing four hours as our threshold, so that any gap of time between sequential pickups longer than that time will be considered two separate shifts, and the intermediate time will be considered a break where the driver was not accepting new passengers:

```
def split(t1: Trip, t2: Trip): Boolean = {
  val p1 = t1.pickupTime
  val p2 = t2.pickupTime
  val d = new Duration(p1, p2)
  d.getStandardHours >= 4
}
```

Armed with our secondary key function and splitting function, we can perform the grouping and sorting. Because this operation triggers a shuffle and a fair bit of computation, and we'll need to use the results more than once, we cache the results:

```
val sessions = groupByKeyAndSortValues(
  taxiDone, secondaryKeyFunc, split, 30)
sessions.cache()
```

The result is an RDD[(String, List[Trip])], where all of the trips belong to the same shift for the same driver, and the trips are sorted by time.

Executing a sessionization pipeline is an expensive operation, and the sessionized data is often useful for many different analysis tasks that we might want to perform. In settings where one might want to pick up on the analysis later or collaborate with other data scientists, it's a good idea to amortize the cost of sessionizing a large data set by only performing the sessionization once, and then writing the sessionized data to HDFS so that it can be used to answer lots of different questions. Performing sessionization once is also a good way to enforce standard rules for session definitions across the entire data science team, which has the same benefits for ensuring apples-to-apples comparisons of results.

At this point, we are ready to analyze our sessions data to see how long it takes for a driver to find his next fare after a dropoff in a particular borough. We will create a boroughDuration method that takes two instances of the Trip class and computes both the borough of the first trip and the Duration between the dropoff time of the first trip and the pickup time of the second:

```
def boroughDuration(t1: Trip, t2: Trip) = {
  val b = borough(t1)
  val d = new Duration(
    t1.dropoffTime,
    t2.pickupTime)
  (b, d)
}
```

We want to apply our new function to all sequential pairs of trips inside of our ses sions RDD. Although we could write a for loop to do this, we can also use the slid ing method of the Scala Collections API to get the sequential pairs in a more functional way:

```
val boroughDurations: RDD[(Option[String], Duration)] =
  sessions.values.flatMap(trips => {
    val iter: Iterator[Seq[Trip]] = trips.sliding(2)
    val viter = iter.filter(_.size == 2)
    viter.map(p => boroughDuration(p(0), p(1)))
  }).cache()
```

The filter call on the result of the sliding method ensures that we ignore any sessions that contain only a single trip, and the result of our flatMap over the sessions is an RDD[(Option[String], Duration)] that we can now examine. First, we should do a validation check to ensure that most of the durations are nonnegative:

```
boroughDurations.values.map(_.getStandardHours).
  countByValue().
  toList.
  sorted.
  foreach(println)
...
(-2,2)
(-1,17)
(0,13367875)
(1,347479)
(2,76147)
(3,19511)
```

Only a few of the records have a negative duration, and when we examine them more closely, there don't seem to be any common patterns to them that we could use to understand the source of the erroneous data. We will exclude these records from our analysis of the distribution of durations, which we can compute with the help of Spark's StatCounter class that we have used before:

```
import org.apache.spark.util.StatCounter

boroughDurations.filter {
  case (b, d) => d.getMillis >= 0
}.mapValues(d => {
  val s = new StatCounter()
  s.merge(d.getStandardSeconds)
}).
reduceByKey((a, b) => a.merge(b)).collect().foreach(println)
...

(Some(Bronx),(count: 56951, mean: 1945.79,
  stdev: 1617.69, max: 14116, min: 0))
(None,(count: 57685, mean: 1922.10,
  stdev: 1903.77, max: 14280, min: 0))
(Some(Queens),(count: 557826, mean: 2338.25,
  stdev: 2120.98, max: 14378.000000, min: 0))
(Some(Manhattan),(count: 12505455, mean: 622.58,
  stdev: 1022.34, max: 14310, min: 0))
(Some(Brooklyn),(count: 626231, mean: 1348.675465,
  stdev: 1565.119331, max: 14355, min: 0))
(Some(Staten Island),(count: 2612, mean: 2612.24,
  stdev: 2186.29, max: 13740, min: 0.000000))
```

As we would expect, the data shows that dropoffs in Manhattan have the shortest amount of downtime for drivers at just over 10 minutes. Taxi rides that end in Brooklyn have a downtime of more than twice that, and the relatively few rides that end in Staten Island take a driver an average of almost 45 minutes to get to his next fare.

As the data demonstrates, taxi drivers have a major financial incentive to discriminate among passengers based on their final destination; dropoffs in Staten Island, in particular, involve an extensive amount of downtime for a driver. The NYC Taxi and Limousine Commission has made a major effort over the years to identify this discrimination and has fined drivers who have been caught rejecting passengers because of where they wanted to go. It would be interesting to attempt to examine the data for unusually short taxi rides that could be indicative of a dispute between the driver and the passenger about where the passenger wanted to be dropped off.

Where to Go from Here

Imagine using this same technique on the taxi data to build an application that could recommend the best place for a cab to go after a dropoff, based on the current traffic patterns and the historical record of next-best locations that is contained within this data. You could also look at the information from the perspective of someone trying to catch a cab: given the current time, place, and weather data, what is the probability that I will be able to hail a cab from the street within the next five minutes? This sort of information could be incorporated into applications like Google Maps to help travelers decide when to leave and which travel option they should take.

The Esri API is one of a few different tools that can help us interact with geospatial data from JVM-based languages. Another is GeoTrellis, a geospatial library written in Scala, that seeks to be easily accessible from Spark. A third is GeoTools, a Java-based GIS toolkit.

CHAPTER 9

Estimating Financial Risk through Monte Carlo Simulation

Sandy Ryza

If you want to understand geology, study earthquakes.
If you want to understand the economy, study the Depression.
—Ben Bernanke

Under reasonable circumstances, how much can you expect to lose? This is the quantity that the financial statistic *Value at Risk* (VaR) seeks to measure. Since its development soon after the stock market crash of 1987, VaR has seen widespread use across financial services organizations. The statistic plays a vital role in the management of these institutions—it helps determine how much cash they must hold to meet the credit ratings that they seek. In addition, some use it to more broadly understand the risk characteristics of large portfolios, and others compute it before executing trades to help inform immediate decisions.

Many of the most sophisticated approaches to estimating this statistic rely on computationally intensive simulation of markets under random conditions. The technique behind these approaches, called *Monte Carlo simulation*, involves posing thousands or millions of random market scenarios and observing how they tend to affect a portfolio. Spark is an ideal tool for Monte Carlo simulation, because the technique is naturally massively parallelizable. Spark can leverage thousands of cores to run random trials and aggregate their results. As a general-purpose data transformation engine, it is also adept at performing the pre- and post-processing steps that surround the simulations. It can transform the raw financial data into the model parameters needed to carry out the simulations, as well as support ad-hoc analysis of the results. Its simple programming model can drastically reduce development time compared to more traditional approaches that use HPC environments.

Let's define "how much can you expect to lose" a little more rigorously. VaR is a simple measure of investment risk that tries to provide a reasonable estimate of the maximum probable loss in value of an investment portfolio over the particular time period. A VaR statistic depends on three parameters: a portfolio, a time period, and a p-value. A VaR of 1 million dollars with a 5% p-value and two weeks indicates the belief that the portfolio stands only a 5% chance of losing more than 1 million dollars over two weeks.

We'll also discuss how to compute a related statistic called *Conditional Value at Risk* (CVaR), sometimes known as Expected Shortfall, which the Basel Committee on Banking Supervision has recently proposed as a better risk measure than VaR. A CVaR statistic has the same three parameters as a VaR statistic, but considers the expected loss instead of the cutoff value. A CVaR of 5 million dollars with a 5% *q-value* and two weeks indicates the belief that the average loss in the worst 5% of outcomes is 5 million dollars.

In service of modeling VaR, we'll introduce a few different concepts, approaches, and packages. We'll cover kernel density estimation and plotting with the *breeze-viz* package, sampling from the multivariate normal distribution, and statistics functions from the Apache Commons Math package.

Terminology

This chapter makes use of a set of terms specific to the finance domain. We'll briefly define them here:

Instrument
A tradable asset, such as a bond, loan, option, or stock investment. At any particular time, an instrument is considered to have a *value*, which is the price for which it could be sold.

Portfolio
A collection of instruments owned by a financial institution.

Return
The change in an instrument or portfolio's value over a time period.

Loss
A negative return.

Index
An imaginary portfolio of instruments. For example, the NASDAQ Composite index includes about 3,000 stocks and similar instruments for major US and international companies.

Market factor

A value that can be used as an indicator of macro aspects of the financial climate at a particular time—for example, the value of an index, the Gross Domestic Product of the United States, or the exchange rate between the dollar and the euro. We will often refer to market factors as just *factors*.

Methods for Calculating VaR

So far, our definition of VaR has been fairly open ended. Estimating this statistic requires proposing a model for how a portfolio functions and choosing the probability distribution its returns are likely to take. Institutions employ a variety of approaches for calculating VaR, all of which tend to fall under a few general methods.

Variance-Covariance

Variance-Covariance is by far the simplest and least computationally intensive method. Its model assumes that the return of each instrument is normally distributed, which allows deriving a estimate analytically.

Historical Simulation

Historical Simulation extrapolates risk from historical data by using its distribution directly instead of relying on summary statistics. For example, to determine a 95% VaR for a portfolio, it might look at that portfolio's performance for the last hundred days and estimate the statistic as its value on the fifth-worst day. A drawback of this method is that historical data can be limited and fails to include "what-ifs." The history we have for the instruments in our portfolio may lack market collapses, but we might wish to model what happens to our portfolio in these situations. Techniques exist for making historical simulation robust to these issues, such as introducing "shocks" into the data, but we won't cover them here.

Monte Carlo Simulation

Monte Carlo Simulation, which the rest of this chapter will focus on, tries weakening the assumptions in the previous methods by simulating the portfolio under random conditions. When we can't derive a closed form for a probability distribution analytically, we can often estimate its density function (PDF) by repeatedly sampling simpler random variables that it depends on and seeing how it plays out in aggregate. In its most general form, this method:

- Defines a relationship between market conditions and each instrument's returns. This relationship takes the form of a model fitted to historical data.

- Defines distributions for the market conditions that are straightforward to sample from. These distributions are fitted to historical data.
- Poses *trials* consisting of random market conditions.
- Calculates the total portfolio loss for each trial, and uses these losses to define an empirical distribution over losses. This means that, if we run 100 trials and want to estimate the 5% VaR, we would choose it as the loss from the trial with the fifth-greatest loss. To calculate the 5% CVaR, we would find the average loss over the five worst trials.

Of course, the Monte Carlo method isn't perfect either. The models for generating trial conditions and for inferring instrument performance from them must make simplifying assumptions, and the distribution that comes out won't be more accurate than the models and historical data going in.

Our Model

A Monte Carlo risk model typically phrases each instrument's return in terms of a set of *market factors*. Common market factors might be the value of indexes like the S&P 500, the US GDP, or currency exchange rates. We then need a model that predicts the return of each instrument based on these market conditions. In our simulation, we'll use a simple linear model. By our previous definition of return, a factor return is a change in the value of a market factor over a particular time. For example, if the value of the S&P 500 moves from 2,000 to 2,100 over a time interval, its return would be 100. We'll derive a set of features from simple transformations of the factor returns. That is, the market factor vector m_t for a trial t is transformed by some function φ to produce a feature vector of possible different length f_t:

$$f_t = \phi(m_t)$$

For each instrument, we'll train a model that assigns a weight to each feature. To calculate r_{it}, the return of instrument i in trial t, we use c_i, the intercept term for the instrument; w_{ij}, the regression weight for feature j on instrument i; and f_{tj}, the randomly generated value of feature j in trial t:

$$r_{it} = c_i + \sum_{j=1}^{|w_i|} w_{ij} * f_{tj}$$

This means that the return of each instrument is calculated as the sum of the returns of the market factor features multiplied by their weights for that instrument. We can fit the linear model for each instrument using historical data (also known as doing linear regression). If the horizon of the VaR calculation is two weeks, the regression treats every (overlapping) two-week interval in history as a labeled point.

It's also worth mentioning that we could have chosen a more complicated model. For example, the model need not be linear: it could be a regression tree or explicitly incorporate domain-specific knowledge.

Now that we have our model for calculating instrument losses from market factors, we need a process for simulating the behavior of market factors. A simple assumption is that each market factor return follows a normal distribution. To capture the fact that market factors are often correlated—when NASDAQ is down, the Dow is likely to be suffering as well—we can use a multivariate normal distribution with a non-diagonal covariance matrix:

$$m_t \sim \mathcal{N}(\mu, \Sigma)$$

where μ is a vector of the empirical means of the returns of the factors and Σ is the empirical covariance matrix of the returns of the factors.

As before, we could have chosen a more complicated method of simulating the market or assumed a different type of distribution for each market factor, perhaps using distributions with fatter tails.

Getting the Data

It can be difficult to find large volumes of nicely formatted historical price data, but Yahoo! has a variety of stock data available for download in CSV format. The following script, located in the *risk/data* directory of the repo, will make a series of REST calls to download histories for all the stocks included in the NASDAQ index and place them in a *stocks/* directory:

```
$ ./download-all-symbols.sh
```

We also need historical data for our risk factors. For our factors, we'll use the values of the S&P 500 and NASDAQ indexes, as well as the prices of 30-year treasury bonds and crude oil. The indexes can be downloaded from Yahoo! as well:

```
$ mkdir factors/
$ ./download-symbol.sh ^GSPC factors
$ ./download-symbol.sh ^IXIC factors
```

The treasury bonds and crude oil must be copy/pasted from *Investing.com*.

Preprocessing

At this point, we have data from different sources in different formats. For example, the first few rows of the Yahoo!-formatted data for GOOGL looks like:

```
Date,Open,High,Low,Close,Volume,Adj Close
2014-10-24,554.98,555.00,545.16,548.90,2175400,548.90
2014-10-23,548.28,557.40,545.50,553.65,2151300,553.65
2014-10-22,541.05,550.76,540.23,542.69,2973700,542.69
2014-10-21,537.27,538.77,530.20,538.03,2459500,538.03
2014-10-20,520.45,533.16,519.14,532.38,2748200,532.38
```

And the *Investing.com* history for crude oil price looks like:

```
Oct 24, 2014    81.01   81.95   81.95   80.36   272.51K -1.32%
Oct 23, 2014    82.09   80.42   82.37   80.05   354.84K 1.95%
Oct 22, 2014    80.52   82.55   83.15   80.22   352.22K -2.39%
Oct 21, 2014    82.49   81.86   83.26   81.57   297.52K 0.71%
Oct 20, 2014    81.91   82.39   82.73   80.78   301.04K -0.93%
Oct 19, 2014    82.67   82.39   82.72   82.39   -       0.75%
```

From each source, for each instrument and factor, we want to derive a list of (date, closing price) tuples. Using Java's `SimpleDateFormat`, we can parse dates in the *Investing.com* format:

```
import java.text.SimpleDateFormat

val format = new SimpleDateFormat("MMM d, yyyy")
format.parse("Oct 24, 2014")
res0: java.util.Date = Fri Oct 24 00:00:00 PDT 201
```

The 3,000-instrument histories and 4-factor histories are small enough to read and process locally. This remains the case even for larger simulations with hundreds of thousands of instruments and thousands of factors. The need for a distributed system like Spark comes in when we're actually running the simulations, which can require massive amounts of computation on each instrument.

To read a full *Investing.com* history from local disk:

```
import com.github.nscala_time.time.Imports._
import java.io.File
import scala.io.Source

def readInvestingDotComHistory(file: File):
    Array[(DateTime, Double)] = {
  val format = new SimpleDateFormat("MMM d, yyyy")
  val lines = Source.fromFile(file).getLines().toSeq
  lines.map(line => {
    val cols = line.split('\t')
    val date = new DateTime(format.parse(cols(0)))
    val value = cols(1).toDouble
    (date, value)
```

```
    }).reverse.toArray
  }
```

As in Chapter 8, we use JodaTime and its Scala wrapper NScalaTime to represent our dates, wrapping the `Date` output of `SimpleDateFormat` in a JodaTime `DateTime`.

To read a full Yahoo! history:

```
def readYahooHistory(file: File): Array[(DateTime, Double)] = {
  val format = new SimpleDateFormat("yyyy-MM-dd")
  val lines = Source.fromFile(file).getLines().toSeq
  lines.tail.map(line => {
    val cols = line.split(',')
    val date = new DateTime(format.parse(cols(0)))
    val value = cols(1).toDouble
    (date, value)
  }).reverse.toArray
}
```

Notice that `lines.tail` is useful for excluding the header row. We load all the data and filter out instruments with less than five years of history:

```
val start = new DateTime(2009, 10, 23, 0, 0)
val end = new DateTime(2014, 10, 23, 0, 0)

val files = new File("data/stocks/").listFiles()
val rawStocks: Seq[Array[(DateTime, Double)]] =
  files.flatMap(file => {
    try {
      Some(readYahooHistory(file))
    } catch {
      case e: Exception => None
    }
  }).filter(_.size >= 260*5+10)


val factorsPrefix = "data/factors/"
val factors1: Seq[Array[(DateTime, Double)]] =
  Array("crudeoil.tsv", "us30yeartreasurybonds.tsv").
  map(x => new File(factorsPrefix + x)).
  map(readInvestingDotComHistory)
val factors2: Seq[Array[(DateTime, Double)]] =
  Array("^GSPC.csv", "^IXIC.csv").
  map(x => new File(factorsPrefix + x)).
  map(readYahooHistory)
```

Different types of instruments may trade on different days, or the data may have missing values for other reasons, so it is important to make sure that our different histories align. First, we need to trim all of our time series to the same region in time. Then, we need to fill in missing values. To deal with time series that are missing values at the start and end dates in the time region, we simply fill in those dates with nearby values in the time region:

```
def trimToRegion(history: Array[(DateTime, Double)],
    start: DateTime, end: DateTime): Array[(DateTime, Double)] = {
  var trimmed = history.
    dropWhile(_._1 < start).takeWhile(_._1 <= end) ❶
  if (trimmed.head._1 != start) {
    trimmed = Array((start, trimmed.head._2)) ++ trimmed
  }
  if (trimmed.last._1 != end) {
    trimmed = trimmed ++ Array((end, trimmed.last._2))
  }
  trimmed
}
```

❶ Implicitly takes advantage of the NScalaTime operator overloading for comparing dates

To deal with missing values within a time series, we use a simple imputation strategy that fills in an instrument's price as its most recent closing price before that day. Unfortunately, there is no pretty Scala collections method that can do this for us, so we need to write our own:

```
import scala.collection.mutable.ArrayBuffer

def fillInHistory(history: Array[(DateTime, Double)],
    start: DateTime, end: DateTime): Array[(DateTime, Double)] = {
  var cur = history
  val filled = new ArrayBuffer[(DateTime, Double)]()
  var curDate = start
  while (curDate < end) {
    if (cur.tail.nonEmpty && cur.tail.head._1 == curDate) {
      cur = cur.tail
    }

    filled += ((curDate, cur.head._2))

    curDate += 1.days
    // Skip weekends
    if (curDate.dayOfWeek().get > 5) curDate += 2.days
  }
  filled.toArray
}
```

We apply `trimToRegion` and `fillInHistory` to the data:

```
val stocks = rawStocks.
  map(trimToRegion(_, start, end)).
  map(fillInHistory(_, start, end))

val factors = (factors1 ++ factors2).
  map(trimToRegion(_, start, end)).
  map(fillInHistory(_, start, end))
```

Each element of `stocks` is an array of values at different time points for a particular stock. `factors` has the same structure. All these arrays should have equal length, which we can verify with:

```
(stocks ++ factors).forall(_.size == stocks(0).size)
res17: Boolean = true
```

Determining the Factor Weights

Recall that Value at Risk deals with losses *over a particular time horizon*. We are not concerned with the absolute prices of instruments, but how those prices move over a given length of time. In our calculation, we will set that length to two weeks. The following function makes use of the Scala collections' `sliding` method to transform time series of prices into an overlapping sequence of price movements over two-week intervals. Note that we use 10 instead of 14 to define the window because financial data does not include weekends:

```
def twoWeekReturns(history: Array[(DateTime, Double)])
  : Array[Double] = {
  history.sliding(10).
    map { window =>
      val next = window.last._2
      val prev = window.head._2
      (next - prev) / prev
    }.toArray
}

val stocksReturns = stocks.map(twoWeekReturns)
val factorsReturns = factors.map(twoWeekReturns)
```

With these return histories in hand, we can turn to our goal of training predictive models for the instrument returns. For each instrument, we want a model that predicts its two-week return based on the returns of the factors over the same time period. For simplicity, we will use a linear regression model.

To model the fact that instrument returns may be nonlinear functions of the factor returns, we can include some additional features in our model that we derive from nonlinear transformations of the factor returns. We will try adding two additional features for each factor return: its square and its square root. Our model is still a linear model in the sense that the response variable is a linear function of the features. Some of the features just happen to be determined by nonlinear functions of the factor returns. Keep in mind that this particular feature transformation is meant to demonstrate some of the options available—it shouldn't be perceived as a state-of-the-art practice in predictive financial modeling.

While we will be carrying out many regressions—one for each instrument—the number of features and data points in each regression is small, meaning that we don't need to make use of Spark's distributed linear modeling capabilities. Instead, we'll use the ordinary least squares regression offered by the Apache Commons Math package. While our factor data is currently a `Seq` of histories (each an array of (`DateTime`, `Double`) tuples), `OLSMultipleLinearRegression` expects data as an array of sample points (in our case a two-week interval), so we need to transpose our factor matrix:

```
def factorMatrix(histories: Seq[Array[Double]])
  : Array[Array[Double]] = {
  val mat = new Array[Array[Double]](histories.head.length)
  for (i <- 0 until histories.head.length) {
    mat(i) = histories.map(_(i)).toArray
  }
  mat
}

val factorMat = factorMatrix(factorsReturns)
```

Then we can tack on our additional features:

```
def featurize(factorReturns: Array[Double]): Array[Double] = {
  val squaredReturns = factorReturns.
    map(x => math.signum(x) * x * x)
  val squareRootedReturns = factorReturns.
    map(x => math.signum(x) * math.sqrt(math.abs(x)))
  squaredReturns ++ squareRootedReturns ++ factorReturns
}

val factorFeatures = factorMat.map(featurize)
```

And then fit the linear models:

```
import org.apache.commons.math3.stat.regression.OLSMultipleLinearRegression

def linearModel(instrument: Array[Double],
    factorMatrix: Array[Array[Double]])
  : OLSMultipleLinearRegression = {
  val regression = new OLSMultipleLinearRegression()
  regression.newSampleData(instrument, factorMatrix)
  regression
}

val models = stocksReturns.map(linearModel(_, factorFeatures))
```

We will elide this analysis for brevity, but at this point in any real-world pipeline, it would be useful to understand how well these models fit the data. Because the data points are drawn from time series, and especially because the time intervals are overlapping, it is very likely that the samples are autocorrelated. This means that common measures like R^2 are likely to overestimate how well the models fit the data. The Breusch-Godfrey (*http://en.wikipedia.org/wiki/Breusch%E2%80%93Godfrey_test*) test is a standard test for assessing these effects. One quick way to evaluate a model is to separate a time series into two sets, leaving out enough data points in the middle so that the last points in the earlier set are not autocorrelated with the first points in the later set. Then train the model on one set and look at its error on the other.

To find the model parameters for each instrument, we can use `OLSMultipleLinearRegression`'s `estimateRegressionParameters` method:

```
val factorWeights = models.map(_.estimateRegressionParameters()).
  toArray
```

We now have a 1,867-×-8 matrix where each row is the set of model parameters (coefficients, weights, covariants, regressors, whatever you wish to call them) for an instrument.

Sampling

With our models that map factor returns to instrument returns in hand, we now need a procedure for simulating market conditions by generating random factor returns. That is, we need to decide on a probability distribution over factor return vectors and sample from it. What distribution does the data actually take? It can often be useful to start answering this kind of question visually. A nice way to visualize a probability distribution over continuous data is a density plot that plots the distribution's domain versus its PDF. Because we don't know the distribution that governs the data, we don't have an equation that can give us its density at an arbitrary point, but we can approximate it through a technique called *kernel density estimation*. In a loose way, kernel density estimation is a way of smoothing out a histogram. It centers a probability distribution (usually a normal distribution) at each data point. So a set of two-week-return samples would result in 200 normal distributions, each with a different mean. To estimate the probability density at a given point, it evaluates the PDFs of all the normal distributions at that point and takes their average. The smoothness of a kernel density plot depends on its *bandwidth*, the standard deviation of each of the normal distributions. The GitHub repository comes with a kernel density implementation that works both over RDDs and local collections. For brevity, it is elided here.

breeze-viz is a Scala library that makes it easy to draw simple plots. The following snippet creates a density plot from a set of samples:

```
import com.cloudera.datascience.risk.KernelDensity
import breeze.plot._

def plotDistribution(samples: Array[Double]) {
  val min = samples.min
  val max = samples.max
  val domain = Range.Double(min, max, (max - min) / 100).
    toList.toArray
  val densities = KernelDensity.estimate(samples, domain)

  val f = Figure()
```

```
    val p = f.subplot(0)
    p += plot(domain, densities)
    p.xlabel = "Two Week Return ($)"
    p.ylabel = "Density"
}

plotDistribution(factorsReturns(0))
plotDistribution(factorsReturns(1))
```

Figure 9-1 shows the distribution (probability density function) of two-week returns for the bonds in our history.

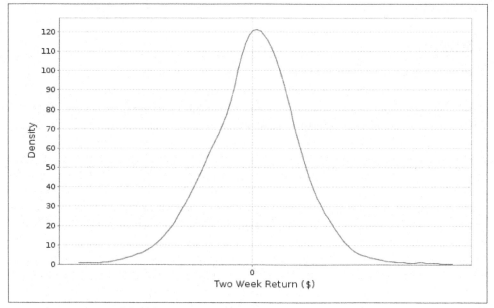

Figure 9-1. Two-week bond returns distribution

Figure 9-2 shows the same for two-week returns of crude oil.

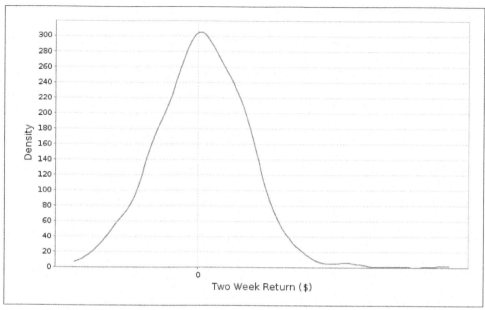

Figure 9-2. Two-week crude oil returns distribution

We will fit a normal distribution to the returns of each factor. Looking for a more exotic distribution, perhaps with fatter tails, that more closely fits the data is often worthwhile. However, for the sake of simplicity, we will avoid tuning our simulation in this way.

The simplest way to sample factors' returns would be to fit a normal distribution to each of the factors and sample from these distributions independently. However, this ignores the fact that market factors are often correlated. If S&P is down, the Dow is likely to be down as well. Failing to take these correlations into account can give us a much rosier picture of our risk profile than its reality. Are the returns of our factors correlated? The Pearson's correlation implementation from Commons Math can help us find out:

```
import org.apache.commons.math3.stat.correlation.PearsonsCorrelation

val factorCor =
  new PearsonsCorrelation(factorMat).getCorrelationMatrix().getData()
println(factorCor.map(_.mkString("\t")).mkString("\n"))
1.0        -0.3472  0.4424    0.4633 ❶
-0.3472   1.0       -0.4777   -0.5096
0.4424    -0.4777   1.0       0.9199
0.4633    -0.5096   0.9199    1.0
```

❶ Digits truncated to fit between the margins

Because we have nonzero elements off the diagonals, it doesn't look like it.

The Multivariate Normal Distribution

The multivariate normal distribution can help here by taking the correlation information between the factors into account. Each sample from a multivariate normal is a vector. Given values for all of the dimensions but one, the distribution of values along that dimension is normal. But, in their joint distribution, the variables are not independent.

The multivariate normal is parameterized with a mean along each dimension and a matrix describing the covariances between each pair of dimensions. With N dimensions, the covariance matrix is N by N, because we want to capture the covariances between each pair of dimensions. When the covariance matrix is diagonal, the multivariate normal reduces to sampling along each dimension independently, but placing nonzero values in the off-diagonals helps capture the relationships between variables.

The Value at Risk literature often describes a step in which the factor weights are transformed (decorrelated) so that sampling can proceed. This is normally accomplished with a Cholesky Decomposition or Eigendecomposition. The Apache Commons Math `MultivariateNormalDistribution` takes care of this step for us under the covers using an Eigendecomposition.

To fit a multivariate normal distribution to our data, first we need to find its sample means and covariances:

```
import org.apache.commons.math3.stat.correlation.Covariance

val factorCov = new Covariance(factorMat).getCovarianceMatrix().
  getData()

val factorMeans = factorsReturns.
  map(factor => factor.sum / factor.size).toArray
```

Then, we can simply create a distribution parameterized with them:

```
import org.apache.commons.math3.distribution.MultivariateNormalDistribution

val factorsDist = new MultivariateNormalDistribution(factorMeans,
  factorCov)
```

To sample a set of market conditions from it:

```
factorsDist.sample()
res1: Array[Double] = Array(-0.05782773255967754, 0.01890770078427768,
  0.029344325473062878, 0.04398266164298203)

factorsDist.sample()
res2: Array[Double] = Array(-0.009840154244155741, -0.01573733572551166,
  0.029140934507992572, 0.028227818241305904)
```

Running the Trials

With the per-instrument models and a procedure for sampling factor returns, we now have the pieces we need to run the actual trials. Because running the trials is very computationally intensive, we will finally turn to Spark to help us parallelize them. In each trial, we want to sample a set of risk factors, use them to predict the return of each instrument, and sum all those returns to find the full trial loss. To achieve a representative distribution, we want to run thousands or millions of these trials.

We have a few choices in how to parallelize the simulation. We can parallelize along trials, instruments, or both. To parallelize along both, we would create an RDD of instruments and an RDD of trial parameters, and then use the `cartesian` transformation to generate an RDD of all the pairs. This is the most general approach, but it has a couple of disadvantages. First, it requires explicitly creating an RDD of trial parameters, which we can avoid by using some tricks with random seeds. Second, it requires a shuffle operation.

Partitioning along instruments would look something like this:

```
val randomSeed = 1496
val instrumentsRdd = ...
def trialLossesForInstrument(seed: Long, instrument: Array[Double])
  : Array[(Int, Double)] = {
  ...
}
instrumentsRdd.flatMap(trialLossesForInstrument(randomSeed, _)).
  reduceByKey(_ + _)
```

With this approach, the data is partitioned across an RDD of instruments, and, for each instrument a `flatMap` transformation computes and yields the loss against every trial. Using the same random seed across all tasks means that we will generate the same sequence of trials. A `reduceByKey` sums together all the losses corresponding to the same trials. A disadvantage of this approach is that it still requires shuffling $O(|$instruments$| * |$trials$|)$ data.

Our model data for our few thousand instruments data is small enough to fit in memory on every executor, and some back-of-the-envelope calculations reveal that this is probably still the case even with a million or so instruments and hundreds of factors. A million instruments times five hundred factors times the eight bytes needed for the double that stores each factor weight equals roughly 4 GB, small enough to fit in each executor on most modern-day cluster machines. This means that a good option is to distribute the instrument data in a broadcast variable. The advantage of each executor having a full copy of the instrument data is that total loss for each trial can be computed on a single machine. No aggregation is necessary.

With the partition-by-trials approach (which we will use), we start out with an RDD of seeds. We want a different seed in each partition so that each partition generates different trials:

```
val parallelism = 1000
val baseSeed = 1496

val seeds = (baseSeed until baseSeed + parallelism)
val seedRdd = sc.parallelize(seeds, parallelism)
```

Random number generation is a time-consuming and CPU-intensive process. While we don't employ this trick here, it can often be useful to generate a set of random numbers in advance and use it across multiple jobs. The same random numbers should *not* be used within a single job, because this would violate the Monte Carlo assumption that the random values are independently distributed. If we were to go this route, we would replace `parallelize` with `textFile` and load a `randomNumbersRdd`.

For each seed, we want to generate a set of trial parameters and observe the effects of these parameters on all the instruments. Let's start from the ground up by writing a function that calculates the return of a single instrument underneath a single trial. We simply apply the linear model that we trained earlier for that instrument. The length of the `instrument` array of regression parameters is one greater than the length of the `trial` array, because the first element of the `instrument` array contains the intercept term:

```
def instrumentTrialReturn(instrument: Array[Double],
    trial: Array[Double]): Double = {
  var instrumentTrialReturn = instrument(0)
  var i = 0
  while (i < trial.length) { ❶
    instrumentTrialReturn += trial(i) * instrument(i+1)
    i += 1
  }
  instrumentTrialReturn
}
```

❶ We use a `while` loop here instead of a more functional Scala construct because this is a performance-critical region

Then, to calculate the full return for a single trial, we simply average over the returns of all the instruments. This assumes that we're holding an equal value of each instrument in the portfolio. A weighted average would be used if we held different amounts of each stock.

```
def trialReturn(trial: Array[Double],
    instruments: Seq[Array[Double]]): Double = {
  var totalReturn = 0.0
  for (instrument <- instruments) {
```

```
        totalReturn += instrumentTrialReturn(instrument, trial)
    }
    totalReturn / instruments.size
}
```

Lastly, we need to generate a bunch of trials in each task. Because choosing random numbers is a big part of the process, it is important to use a strong random number generator that will take a very long time to repeat itself. Commons Math includes a Mersenne twister implementation that is good for this. We use it to sample from a multivariate normal distribution as described previously. Note that we are applying the `featurize` method that we defined before on the generated factor returns in order to transform them into the feature representation used in our models:

```
import org.apache.commons.math3.random.MersenneTwister

def trialReturns(seed: Long, numTrials: Int,
    instruments: Seq[Array[Double]], factorMeans: Array[Double],
    factorCovariances: Array[Array[Double]]): Seq[Double] = {
  val rand = new MersenneTwister(seed)
  val multivariateNormal = new MultivariateNormalDistribution(
    rand, factorMeans, factorCovariances)

  val trialReturns = new Array[Double](numTrials)
  for (i <- 0 until numTrials) {
    val trialFactorReturns = multivariateNormal.sample()
    val trialFeatures = featurize(trialFactorReturns)
    trialReturns(i) = trialReturn(trialFeatures, instruments)
  }
  trialReturns
}
```

With our scaffolding complete, we can use it to compute an RDD where each element is the total return from a single trial. Because the instrument data (matrix including a weight on each factor feature for each instrument) is large, we use a broadcast variable for it. This ensures that it only needs to be deserialized once per executor:

```
val numTrials = 10000000
val bFactorWeights = sc.broadcast(factorWeights)

val trials = seedRdd.flatMap(
  trialReturns(_, numTrials / parallelism,
    bFactorWeights.value, factorMeans, factorCov))
```

If you recall, the whole reason we've been messing around with all these numbers was to calculate VaR. `trials` now forms an empirical distribution over portfolio returns. To calculate 5% VaR, we need to find a return that we expect to underperform 5% of the time, and a return that we expect to outperform 5% of the time. With our empirical distribution, this is as simple as finding the value that 5% of trials are worse than and 95% of trials are better than. We can accomplish this using the `takeOrdered` action to pull the worst 5% of trials into the driver. Our VaR is the return of the best trial in this subset:

```scala
def fivePercentVaR(trials: RDD[Double]): Double = {
  val topLosses = trials.takeOrdered(math.max(trials.count().toInt / 20, 1))
  topLosses.last
}

val valueAtRisk = fivePercentVaR(trials)
valueAtRisk: Double = -0.1468829958280655
```

We can find the CVaR with a nearly identical approach. Instead of taking the best trial return from the worst 5% of trials, we take the average return from that set of trials:

```scala
def fivePercentCVaR(trials: RDD[Double]): Double = {
  val topLosses = trials.takeOrdered(math.max(trials.count().toInt / 20, 1))
  topLosses.sum / topLosses.length
}

val conditionalValueAtRisk = fivePercentCVaR(trials)
conditionalValueAtRisk: Double = -0.3040739599830849
```

Visualizing the Distribution of Returns

In addition to calculating VaR at a particular confidence level, it can be useful to look at a fuller picture of the distribution of returns. Are they normally distributed? Do they spike at the extremities? As we did for the individual factors, we can plot an estimate of the probability density function for the joint probability distribution using kernel density estimation (see Figure 9-3). Again, the supporting code for calculating the density estimates in a distributed fashion (over RDDs) is included in the GitHub repository accompanying this book:

```scala
def plotDistribution(samples: RDD[Double]) {
  val stats = samples.stats()
  val min = stats.min
  val max = stats.max
  val domain = Range.Double(min, max, (max - min) / 100)
    .toList.toArray
  val densities = KernelDensity.estimate(samples, domain)

  val f = Figure()
  val p = f.subplot(0)
  p += plot(domain, densities)
  p.xlabel = "Two Week Return ($)"
  p.ylabel = "Density"
}

plotDistribution(trials)
```

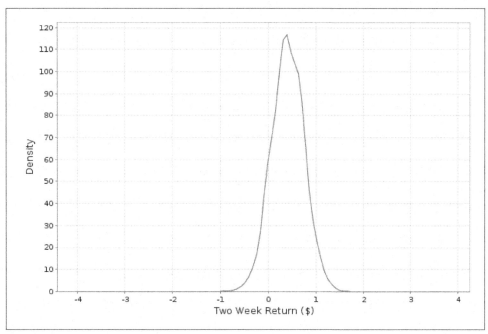

Figure 9-3. Two-week returns distribution

Evaluating Our Results

How do we know whether our estimate is a good estimate? How do we know whether we should simulate with a larger number of trials? In general, the error in a Monte Carlo simulation should be proportional to $1/\sqrt{n}$. This means that, in general, quadrupling the number of trials should approximately cut the error in half.

A nice way to get a confidence interval on our VaR statistic is through bootstrapping. We achieve a bootstrap distribution over the VaR by repeatedly sampling with replacement from the set of portfolio returns that are the results of our trials. Each time, we take a number of samples equal to the full size of the trials set and compute a VaR from those samples. The set of VaRs computed from all the times form an empirical distribution, and we can get our confidence interval by simply looking at its quantiles.

The following is a function that will compute a bootstrapped confidence interval for any statistic (given by the `computeStatistic` argument) of an RDD. Notice its use of Spark's `sample` where we pass `true` for its first argument `withReplacement`, and 1.0 for its second argument to collect a number of samples equal to the full size of the data set:

```
def bootstrappedConfidenceInterval(
    trials: RDD[Double],
```

```
    computeStatistic: RDD[Double] => Double,
    numResamples: Int,
    pValue: Double): (Double, Double) = {
  val stats = (0 until numResamples).map { i =>
    val resample = trials.sample(true, 1.0)
    computeStatistic(resample)
  }.sorted
  val lowerIndex = (numResamples * pValue / 2).toInt
  val upperIndex = (numResamples * (1 - pValue / 2)).toInt
  (stats(lowerIndex), stats(upperIndex))
}
```

Then we call this function, passing in the `fivePercentVaR` function we defined earlier that computes the VaR from an RDD of trials:

```
bootstrappedConfidenceInterval(trials, fivePercentVaR, 100, .05)
(-0.14729359672067843,-0.146524102417069)
```

We can bootstrap the CVaR as well:

```
bootstrappedConfidenceInterval(trials, fivePercentCVaR, 100, .05)
(-0.3048383366371745,-0.3032050872609137)
```

The confidence interval helps us understand how confident our model is in its result, but it does little to help us understand how well our model matches reality. Backtesting on historical data is a good way to check the quality of a result. One common test for VaR is Kupiec's proportion-of-failures (POF) test. It considers how the portfolio performed at many historical time intervals and counts the number of times that the losses exceeded the VaR. The null hypothesis is that the VaR is reasonable, and a sufficiently extreme test statistic means that the VaR estimate does not accurately describe the data. The test statistic, which relies on p, the confidence level parameter of the VaR calculation; x, the number of historical intervals over which the losses exceeded the VaR; and T, the total number of historical intervals considered, is computed as:

$$-2 \ln \left(\frac{(1-p)^{T-x} p^x}{\left(1 - \frac{x}{T}\right)^{T-x} \left(\frac{x}{T}\right)^x} \right)$$

The following computes the test statistic on our historical data. We expand out the logs for better numerical stability:

$$-2\left((T-x) \ln (1-p) + x \ln (p) - (T-x) \ln \left(1 - \frac{x}{T}\right) - x \ln \left(\frac{x}{T}\right)\right)$$

```
var failures = 0
for (i <- 0 until stocksReturns(0).size) {
  val loss = stocksReturns.map(_(i)).sum / stocksReturns.size
  if (loss < valueAtRisk) {
```

```
    failures += 1
  }
}
failures
...
1

val total = stocksReturns.size
val confidenceLevel = 0.05
val failureRatio = failures.toDouble / total
val logNumer = (total - failures) * math.log1p(-confidenceLevel) +
  failures * math.log(confidenceLevel)
val logDenom = (total - failures) * math.log1p(-failureRatio) +
  failures * math.log(failureRatio)
val testStatistic = -2 * (logNumer - logDenom)
...
180.3543986286574
```

If we assume the null hypothesis that the VaR is reasonable, then this test statistic is drawn from a chi-squared distribution with a single degree of freedom. We can use the Commons Math `ChiSquaredDistribution` to find the p-value accompanying our test statistic value:

```
import org.apache.commons.math3.distribution.ChiSquaredDistribution
```

```
1 - new ChiSquaredDistribution(1.0).cumulativeProbability(testStatistic)
```

This gives us a tiny p-value, meaning we do have sufficient evidence to reject the null hypothesis that the model is reasonable. While the fairly tight confidence intervals we computed earlier indicate that our model is internally consistent, the test result indicates that it doesn't correspond well to observed reality. Looks like we need to improve it a little…

Where to Go from Here

The model laid out in this exercise is a very rough first cut of what would be used in an actual financial institution. In building an accurate VaR model, a few steps that we glossed over are very important. Curating the set of market factors can make or break a model, and it is not uncommon for financial institutions to incorporate hundreds of factors in their simulations. Picking these factors requires both running numerous experiments on historical data and a heavy dose of creativity. Choosing the predictive model that maps market factors to instrument returns is also important. Although we used a simple linear model, many calculations use nonlinear functions or simulate the path over time with Brownian motion. Lastly, it is worth putting care into the distribution used to simulate the factor returns. Kolmogorov-Smirnoff tests and chi-squared tests are useful for testing an empirical distribution's normality. Q-Q plots are useful for comparing distributions visually. Usually, financial risk is better mirrored by a distribution with fatter tails than the normal that we used. Mixtures of normal distributions is one good way to achieve these fatter tails. "Financial Economics, Fat-tailed Distributions" (*http://bit.ly/1ACazwy*), an article by Markus Haas and Christian Pigorsch, provides a nice reference on some of the other fat-tailed distributions out there.

Banks use Spark and large-scale data processing frameworks for calculating VaR with historical methods as well. "Evaluation of Value-at-Risk Models Using Historical Data" (*http://nyfed.org/1ACaI2O*), by Darryll Hendricks, provides a good overview and performance comparison of historical VaR methods.

Monte Carlo risk simulations can be used for more than calculating a single statistic. The results can be used to proactively reduce the risk of a portfolio by shaping investment decisions. For example, if, in the trials with the poorest returns, a particular set of instruments tends to come up losing money repeatedly, we might consider dropping those instruments from the portfolio or adding instruments that tend to move in the opposite direction from them.

CHAPTER 10

Analyzing Genomics Data and the BDG Project

Uri Laserson

> *So we need to shoot our SCHPON [...] into the void.*
> —George M. Church

The advent of next-generation DNA sequencing (NGS) technology is rapidly transforming the life sciences into a data-driven field. However, making the best use of this data is butting up against a traditional computational ecosystem that builds on difficult-to-use, low-level primitives for distributed computing (e.g., DRMAA or MPI) and a jungle of semi-structured text-based file formats.

This chapter will serve three primary purposes. First, we introduce the general Spark user to a new set of Hadoop-friendly serialization and file formats (Avro and Parquet) that greatly simplify many problems in data management. We broadly promote the use of these serialization technologies to achieve compact binary representations, service-oriented architectures, and language cross-compatibility. Second, we show the experienced bioinformatician how to perform typical genomics tasks in the context of Spark. Specifically, we will use Spark to manipulate large quantities of genomics data to process and filter data, build a transcription factor binding site prediction model, and join ENCODE genome annotations against the 1000 Genome project variants. Finally, this chapter will serve as a tutorial to the ADAM project, which comprises a set of genomics-specific Avro schemas, Spark-based APIs, and command-line tools for large-scale genomics analysis. Among other applications, ADAM provides a natively distributed implementation of the GATK best practices using Hadoop and Spark.

The genomics portions of this chapter are targeted at experienced bioinformaticians familiar with typical problems. However, the data serialization portions should be useful to anyone who is processing large amounts of data.

Decoupling Storage from Modeling

Bioinformaticians spend a disproportionate amount of time worrying about file formats—*.fasta, .fastq, .sam, .bam, .vcf, .gvcf, .bcf, .bed, .gff, .gtf, .narrowPeak, .wig, .bigWig, .bigBed, .ped, .tped*, to name a few—not to mention the scientists who feel it is necessary to specify their own custom format for their own custom tool. On top of that, many of the format specifications are incomplete or ambiguous (which makes it hard to ensure implementations are consistent or compliant) and specify ASCII-encoded data. ASCII data is very common in bioinformatics, but it is inefficient and compresses relatively poorly—this is starting to be addressed by community efforts to improve the specs, like *https://github.com/samtools/hts-specs*. In addition, the data must always be parsed, necessitating additional compute cycles. It is particularly troubling because all of these file formats essentially store just a few common object types: an aligned sequence read, a called genotype, a sequence feature, and a phenotype. (The term "sequence feature" is slightly overloaded in genomics, but in this chapter we mean it in the sense of an element from a track of the UCSC genome browser.) Libraries like biopython (*http://biopython.org/*) are popular because they are chock-full-o'-parsers (e.g., Bio.SeqIO) that attempt to read all the file formats into a small number of common in-memory models (e.g., Bio.Seq, Bio.SeqRecord, Bio.SeqFeature).

We can solve all of these problems in one shot using a serialization framework like Apache Avro. The key lies in Avro's separation of the data model (i.e., an explicit schema) from the underlying storage file format and also the language's in-memory representation. Avro specifies how data of a certain type should be communicated between processes, whether that's between running processes over the Internet, or a process trying to write the data into a particular file format. For example, a Java program that uses Avro can write the data into multiple underlying file formats that are all compatible with Avro's data model. This allows each process to stop worrying about compatibility with multiple file formats: the process only needs to know how to read Avro, and the filesystem needs to know how to supply Avro.

Let's take the sequence feature as an example. We begin by specifying the desired schema for the object using the Avro interface definition language (IDL):

```
enum Strand {
  Forward,
  Reverse,
  Independent
}
```

```
record SequenceFeature {
  string featureId;
  string featureType; ❶
  string chromosome;
  long startCoord;
  long endCoord;
  Strand strand;
  double value;
  map<string> attributes;
}
```

❶ For example, "conservation," "centipede," "gene"

This data type could be used to encode, for example, conservation level, the presence of a promoter or ribosome binding site, a transcription factor binding site, and so on. One way to think about it is a binary version of JSON, but more restricted and with much higher performance. Given a particular data schema, the Avro spec then determines the precise binary encoding for the object, so that it can be easily communicated between processes (even if written in different programing languages), over the network, or onto disk for storage. The Avro project includes modules for processing Avro-encoded data from many languages, including Java, C/C++, Python, and Perl; after that, the language is free to store the object in memory in whichever way is deemed most advantageous. The separation of data modeling from the storage format provides another level of flexibility/abstraction; Avro data can be stored as Avro-serialized binary objects (Avro container file), in a columnar file format for fast queries (Parquet file), or as text JSON data for maximum flexibility (minimum efficiency). Finally, Avro supports schema evolvability, allowing the user to add new fields as they become necessary, while all the software gracefully deals with new/old versions of the schema.

Overall, Avro is an efficient binary encoding that allows you to easily specify evolvable data schemas, process the same data from many programming languages, and store the data using many formats. Deciding to store your data using Avro schemas frees you from perpetually working with more and more custom data formats, while simultaneously increasing the performance of your computations.

Serialization/RPC Frameworks

There exist a large number of serialization frameworks in the wild. The most commonly used frameworks in the big data community are Apache Avro, Apache Thrift, and Google's Protocol Buffers. At the core, they all provide an interface definition language for specifying the schemas of object/message types, and they all compile into a variety of programming languages. On top of IDL, which is supported by Protocol Buffers, Thrift also adds a way to specify RPCs. (Google also has an RPC mechanism called Stubby, but it has not been open sourced.) Finally, on top of IDL and RPC, Avro adds a file format specification for storing the data on-disk. It's difficult to make generalizations about which framework is appropriate in what circumstances, because they all support different languages and have different performance characteristics for the various languages.

The particular `SequenceFeature` model used in the preceding example is a bit simplistic for real data, but the Big Data Genomics (BDG) project (*http://bdgenomics.org/*) has already defined Avro schemas to represent the following objects, as well as many others:

- `AlignmentRecord` for reads
- `Pileup` for base observations at particular positions
- `Variant` for known genome variants and metadata
- `Genotype` for a called genotype at a particular locus
- `Feature` for a sequence feature (annotation on a genome segment)

The actual schemas can be found in the `bdg-formats` GitHub repo (*https://github.com/bigdatagenomics/bdg-formats*). The Global Alliance for Genomics and Health is also starting to develop its own set of Avro schemas (*https://github.com/ga4gh/schemas*). Hopefully this will not turn into its own *http://xkcd.com/927/* situation, where there is a proliferation of competing Avro schemas. Even so, Avro provides many performance and data modeling benefits over the custom ASCII status quo. In the remainder of the chapter, we'll use some of the BDG schemas to accomplish some typical genomics tasks.

Ingesting Genomics Data with the ADAM CLI

 This chapter makes heavy use of the ADAM project for genomics on Spark. The project is under heavy development, including the documentation. If you run into problems, make sure to check the latest README files on GitHub, the GitHub issue tracker, or the `adam-developers` mailing list.

BDG's core set of genomics tools is called ADAM. Starting from a set of mapped reads, this core includes tools that can perform mark-duplicates, base quality score recalibration, indel realignment, and variant calling, among other tasks. ADAM also contains a command-line interface that wraps the core for ease of use. In contrast to HPC, these command-line tools know about Hadoop and HDFS, and many of them can automatically parallelize across a cluster without having to split files or schedule jobs manually.

We'll start by building `adam` like the README tells us to:

```
git clone -b adam-parent-0.16.0 \
  https://github.com/bigdatagenomics/adam.git
cd adam
export "MAVEN_OPTS=-Xmx512m -XX:MaxPermSize=128m"
mvn clean package -DskipTests
```

ADAM comes with a submission script that facilitates interfacing with Spark's `spark-submit` script; the easiest way to use it is probably to alias it:

```
export $ADAM_HOME=path/to/adam
alias adam-submit="$ADAM_HOME/bin/adam-submit"
```

As noted in the README, additional JVM options can be set through `$JAVA_OPTS`, or check the `appassembler` docs for more info. At this point, you should be able to run ADAM from the command line and get the usage message:

```
$ adam-submit
...


        e          888~-_              e          e   e
       d8b         888   \            d8b        d8b d8b
      /Y88b        888   |           /Y88b       d888bdY88b
     /  Y88b       888   |          /  Y88b     / Y88Y Y888b
    /____Y88b      888   /         /____Y88b   /   YY   Y888b
   /      Y88b     888_-~         /      Y88b /         Y888b


Choose one of the following commands:

ADAM ACTIONS
          compare : Compare two ADAM files based on read name
        findreads : Find reads that match particular individual
                    or comparative criteria
            depth : Calculate the depth from a given ADAM file,
                    at each variant in a VCF
      count_kmers : Counts the k-mers/q-mers from a read
                    dataset.
aggregate_pileups : Aggregate pileups in an ADAM reference-
                    oriented file
        transform : Convert SAM/BAM to ADAM format and
                    optionally perform read pre-processing
                    transformations
           plugin : Executes an ADAMPlugin
              [etc.]
```

We'll start by taking a *.bam* file containing some mapped NGS reads, converting them to the corresponding BDG format (`AlignedRecord` in this case), and saving them to HDFS. First, we get our hands on a suitable *.bam* file and put it in HDFS:

```
# Note: this file is 16 GB
curl -O ftp://ftp.ncbi.nih.gov/1000genomes/ftp/phase3/data\
/HG00103/alignment/HG00103.mapped.ILLUMINA.bwa.GBR\
.low_coverage.20120522.bam
```

```
# or using Aspera instead (which is *much* faster)
ascp -i path/to/asperaweb_id_dsa.openssh -QTr -l 10G \
anonftp@ftp.ncbi.nlm.nih.gov:/1000genomes/ftp/data/HG00103\
/alignment/HG00103.mapped.ILLUMINA.bwa.GBR\
.low_coverage.20120522.bam .

hadoop fs -put HG00103.mapped.ILLUMINA.bwa.GBR\
.low_coverage.20120522.bam /user/ds/genomics
```

We can then use the ADAM `transform` command to convert the *.bam* file to Parquet format (described in "Parquet Format and Columnar Storage" on page 204). This would work both on a cluster and in `local` mode:

```
adam-submit \
    transform \ ❶
    /user/ds/genomics/HG00103.mapped.ILLUMINA.bwa.GBR\
.low_coverage.20120522.bam \ ❷
    /user/ds/genomics/reads/HG00103
```

❶ The ADAM command itself

❷ The rest of the arguments are specific to the `transform` command

This should kick off a pretty large amount of output to the console, including the URL to track the progress of the job. Let's see what we've generated:

```
$ hadoop fs -du -h /user/ds/genomics/reads/HG00103
0        /user/ds/genomics/reads/HG00103/_SUCCESS
516.9 K  /user/ds/genomics/reads/HG00103/_metadata
101.8 M  /user/ds/genomics/reads/HG00103/part-r-00000.gz.parquet
101.7 M  /user/ds/genomics/reads/HG00103/part-r-00001.gz.parquet
[...]
104.9 M  /user/ds/genomics/reads/HG00103/part-r-00126.gz.parquet
12.3 M   /user/ds/genomics/reads/HG00103/part-r-00127.gz.parquet
```

The resulting data set is the concatenation of all the files in the */user/ds/genomics/reads/HG00103/* directory, where each *part-*.parquet* file is the output from one of the Spark tasks. You'll also notice that the data has been compressed more efficiently than the initial *.bam* file (which is gzipped underneath) thanks to the columnar storage:

```
$ hadoop fs -du -h "/user/ds/genomics/HG00103.*.bam"
15.9 G  /user/ds/genomics/HG00103. [...] .bam

$ hadoop fs -du -h -s /user/ds/genomics/reads/HG00103
12.6 G  /user/ds/genomics/reads/HG00103
```

Let's see what one of these objects looks like in an interactive session. First we start up the Spark shell using the ADAM helper script. It takes the same arguments/options as the default Spark scripts, but loads all of the JARs that are necessary. In the following example, we are running Spark on YARN:

```
export SPARK_HOME=/path/to/spark
$ADAM_HOME/bin/adam-shell

...
14/09/11 17:44:36 INFO SecurityManager: [...]
14/09/11 17:44:36 INFO HttpServer: Starting HTTP Server
Welcome to
      ____              __
     / __/__  ___ _____/ /__
    _\ \/ _ \/ _ `/ __/  '_/
   /___/ .__/\_,_/_/ /_/\_\   version 1.2.1
      /_/

Using Scala version 2.10.4
  (Java HotSpot(TM) 64-Bit Server VM, Java 1.7.0_67)
[...lots of additional logging around setting up the YARN app...]

scala>
```

Note that when you're working on YARN, the interactive Spark shell requires yarn-client mode, so that the driver is executed locally. It may also be necessary to set either HADOOP_CONF_DIR or YARN_CONF_DIR appropriately. Now we'll load the aligned read data as an RDD[AlignmentRecord]:

```
import org.apache.spark.rdd.RDD
import org.bdgenomics.adam.rdd.ADAMContext._
import org.bdgenomics.formats.avro.AlignmentRecord

val readsRDD: RDD[AlignmentRecord] = sc.adamLoad(
  "/user/ds/genomics/reads/HG00103")
readsRDD.first()
```

This prints a lot of logging output (Spark and Parquet love to log) along with the result itself:

```
res0: org.bdgenomics.formats.avro.AlignmentRecord =
{"contig":
 {"contigName": "X", "contigLength": 155270560,
  "contigMD5": "7e0e2e580297b7764e31dbc80c2540dd",
  "referenceURL": "ftp:\/\/ftp.1000genomes.ebi.ac.uk\/...",
  "assembly": null, "species": null},
 "start": 50194838, "end": 50194938, "mapq": 60,
 "readName": "SRR062642.27455291",
 "sequence": "TGACTCTGATGTTAAGATGCATTGTT...",
 "qual": ".LMMQPRQQPRQPILRQQRRIQQRQ...", "cigar": "100M",
 "basesTrimmedFromStart": 0, "basesTrimmedFromEnd": 0,
 "readPaired": true, "properPair": true, "readMapped":...}
```

(This output has been modified to fit the page.) You may get a different read, because the partitioning of the data may be different on your cluster, so there is no guarantee which read will come back first.

Now we can interactively ask questions about our data set, all while executing the computations themselves across a cluster in the background. How many reads do we have in this data set?

```
readsRDD.count()
...
14/09/11 18:26:05 INFO SparkContext: Starting job: count [...]
...
res16: Long = 160397565
```

Do the reads in this data set derive from all human chromosomes?

```
val uniq_chr = (readsRDD
  .map(_.contig.contigName.toString)
  .distinct()
  .collect())
uniq_chr.sorted.foreach(println)
...
1
10
11
12
[...]
GL000249.1
MT
NC_007605
X
Y
hs37d5
```

Yep. Let's analyze the statement a little more closely:

```
val uniq_chr = (readsRDD ❶
  .map(_.contig.contigName.toString) ❷
  .distinct() ❸
  .collect()) ❹
```

❶ RDD[AlignmentRecord]: Contains all our data

❷ RDD[String]: From each AlignmentRecord object, we extract the contig name, and convert to a String

❸ RDD[String]: This will cause a reduce/shuffle to aggregate all the distinct contig names; should be small, but still an RDD

❹ Array[String]: This triggers the computation and brings the data in the RDD back to the client app (the shell)

Say we are carrier screening an individual for cystic fibrosis using next-generation sequencing and our genotype caller gave us something that looks like a premature stop codon, but it's not present in HGMD (*http://www.hgmd.cf.ac.uk/*), nor is it in the

Sickkids CFTR database (*http://www.genet.sickkids.on.ca/*). We want to go back to the raw sequencing data to see if the potentially deleterious genotype call is a false positive. To do so, we need to manually analyze all the reads that map to that variant locus, say, chromosome 7 at 117149189 (see Figure 10-1):

```
val cftr_reads = (readsRDD
  .filter(_.contig.contigName.toString == "7")
  .filter(_.start <= 117149189)
  .filter(_.end > 117149189)
  .collect())
cftr_reads.length // cftr_reads is a local Array[AlignmentRecord]
...
res2: Int = 9
```

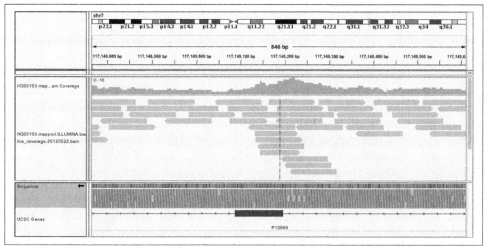

Figure 10-1. IGV visualization of the HG00103 at chr7:117149189 in the CFTR gene

It is now possible to manually inspect these nine reads, or process them through a custom aligner, for example, and check whether the reported pathogenic variant is a false positive. Exercise for the reader: what is the average coverage on chromosome 7? (It's definitely too low for reliably making a genotype call at a given position.)

Say we're running a clinical lab that is performing such carrier screening as a service to clinicians. Archiving the raw data using Hadoop ensures that the data stays relatively warm (compared with, say, tape archive). In addition to having a reliable system for actually performing the data processing, we can easily access all of the past data for quality control (QC) or for cases where there need to be manual interventions, like the CFTR example presented earlier. In addition to the rapid access to the totality of the data, the centrality also makes it easy to perform large analytical studies, like population genetics, large-scale QC analyses, and so on.

Parquet Format and Columnar Storage

In the previous section, we saw how we can manipulate a potentially large amount of sequencing data without worrying about the specifics of the underlying storage or the parallelization of the execution. However, it's worth noting that the ADAM project makes use of the Parquet file format, which confers some considerable performance advantages that we introduce here.

Parquet is an open source file format specification and a set of reader/writer implementations that we recommend for general use for data that will be used in analytical queries (write once, read many times). It is largely based on the underlying data storage format used in Google's Dremel system (see "Dremel: Interactive Analysis of Web-scale Datasets" (*http://research.google.com/pubs/archive/36632.pdf*) Proc. VLDB, 2010, by Melnik et al.), and has a data model that is compatible with Avro, Thrift, and Protocol Buffers. Specifically, it supports most of the common database types (int, double, string, etc.), along with arrays and records, including nested types. Significantly, it is a columnar file format, meaning that values for a particular column from many records are stored contiguously on disk (see Figure 10-2). This physical data layout allows for far more efficient data encoding/compression, and significantly reduces query times by minimizing the amount of data that must be read/deserialized (*http://the-paper-trail.org/blog/columnar-storage/*). Parquet supports specifying different encoding/compression schemes for each column, and for each column supports run-length encoding, dictionary encoding, and delta encoding.

Another useful feature of Parquet for increasing performance is "predicate push-down." A "predicate" is some expression or function that evaluates to `true` or `false` based on the data record (or equivalently, the expressions in a SQL `WHERE` clause). In our earlier CFTR query, Spark had to deserialize/materialize the entirety of every single `AlignmentRecord` before deciding whether or not it passes the predicate. This leads to a significant amount of wasted I/O and CPU time. The Parquet reader implementations allow us to provide a predicate class that only deserializes the necessary columns for making the decision, before materializing the full record.

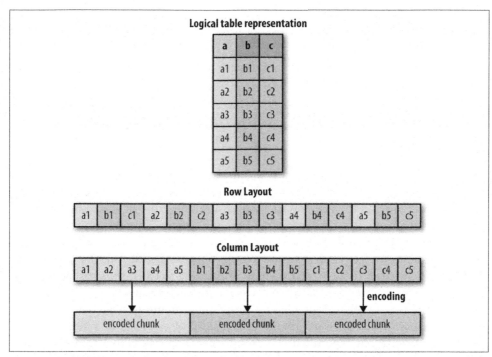

Figure 10-2. Differences between a row-major and column-major data layout

For example, to implement our CFTR query using predicate pushdown, we must first define a suitable predicate class that tests whether the AlignmentRecord is in the target locus:

```
import org.bdgenomics.adam.predicates.ColumnReaderInput._
import org.bdgenomics.adam.predicates.ADAMPredicate
import org.bdgenomics.adam.predicates.RecordCondition
import org.bdgenomics.adam.predicates.FieldCondition

class CftrLocusPredicate extends ADAMPredicate[AlignmentRecord] {
  override val recordCondition = RecordCondition[AlignmentRecord](
    FieldCondition(
      "contig.contigName", (x: String) => x == "chr7"),
    FieldCondition(
      "start", (x: Long) => x <= 117149189),
    FieldCondition(
      "end", (x: Long) => x >= 117149189))
}
```

Note that for the predicate to work, the Parquet reader must instantiate the class itself. This means we must compile this code into a JAR and make it available to the executors by adding it to the Spark classpath. After that's done, the predicate can be used like so:

```
val cftr_reads = sc.adamLoad[AlignmentRecord, CftrLocusPredicate](
  "/user/ds/genomics/reads/HG00103",
  Some(classOf[CftrLocusPredicate])).collect()
```

This should execute faster because it no longer must materialize all of the `Alignmen tRecord` objects.

Predicting Transcription Factor Binding Sites from ENCODE Data

In this example, we will use publicly available sequence feature data to build a simple model for transcription factor binding. Transcription factors (TFs) are proteins that bind to specific sites in the genome and help control the expression of different genes. As a result, they are critical in determining the phenotype of a particular cell, and are involved in many physiological and disease processes. ChIP-seq is an NGS-based assay that allows the genome-wide characterization of binding sites for a particular TF in a particular cell/tissue type. However, in addition to ChIP-seq's cost and technical difficulty, it requires a separate experiment for each tissue/TF pair. In contrast, DNase-seq is an assay that finds regions of open-chromatin genome-wide, and only needs to be performed once per tissue type. Instead of assaying TF binding sites by performing a ChIP-seq experiment for each tissue/TF combination, we'd like to predict TF binding sites in a new tissue type assuming only the availability of DNase-seq data.

In particular, we will be predicting the binding sites for the CTCF transcription factor using DNase-seq data along with known sequence motif data (from HT-SELEX (*http://dx.doi.org/10.1016/j.cell.2012.12.009*)) and other data from the publicly available ENCODE data set (*https://www.encodeproject.org/*). We have chosen six different cell types that have available DNase-seq and CTCF ChIP-seq data. A training example will be a DNase hypersensitivity (HS) peak, and the label will be derived from the ChIP-seq data.

We will be using data from the following cell lines:

GM12878
    Commonly studied lymphoblastoid cell line

K562
    Female chronic myelogenous leukemia

BJ
    Skin fibroblast

HEK293
    Embryonic kidney

H54

Glioblastoma

HepG2

Hepatocellular carcinoma

First, we download the DNase data for each cell line in *.narrowPeak* format:

```
hadoop fs -mkdir /user/ds/genomics/dnase
curl -s -L <...DNase URL...> \ ❶
  | gunzip \ ❷
  | hadoop fs -put - /user/ds/genomics/dnase/sample.DNase.narrowPeak
[...]
```

❶ See accompanying code repo for actual curl commands

❷ Streaming decompression

Next, we download the ChIP-seq data for the CTCF transcription factor, also in *.narrowPeak* format, and the GENCODE data, in GTF format:

```
hadoop fs -mkdir /user/ds/genomics/chip-seq
curl -s -L <...ChIP-seq URL...> \ ❶
  | gunzip \
  | hadoop fs -put - /user/ds/genomics/chip-seq/samp.CTCF.narrowPeak
[...]
```

❶ See accompanying code repo for actual curl commands

Note how we unzip the stream of data with `gunzip` on the way to depositing it in HDFS. Now we download a few additional data sets from which we'll derive features for prediction:

```
# the hg19 human genome reference sequence
curl -s -L -O \
  "http://hgdownload.cse.ucsc.edu/goldenPath/hg19/bigZips/hg19.2bit"
```

Finally, the conservation data is available in fixed wiggle format, which is difficult to read as a splittable file. It is not possible to predict how far back in a file a particular task must read in order to obtain the metadata about the contig coordinates. Therefore, we convert the *.wigFix* data to BED format on the way into HDFS as well:

```
hadoop fs -mkdir /user/ds/genomics/phylop
for i in $(seq 1 22); do
    curl -s -L <...phyloP.chr$i URL...> \ ❶
        | gunzip \
        | adam-submit wigfix2bed \
        | hadoop fs -put - "/user/ds/genomics/phylop/chr$i.phyloP.bed"
done
[...]
```

❶ See accompanying code repo for actual curl commands

Finally, we perform a one-time conversion of the phyloP data from the text-based *.bed* format to Parquet in a Spark shell:

```
(sc
  .adamBEDFeatureLoad("/user/ds/genomics/phylop_text")
  .adamSave("/user/ds/genomics/phylop"))
```

From all of this raw data, we want to generate a training set with a schema like the following:

1. DNase HS peak ID
2. Chromosome
3. Start
4. End
5. Highest TF motif PWM score
6. Average phyloP conservation score
7. Maximum phyloP conservation score
8. Minimum phyloP conservation score
9. Distance to closest transcription start site (TSS)
10. TF identity (always "CTCF" in this case)
11. Cell line
12. TF binding status (boolean; the target variable)

Now we generate the data set that can be used to create the RDD[LabeledPoint]. We need to generate the data for multiple cell lines, so we will define an RDD for each cell line and concatenate them at the end:

❶

```
val cellLines = Vector(
  "GM12878", "K562", "BJ", "HEK293", "H54", "HepG2")
val dataByCellLine = cellLines.map(cellLine => { ❷
  ❸
})

❹
```

❶ Load the necessary annotation data

❷ For each cell line…

❸ ...generate an RDD suitable for conversion to RDD[LabeledPoint]

❹ Concatenate the RDDs and carry through into MLlib, for example

Before we start, we load some data that will be used throughout the computation, including conservation, transcription start sites, the human genome reference sequence, and the CTCF PWM as derived from HT-SELEX (*http://dx.doi.org/ 10.1016/j.cell.2012.12.009*):

```
// Load the human genome reference sequence
val bHg19Data = sc.broadcast(
  new TwoBitFile(
    new LocalFileByteAccess(
      new File("/user/ds/genomics/hg19.2bit"))))

val phylopRDD = (sc.adamLoad[Feature, Nothing]("/user/ds/genomics/phylop")
  // clean up a few irregularities in the phylop data
  .filter(f => f.getStart <= f.getEnd))

val tssRDD = (sc.adamGTFFeatureLoad(
    "/user/ds/genomics/gencode.v18.annotation.gtf")
  .filter(_.getFeatureType == "transcript")
  .map(f => (f.getContig.getContigName, f.getStart)))

val bTssData = sc.broadcast(tssRDD
  // group by contig name
  .groupBy(_._1)
  // create Vector of TSS sites for each chromosome
  .map(p => (p._1, p._2.map(_._2.toLong).toVector))
  // collect into local in-memory structure for broadcasting
  .collect().toMap)

// CTCF PWM from http://dx.doi.org/10.1016/j.cell.2012.12.009
val bPwmData = sc.broadcast(Vector(
  Map('A'->0.4553,'C'->0.0459,'G'->0.1455,'T'->0.3533),
  Map('A'->0.1737,'C'->0.0248,'G'->0.7592,'T'->0.0423),
  Map('A'->0.0001,'C'->0.9407,'G'->0.0001,'T'->0.0591),
  Map('A'->0.0051,'C'->0.0001,'G'->0.9879,'T'->0.0069),
  Map('A'->0.0624,'C'->0.9322,'G'->0.0009,'T'->0.0046),
  Map('A'->0.0046,'C'->0.9952,'G'->0.0001,'T'->0.0001),
  Map('A'->0.5075,'C'->0.4533,'G'->0.0181,'T'->0.0211),
  Map('A'->0.0079,'C'->0.6407,'G'->0.0001,'T'->0.3513),
  Map('A'->0.0001,'C'->0.9995,'G'->0.0002,'T'->0.0001),
  Map('A'->0.0027,'C'->0.0035,'G'->0.0017,'T'->0.9921),
  Map('A'->0.7635,'C'->0.0210,'G'->0.1175,'T'->0.0980),
  Map('A'->0.0074,'C'->0.1314,'G'->0.7990,'T'->0.0622),
  Map('A'->0.0138,'C'->0.3879,'G'->0.0001,'T'->0.5981),
  Map('A'->0.0003,'C'->0.0001,'G'->0.9853,'T'->0.0142),
  Map('A'->0.0399,'C'->0.0113,'G'->0.7312,'T'->0.2177),
  Map('A'->0.1520,'C'->0.2820,'G'->0.0082,'T'->0.5578),
  Map('A'->0.3644,'C'->0.3105,'G'->0.2125,'T'->0.1127)))
```

Now we define some utility functions that will be used in the feature generation, including the labeling, PWM scoring, and TSS distance:

```
// fn for finding closest transcription start site
// naive...make this better
def distanceToClosest(loci: Vector[Long], query: Long): Long = {
  loci.map(x => abs(x - query)).min
}

// compute a motif score based on the TF PWM
def scorePWM(ref: String): Double = {
  val score1 = ref.sliding(bPwmData.value.length).map(s => {
    s.zipWithIndex.map(p => bPwmData.value(p._2)(p._1)).product
  }).max
  val rc = SequenceUtils.reverseComplement(ref)
  val score2 = rc.sliding(bPwmData.value.length).map(s => {
    s.zipWithIndex.map(p => bPwmData.value(p._2)(p._1)).product
  }).max
  max(score1, score2)
}

// functions for labeling the DNase peaks as binding sites or not;
// compute overlaps between an interval and a set of intervals
// naive impl - this only works because we know the ChIP-seq peaks
// are non-overlapping (how do we verify this? exercise for the
// reader)
def isOverlapping(i1: (Long, Long), i2: (Long, Long)) =
  (i1._2 > i2._1) && (i1._1 < i2._2)

def isOverlappingLoci(loci: Vector[(Long, Long)],
                      testInterval: (Long, Long)): Boolean = {
  @tailrec
  def search(m: Int, M: Int): Boolean = {
    val mid = m + (M - m) / 2
    if (M <= m) {
      false
    } else if (isOverlapping(loci(mid), testInterval)) {
      true
    } else if (testInterval._2 <= loci(mid)._1) {
      search(m, mid)
    } else {
      search(mid + 1, M)
    }
  }
  search(0, loci.length)
}
```

Finally, we define the body of the "loop" for computing the data on each cell line. Note how we read the text representations of the ChIP-seq and DNase data, because the data sets are not so large that they will hurt performance.

First, we load the DNase and ChIP-seq data as RDDs:

```
val dnaseRDD = sc.adamNarrowPeakFeatureLoad(
  s"/user/ds/genomics/dnase/$cellLine.DNase.narrowPeak")
val chipseqRDD = sc.adamNarrowPeakFeatureLoad(
  s"/user/ds/genomics/chip-seq/$cellLine.ChIP-seq.CTCF.narrowPeak")
```

Then we define the function that will generate the target labels on the DNase features as either "binding" or "not binding." This function requires access to all the ChIP-seq peaks together, so we process the raw ChIP-seq data into an in-memory data structure and broadcast it to all the nodes, as the broadcast variable bBindingData:

```
val bBindingData = sc.broadcast(
  chipseq
    // group peaks by chromosome
    .groupBy(_.getContig.getContigName.toString) ❶
    // for each chr, for each ChIP-seq peak, extract start/end
    .map(p => (p._1, p._2.map(f =>
      (f.getStart: Long, f.getEnd: Long)))) ❷
    // for each chr, sort the peaks (non-overlapping)
    .map(p => (p._1, p._2.toVector.sortBy(x => x._1))) ❸
    // collect them back into a local in-memory data structure for
    // broadcasting
    .collect().toMap)
```

❶ RDD[(String, Iterable[Feature])]

❷ RDD[(String, Iterable[(Long, Long)])]

❸ RDD[(String, Vector[(Long, Long)])]

This operation provides us with a Map where the key is the chromosome name and the value is a Vector of nonoverlapping (start, end) pairs sorted by position. Now we define the actual labeling function:

```
def generateLabel(f: Feature) = {
  val contig = f.getContig.getContigName
  if (!bBindingData.value.contains(contig)) {
    false
  } else {
    val testInterval = (f.getStart: Long, f.getEnd: Long)
    isOverlappingLoci(bBindingData.value(contig), testInterval)
  }
}
```

To compute the conservation features (using the phyloP data), we must join the DNase peaks with the phyloP data. Because we are joining intervals, we will use the BroadcastRegionJoin implementation in ADAM, which collects one side of the join (in this case, the smaller DNase data), computes nonoverlapping regions, and then implements a replicated join by broadcasting the collected data:

```
val dnaseWithPhylopRDD = (
  BroadcastRegionJoin.partitionAndJoin(sc, dnaseRDD, phylopRDD)
```

```
// group the conservation values by DNase peak
.groupBy(x => x._1.getFeatureId)
// compute conservation stats on each peak
.map(x => {
  val y = x._2.toSeq
  val peak = y(0)._1
  val values = y.map(_._2.getValue)
  // compute phylop features
  val avg = values.reduce(_ + _) / values.length
  val m = values.max
  val M = values.min
  (peak.getFeatureId, peak, avg, m, M)
}))
```

Now we compute the final set of features on each DNase peak, including the target variable:

```
// generate the final set of tuples
dnaseWithPhylopRDD.map(tup => {
  val peak = tup._2
  val featureId = peak.getFeatureId
  val contig = peak.getContigName.getContigName
  val start = peak.getStart
  val end = peak.getEnd
  val score = scorePWM(
    bHg19Data.value.extract(ReferenceRegion(peak)))
  val avg = tup._3
  val m = tup._4
  val M = tup._5
  val closest_tss = min(
    distanceToClosest(bTssData.value(contig), peak.getStart),
    distanceToClosest(bTssData.value(contig), peak.getEnd))
  val tf = "CTCF"
  val line = cellLine
  val bound = generateLabel(peak)
  (featureId, contig, start, end, score, avg, m, M, closest_tss,
    tf, line, bound)
})
```

This final RDD is computed in each pass of the loop over the cell lines. Finally, we union each RDD from each cell line, and cache this data in memory in preparation for training models off of it:

```
val preTrainingData = dataByCellLine.reduce(_ ++ _)
preTrainingData.cache()

preTrainingData.count() // 801263
preTrainingData.filter(_._12 == true).count() // 220285
```

At this point, the data in `preTrainingData` can be normalized and converted into an `RDD[LabeledPoint]` for training a classifier, as described in Chapter 4. Note that you should perform cross-validation, where in each fold, you hold out the data from one of the cell lines.

Querying Genotypes from the 1000 Genomes Project

In this example, we will be ingesting the full 1000 Genomes genotype data set. First we will download the raw data directly into HDFS, unzipping in-flight, and then run an ADAM job to convert the data to Parquet. The following example command should be executed for all chromosomes, and can be parallelized across the cluster:

```
curl -s -L ftp://.../1000genomes/.../chr1.vcf.gz \ ❶
  | gunzip \
  | hadoop fs -put - /user/ds/genomics/1kg/vcf/chr1.vcf ❷

export SPARK_JAR_PATH=hdfs:///path/to/spark.jar
adam/bin/adam-submit --conf spark.yarn.jar=$SPARK_JAR_PATH \
  vcf2adam \ ❸
  -coalesce 5 \
  /user/ds/genomics/1kg/vcf/chr1.vcf \
  /user/ds/genomics/1kg/parquet/chr1
```

❶ See the accompanying repo for the actual curl commands

❷ Copy the text VCF file into Hadoop

❸ Run the VCF to ADAM (Parquet) conversion cluster-wide

Note how we specify -coalesce 5; this will ensure that the map tasks will compact the data into a smaller number of large Parquet files. Then, from an ADAM shell, we load and inspect an object like so:

```
import org.bdgenomics.adam.rdd.ADAMContext._
import org.bdgenomics.formats.avro.Genotype

val genotypesRDD = sc.adamLoad[Genotype, Nothing](
  "/user/ds/genomics/1kg/parquet")
val gt = genotypesRDD.first()
...
```

Say we want to compute the minor allele frequency across all our samples for each variant genome-wide that overlaps a CTCF binding site. We essentially must join our CTCF data from the previous section with the genotype data from the 1000 Genomes project:

```
val ctcfRDD = sc.adamNarrowPeakFeatureLoad(
  "/user/ds/genomics/chip-seq/GM12878.ChIP-seq.CTCF.narrowPeak")
val filtered = (BroadcastRegionJoin.partitionAndJoin(
  sc, ctcfRDD, genotypesRDD) ❶
  .map(_._2)) ❷
```

❶ `BroadcastRegionJoin`'s inner join also accomplishes the filtering

❷ This mapper finally produces an `RDD[Genotype]`

We also need a function that will take a `Genotype` and compute the counts of the reference/alternate alleles:

```
def genotypeToAlleleCounts(gt: Genotype): (Variant, (Int, Int)) = {
  val counts = gt.getAlleles.map(allele match {
    case GenotypeAllele.Ref => (1, 0)
    case GenotypeAllele.Alt => (0, 1)
    case _ => (0, 0)
  }).reduce((x, y) => (x._1 + y._1, x._2 + y._2))
  (gt.getVariant, (counts._1, counts._2))
}
```

Finally, we generate the `RDD[(Variant, (Int, Int))]` and perform the aggregation:

```
val counts = filtered.map(genotypeToAlleleCounts)
val countsByVariant = counts.reduceByKey(
  (x, y) => (x._1 + y._1, x._2 + y._2))
val mafByVariant = countsByVariant.map(tup => {
  val (v, (r, a)) = tup
  val n = r + a
  (v, math.min(r, a).toDouble / n)
})
```

Traversing the entire data set is a sizable operation. Because we're only accessing a few fields from the genotype data, it would certainly benefit from predicate pushdown and projection, which we leave as an exercise to the reader.

Where to Go from Here

Many computations in genomics fit nicely into the Spark computational paradigm. When you're performing ad hoc analysis, the most valuable contribution that projects like ADAM provide is the set of Avro schemas that represents the underlying analytical objects (along with the conversion tools). We saw how once data is converted into the corresponding Avro schemas, many large-scale computations become relatively easy to express and distribute.

While there may still be a dearth of tools for performing scientific research on Hadoop/Spark, there do exist a few projects that could help avoid reinventing the wheel. We explored the core functionality implemented in ADAM, but the project already has implementations for the entire GATK best-practices pipeline, including BQSR, indel realignment, and deduplication. In addition to ADAM, many institutions have signed on to the Global Alliance for Genomics and Health, which has started to generate schemas of its own for genomics analysis. The Hammerbacher lab at Mount Sinai School of Medicine has also developed Guacamole, a suite of tools

---

mainly aimed at somatic variant calling for cancer genomics. All of these tools are open source with liberal Apache v2 licenses, so if you start using them in your own work, please consider contributing improvements!

CHAPTER 11

Analyzing Neuroimaging Data with PySpark and Thunder

Uri Laserson

We are not interested in the fact that the brain has the consistency of cold porridge.
—Alan Turing

Advances in imaging equipment and automation have led to a glut of data on the function of the brain. While past experiments might have generated time series data from only a handful of electrodes in the brain, or a small number of static images of brain slices, technologies today can sample brain activity from a large number of neurons in a large region while organisms are actively behaving. Indeed, the Obama administration has endorsed the BRAIN initiative, which has lofty technology development goals to enable, for example, simultaneously recording the electrical activity of every neuron of the mouse brain over an extended period of time. While breakthroughs in measurement technology are certainly necessary, the amount of data generated will create completely new paradigms for biology.

In this chapter, we will introduce the PySpark API (*http://spark.apache.org/docs/latest/api/python/*) for interacting with Spark through Python, as well as the Thunder project (*http://thefreemanlab.com/thunder/*), which is developed on top of PySpark for processing large amounts of time series data in general, and neuroimaging data in particular. PySpark is a particularly flexible tool for exploratory big data analysis, because it integrates well with the rest of the PyData ecosystem, including matplotlib for visualization, and even IPython Notebook (Jupyter) for "executable documents."

We will marshal these tools for the task of understanding some of the structure of zebrafish brains. Using Thunder, we will cluster different regions of the brain (representing groups of neurons) to discover patterns of activity as the zebrafish behaves over time.

Overview of PySpark

Python is a favorite tool for many data scientists (*http://bit.ly/186ShId*), due to its high-level syntax and extensive library of packages, among other things. The Spark ecosystem has recognized Python's importance in the data analytics milieu, and has begun to invest in a Python API for using Spark, despite Python's historical difficulties integrating with the JVM.

Python for Scientific Computing and Data Science

Python has become a favorite tool for scientific computing and data science. It is now being used for many applications that would have traditionally used MATLAB, R, or Mathematica. The reasons include the following:

- Python is a high-level language that is easy to use and learn.
- It has an extensive library system ranging from niche numerical calculations to web-scraping utilities to data visualization tools.
- It interfaces easily with C/C++ code, allowing access to high-performance libraries, including BLAS/LAPACK/ATLAS.

Some libraries to keep in mind in particular include:

`numpy/scipy/matplotlib`
These libraries recapitulate typical MATLAB functionality, including fast array operations, scientific functions, and a widely used MATLAB-inspired plotting library.

`pandas`
This library provides functionality similar to R's `data.frame`, and oftentimes with much higher performance to boot.

`scikit-learn/statsmodels`
These libraries provide high-quality implementations of machine learning algorithms (e.g., classification/regression, clustering, matrix factorization) and statistical models.

`nltk`
A popular library for natural language processing.

You can find a large list of many other available libraries at *https://github.com/vinta/awesome-python*.

Start PySpark just like Spark:

```
export IPYTHON=1 # PySpark can use the IPython shell
pyspark --master ... --num-executors ...  ❶
```

❶ pyspark takes the same Spark arguments as `spark-submit` and `spark-shell`

We can submit Python scripts using `spark-submit`, which will detect the *.py* extension on our scripts. PySpark supports the use of the IPython shell by setting the environment variable `IPYTHON=1`, which is something we recommend universally. When the Python shell starts, it creates a Python `SparkContext` object through which we interact with the cluster. Once the `SparkContext` is available, the PySpark API is very similar to the Scala API. For example, to load some CSV data:

```
raw_data = sc.textFile('path/to/csv/data') # RDD[string]
# filter, split on comma, parse floats to get a RDD[list[float]]
data = (raw_data
    .filter(lambda x: x.startswith("#"))
    .map(lambda x: map(float, x.split(','))))
data.take(5)
```

Just like in the Scala API, we load a text file, filter out rows that start with #, and parse the CSV data into a list of `float` values. The Python functions passed to, for example, `filter` and `map`, are very flexible. They must take a Python object and return a Python object (in the case of `filter`, the return value is interpreted as a boolean). The only restrictions are that the Python function objects must be serializable with `cloudpickle` (which includes anonymous lambda functions), and any necessary modules referenced in the closures must be available on the `PYTHONPATH` of the executor Python processes. To ensure the availability of referenced modules, either the modules must be installed cluster-wide and available on the `PYTHONPATH` of the executor Python processes, or the corresponding module ZIP/EGG files must be explicitly distributed around by Spark, which will then add them to the `PYTHONPATH`. This latter functionality can be accomplished by a call to `sc.addPyFile()`.

The PySpark RDDs are just RDDs of Python objects: like Python lists, they can store objects with mixed types (because underneath, all the objects are instances of `PyObject`).

The PySpark API can lag behind the Scala API to a certain extent, so in some cases, features become available in Scala more rapidly. However, in addition to the core API, there already exists a Python API to MLlib, for example, which is used in Thunder.

PySpark Internals

It is useful to understand a bit about how PySpark is implemented in order to simplify debugging and also to be conscious of possible performance pitfalls (see Figure 11-1).

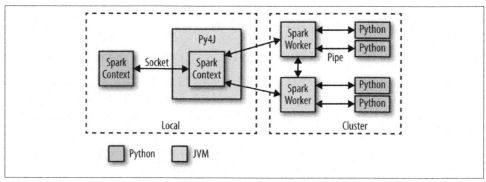

Figure 11-1. PySpark internal architecture

When PySpark's Python interpreter starts, it also starts a JVM with which it communicates through a socket. PySpark uses the Py4J project to handle this communication. The JVM functions as the actual Spark driver, and loads a `JavaSparkContext` that communicates with the Spark executors across the cluster. Python API calls to the `SparkContext` object are then translated into Java API calls to the `JavaSparkContext`. For example, the implementation of PySpark's `sc.textFile()` dispatches a call to the `.textFile` method of the `JavaSparkContext`, which ultimately communicates with the Spark executor JVMs to load the text data from HDFS.

The Spark executors on the cluster start a Python interpreter for each core, with which they communicate data through a pipe when they need to execute user code. A Python RDD in the local PySpark client corresponds to a `PythonRDD` object in the local JVM. The data associated with the RDD actually lives in the Spark JVMs as Java objects. For example, running `sc.textFile()` in the Python interpreter will call the `JavaSparkContext`s `textFile` method, which loads the data as Java `String` objects in the cluster. Similarly, loading a Parquet/Avro file using `newAPIHadoopFile` will load the objects as Java Avro objects.

When an API call is made on the Python RDD, any associated code (e.g., Python lambda function) is serialized via cloudpickle and distributed to the executors. The data is then converted from Java objects to a Python-compatible representation (e.g., pickle objects) and streamed to executor-associated Python interpreters through a pipe. Any necessary Python processing is executed in the interpreter, and the resulting data is stored back as an RDD (as pickle objects by default) in the JVMs.

Python's built-in support for serializing executable code is not as powerful as Scala's. As a result, the authors of PySpark had to use a custom module called "cloudpickle" built by the now defunct PiCloud.

Setting Up PySpark with IPython Notebook (Jupyter)

IPython Notebook is a fantastic environment for exploratory analytics and for use as a computational "lab notebook." It allows the user to integrate text, images, and executable code (in Python and now other languages), and also supports a hosted platform, among other features. While IPython Notebook works well with Spark, it requires some care to configure correctly because PySpark must be initialized in a particular way. Refer to this blog post for details: *http://bit.ly/186UfIE*.

Overview and Installation of the Thunder Library

Thunder Examples and Documentation

The Thunder package has excellent documentation and tutorials. The following examples draw from the provided data sets and tutorials.

Thunder is a Python tool set for processing large amounts of spatial/temporal data sets (i.e., large multidimensional matrices) on Spark. It makes heavy use of NumPy for matrix computations and also the MLlib library for distributed implementations of some statistical techniques. Python also makes it very flexible and accessible to a broad audience. In the following section, we introduce the Thunder API, and attempt to classify some neural traces into a set of patterns using MLlib's K-means implementation as wrapped by Thunder and PySpark.

Thunder requires Spark, as well as the Python libraries NumPy, SciPy, matplotlib, and scikit-learn. Installing Thunder can be as easy as `pip install thunder-python`, though it requires checking out the Git repo itself in order to use anything other than Spark 1.1 and Hadoop 1.x (see the following box). Thunder also includes scripts for easily deploying on Amazon EC2, and has also been demonstrated on traditional HPC environments.

Using Thunder with Different Versions of Hadoop/Spark

At the time of this writing, Thunder is by default built against the Hadoop 1.x API, without any direct support for building against the Hadoop 2.x API (necessary for running against YARN, for example). Installing Thunder via `pip` will also include a prebuilt Thunder JAR compiled against Hadoop 1.x and Spark 1.1. To build against

Hadoop 2.x, change the *scala/build.sbt* file in the Thunder repo to reflect the desired version of Hadoop. The Thunder Hadoop version should match the Spark Hadoop version (which can also be changed in the SBT file).

After installation, and setting the `SPARK_HOME` environment variable, we can invoke the Thunder shell like so:

```
$ export IPYTHON=1 # recommended as usual
$ thunder

[...some logging output...]
Welcome to
      ____              __
     / __/__  ___ _____/ /__
    _\ \/ _ \/ _ `/ __/  '_/
   /__ / .__/\_,_/_/ /_/\_\   version 1.1.0
      /_/

Using Python version 2.7.6 (default, Apr  9 2014 11:54:50)
SparkContext available as sc.

Running thunder version 0.5.0_dev
A thunder context is available as tsc

In [1]:
```

This shows us that the `thunder` command is basically wrapping the PySpark shell. Similarly to PySpark, the start of most computations is the `ThunderContext` variable `tsc`, which wraps the Python `SparkContext` with Thunder-specific functionality.

Loading Data with Thunder

Thunder was designed especially with neuroimaging data sets in mind. Therefore, it is geared toward analyzing data from large sets of images that are often captured over time.

Let's start by loading some images of zebrafish brains from an example data set provided in the Thunder repository, at *python/thunder/utils/data/fish/tif-stack* (*http://bit.ly/1ebiad5*). For the purposes of demonstration, the examples presented are performed on enormously downsampled data. Full-scale data sets are available on AWS via—for example, the `ThunderContext.loadExampleEC2()` function. The zebrafish is a commonly used model organism in biology research. It is small, reproduces quickly, and is used as a model for vertebrate development. It's also interesting because it has exceptionally fast regenerative capabilities. In the context of neuroscience, the zebrafish makes a great model because it is transparent and the brain is small enough that it is essentially possible to image it entirely at a high-enough resolution to distinguish individual neurons. Here is the code to load the data set:

```
path_to_images = (
    'path/to/thunder/python/thunder/utils/data/fish/tif-stack')
imagesRDD = tsc.loadImages(path_to_images,
    inputformat='tif-stack') ❶

print imagesRDD
print imagesRDD.rdd
...
<thunder.rdds.images.Images object at 0x109aa59d0>
PythonRDD[8] at RDD at PythonRDD.scala:43
```

❶ tif-stack is a format where each file contains multiple planes in a z-dimension

This created an Images object that ultimately wraps an RDD, accessible as imagesRDD.rdd. The Images object exposes the relevant similar functionality (like count, take, etc.) as well. The objects stored in Images are key-value pairs:

```
print imagesRDD.first()
...
(0, array([[[26, 25],
        [26, 25],
        [26, 25],
        ...,
        [26, 26],
        [26, 26],
        [26, 26]],

       ...,
       [[25, 25],
        [25, 25],
        [25, 25],
        ...,
        [26, 26],
        [26, 26],
        [26, 26]]], dtype=uint8))
```

The key 0 corresponds to the zeroth image in the set (they are ordered lexicographically from the data directory), and the value is a NumPy array corresponding to the image. All of the core data types in Thunder are ultimately backed by Python RDDs of key-value pairs, where the keys are typically some kind of tuple and the values are NumPy arrays. The keys and values always have a homogeneous type across the RDD, even though PySpark generally allows RDDs of heterogeneous collections. Because of the homogeneity, the Images object exposes a .dims property describing the underlying images:

```
print imagesRDD.first()[1].shape ❶
...
(76, 87, 2) ❸

print imagesRDD.dims ❷
...
Dimensions: min=(0, 0, 0), max=(75, 86, 1), count=(76, 87, 2)
```

```
print imagesRDD.nimages
...
20
```

❶ The shape of the NumPy array of the first key-value pair

❷ A Thunder `Dimensions` object corresponding to the data in this RDD

❸ Each "image" in the RDD is actually a stack of two 76 × 87 images

Our data set is composed of 20 "images" where each image is a 76 × 87 × 2 stack. Thunder provides a `Dimensions` object for keeping track of the shape of the data in the RDD.

Pixels, Voxels, and Stacks

"Pixel" is a portmanteau of "picture element." Digital images can be modeled as simple two-dimensional (2D) matrices of intensity values, and each element in the matrix is a pixel. (A color image would require three of these matrices, one each for a red, green, and blue channel.) However, because the brain is a three-dimensional object, a single 2D slice is not nearly enough to capture its activity. To address this, multiple techniques will either acquire multiple 2D images in different planes on top of each other (a z-stack), and some will even generate 3D information directly (e.g., light field microscopy). This ultimately produces a 3D matrix of intensity values, where each value represents a "volume element," or "voxel." Consistent with this, Thunder models all images as 2D or 3D matrices, depending on the specific data type, and can read file formats like *.tiff* that can natively represent 3D stacks.

One of the features of working in Python is that we can easily visualize our data while working with the RDDs, in this case using the venerable matplotlib library (see Figure 11-2):

```python
import matplotlib.pyplot as plt
img = imagesRDD.values().first()
plt.imshow(img[:, : ,0], interpolation='nearest', aspect='equal',
    cmap='gray')
```

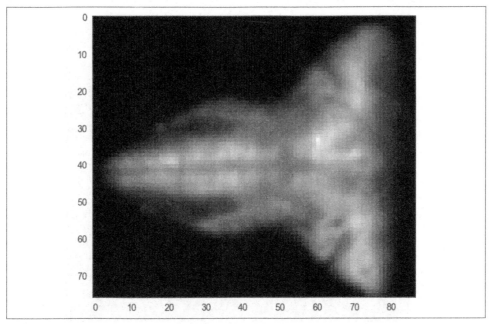

Figure 11-2. A single slice from the raw zebrafish data

The `Images` API offers useful methods for working with the image data in a distributed fashion—for example, to subsample each image down (see Figure 11-3):

```
subsampled = imagesRDD.subsample((5, 5, 1)) ❶
plt.imshow(subsampled.first()[1][:, : ,0], interpolation='nearest',
    aspect='equal', cmap='gray')
print subsampled.dims
...
Dimensions: min=(0, 0, 0), max=(15, 17, 1), count=(16, 18, 2)
```

❶ The stride to subsample each dimension; note that this is an RDD operation, so it returns immediately, waiting for an RDD action to trigger computation

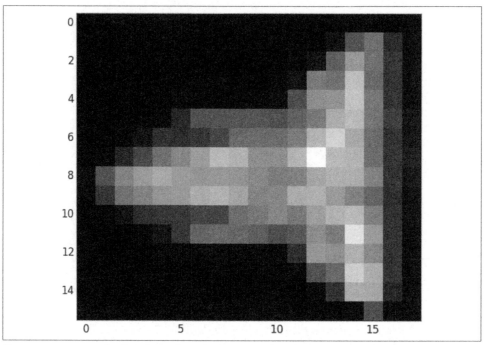

Figure 11-3. A single slice from the subsampled zebrafish data

While analyzing the collection of images may be useful for certain operations (e.g., normalizing images in certain ways), it's difficult to take the temporal relationship of the images into account. To do so, we'd rather work with the image data as a collection of pixel/voxel time series. This is exactly what the Thunder `Series` object is for, and there is an easy way to convert:

```
seriesRDD = imagesRDD.toSeries()
```

This operation executes a large-scale reorganization of the data into a `Series` object, which is an RDD of key-value pairs where the key is a tuple of the coordinates of each image (i.e., the voxel identifier) and the value is a one-dimensional NumPy array corresponding to the time series of values:

```
print seriesRDD.dims
print seriesRDD.index
print seriesRDD.count()
...
Dimensions: min=(0, 0, 0), max=(75, 86, 1), count=(76, 87, 2)
[ 0  1  2  3  4  5  6  7  8  9 10 11 12 13 14 15 16 17 18 19]
13224
```

Whereas `imagesRDD` was a collection of 20 images with dimensions (76 × 87 × 2), `seriesRDD` is a collection of 13,224 (76 × 87 × 2) time series of length 20. Also note that executing `seriesRDD.dims` induces a job, because we can only compute the dimensions by analyzing all of the key values of the `Series` object. The `ser iesRDD.index` property is a Pandas-style index that can be used to reference each of the arrays. Because our original images were three-dimensional, the keys are 3-tuples:

```
print seriesRDD.rdd.takeSample(False, 1, 0)[0]
...
((30, 84, 1), array([35, 35, 35, 35, 35, 35, 35, 35, 34, 34,
        34, 35, 35, 35, 35, 35, 35, 35, 35, 35], dtype=uint8))
```

The `Series` API offers many methods for performing computations across the time series, either at the per-series level or across all series. For example:

```
print seriesRDD.max()
...
array([158, 152, 145, 143, 142, 141, 140, 140, 139, 139, 140, 140,
        142, 144, 153, 168, 179, 185, 185, 182], dtype=uint8)
```

computes the maximum value across all voxels at each time point, while:

```
stddevRDD = seriesRDD.seriesStdev()
print stddevRDD.take(3)
print stddevRDD.dims ❶
...
[((0, 0, 0), 0.4), ((1, 0, 0), 0.0), ((2, 0, 0), 0.0)]
Dimensions: min=(0, 0, 0), max=(75, 86, 1), count=(76, 87, 2)
```

computes the standard deviation of each time series and returns the result as an RDD, preserving all the keys.

❶ This property is intelligently inherited from the parent RDD, so this time there is no Spark calculation because we've computed the `Dimension` for `seriesRDD`

We can also locally repack the `Series` into the shape of the `Dimension` ($76 \times 87 \times 2$ in this case):

```
repacked = stddevRDD.pack()
plt.imshow(repacked[:,:,0], interpolation='nearest', cmap='gray',
    aspect='equal')
print type(repacked)
print repacked.shape
...
<type 'numpy.ndarray'>
(76, 87, 2)
```

This allows us to plot the standard deviation of each voxel using the same spatial relationships (see Figure 11-4). We should take care to make sure that we're not trying to return too much data to the client, because it will consume significant network and memory resources.

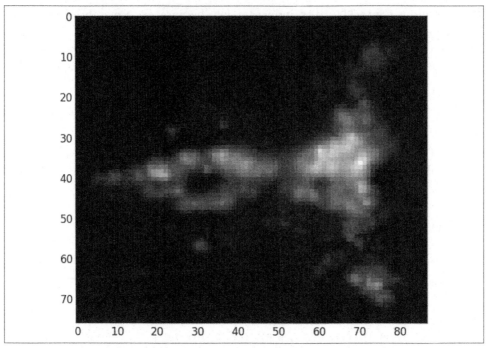

Figure 11-4. Standard deviation of each voxel in the raw zebrafish data

Alternatively, we can look at the centered time series directly, by plotting a subset of them (see Figure 11-5):

```
plt.plot(seriesRDD.center().subset(50).T)
```

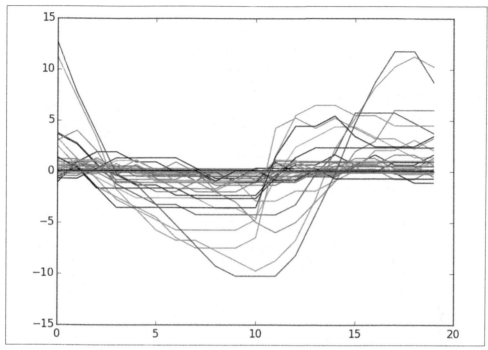

Figure 11-5. A random subset of 50 of the centered time series

It's also very easy to apply any user-defined function to each series (including lambda functions), using the `apply` method, which calls the RDD's `.values().map()` underneath:

```
seriesRDD.apply(lambda x: x.argmin())
```

Thunder Core Data Types

More generally, the two core data types in Thunder, `Series` and `Images`, both inherit from the `Data` class, which wraps a Python RDD object and exposes part of the RDD API. The `Data` class models RDDs of key-value pairs, where the key represents some type of semantic identifier (e.g., a tuple of coordinates in space), and the value is a NumPy array of actual data. For the `Images` object, the key could be a time point, for example, and the value is the image at that time point formatted as a NumPy array. For the `Series` object, the key might be an n-dimensional tuple with the coordinates of the corresponding voxel, while the value is a one-dimensional NumPy array representing the time series of measurements at that voxel. All the arrays in `Series` must have the same dimensions. Some useful bits of the objects' APIs are summarized here:

```
class Data:
    property dtype:
        # The dtype of the numpy array in this RDD's value slot
```

```
    # lots of RDD methods, like first(), count(), cache(), etc.

    # methods for aggregating across arrays, like mean(),
    # variance(), etc., that keep the dtype constant

class Series(Data):
    property dims:
        # lazily computes Dimension object with information about
        # the spatial dimensions encoded in the keys of this RDD

    property index:
        # a set of indices into each array, in the style of a
        # Pandas Series object

    # lots of methods to process all of the 1D arrays in parallel
    # across the cluster, like normalize(), detrend(), select(),
    # and apply(), that keep the dtype constant

    # methods for parallel aggregations, like seriesMax(),
    # seriesStdev(), etc., that change the dtype

    def pack():
        # collects the data at the client and repacks from the
        # sparse representation in the RDD to a dense
        # representation as a NumPy array with shape corresponding
        # to dims

class Images(Data):
    property dims:
        # the Dimension object corresponding to the NumPy shape
        # parameter of each value array

    property nimages:
        # number of images in RDD; lazily executes an RDD count
        # operation

    # multiple methods for aggregating across images or processing
    # them in parallel, like maxProjection(), subsample(),
    # subtract(), and apply()

    def toSeries():
        # reorganize data as a Series object
```

We can typically represent the same data set as either an `Images` or `Series` object, converting between the two through a (possibly expensive) shuffle operation (analogous to switching between row-major and column-major representations).

Data for Thunder can be persisted as a set of images, with the ordering encoded by lexicographic ordering of the individual image filenames; or the data can be persisted as a set of binary 1D arrays for `Series` objects. See the documentation for more details.

Categorizing Neuron Types with Thunder

In this example, we'll use the K-means algorithm to cluster the various fish time series into multiple clusters in an attempt to describe the classes of neural behavior. We will use data already persisted as `Series` data packaged in the repo that is larger than the image data used previously. However, the spatial resolution of this data is still too low to define individual neurons.

First we load the data:

```
seriesRDD = tsc.loadSeries(
    'path/to/thunder/python/thunder/utils/data/fish/bin')
print seriesRDD.dims
print seriesRDD.index
...
Dimensions: min=(0, 0, 0), max=(75, 86, 1), count=(76, 87, 2)
[  0   1   2   3   4   5   6   ...   234 235 236 237 238 239]
```

We see this represents images with the same dimensions as earlier, but with 240 time points instead of 20. We must normalize our features to get the best clustering:

```
normalizedRDD = seriesRDD.normalize(baseline='mean') ❶
```

❶ The `baseline=mean` option we specified is actually not documented. The Thunder code is quite clear, and in multiple cases, there may be hidden functionality that expresses what we want.

Let's plot a few of the series to see what they look like. Thunder allows us to take a random subset of the RDD and filter only collection elements that meet a certain criterion, like minimum standard deviation by default. To choose a good value for the threshold, let's first compute the stddev of each series and plot a histogram of a 10% sample of the values (see Figure 11-6):

```
stddevs = (normalizedRDD
    .seriesStdev()
    .values()
    .sample(False, 0.1, 0)
    .collect())
plt.hist(stddevs, bins=20)
```

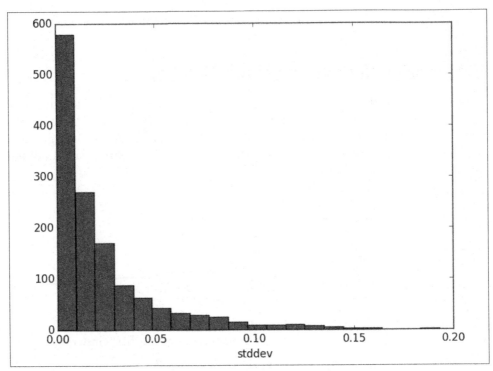

Figure 11-6. Distribution of the standard deviations of the voxels

With this in mind, we'll choose a threshold of 0.1 to look at the most "active" series (see Figure 11-7):

```
plt.plot(normalizedRDD.subset(50, thresh=0.1, stat='std').T)
```

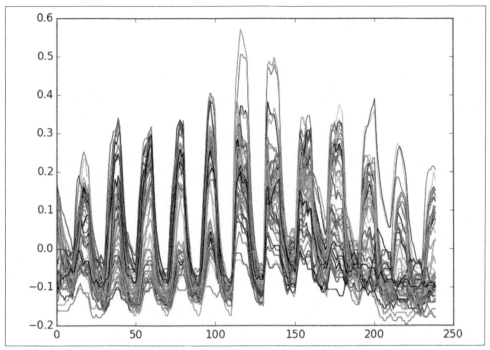

Figure 11-7. Fifty of the most active time series, based on standard deviation

Now that we have a feel for the data, let's finally cluster the voxels into the various patterns of behavior. Thunder has implemented a scikit-learn-style API for working with RDDs. In some cases, Thunder contains its own implementations (e.g., the matrix factorization code). In this case, Thunder's K-means abstraction calls out to the MLlib Python API. We will perform K-means for multiple values of *k*:

```
from thunder import KMeans
ks = [5, 10, 15, 20, 30, 50, 100, 200]
models = []
for k in ks:
    models.append(KMeans(k=k).fit(normalizedRDD))
```

Now we'll compute two simple error metrics on each of the clusterings. The first will simply be the sum across all time series of the Euclidean distance from the time series to its cluster center. The second will be a built-in metric of the KMeansModel object:

```
def model_error_1(model):
    def series_error(series):
        cluster_id = model.predict(series)
        center = model.centers[cluster_id]
        diff = center - series
        return diff.dot(diff) ** 0.5

    return (normalizedRDD
```

```
        .apply(series_error)
        .sum())

def model_error_2(model):
    return 1. / model.similarity(normalizedRDD).sum()
```

We will compute both error metrics for each value of k and plot them (see Figure 11-8):

```
import numpy as np
errors_1 = np.asarray(map(model_error_1, models))
errors_2 = np.asarray(map(model_error_2, models))
plt.plot(
    ks, errors_1 / errors_1.sum(), 'k-o',
    ks, errors_2 / errors_2.sum(), 'b:v')
```

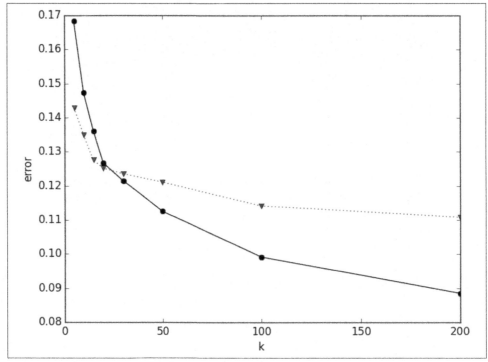

Figure 11-8. K-means error metrics as a function of k (black circles are model_error_1 and blue triangles are model_error_2)

We'd expect these metrics to generally be monotonic with k; it seems like k=20 might be a sharper elbow in the curve. Let's visualize the cluster centers that we've learned from the data (see Figure 11-9):

```
model20 = models[3]
plt.plot(model20.centers.T)
```

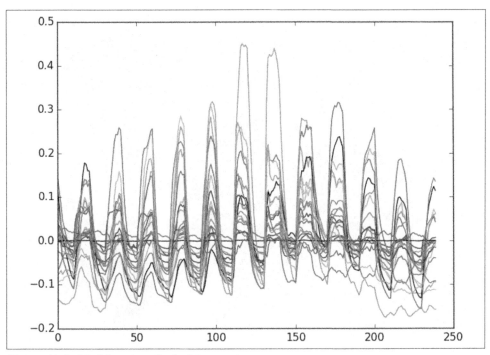

Figure 11-9. Model centers for k=20

It's also easy to plot the images themselves with the voxels colored according to their assigned cluster (see Figure 11-10):

```
from matplotlib.colors import ListedColormap
by_cluster = model20.predict(normalizedRDD).pack()
cmap_cat = ListedColormap(sns.color_palette("hls", 10), name='from_list')
plt.imshow(by_cluster[:, :, 0], interpolation='nearest',
    aspect='equal', cmap='gray')
```

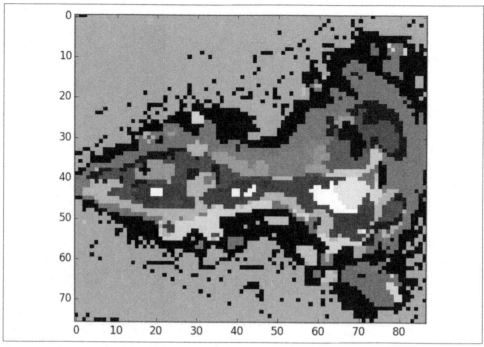

Figure 11-10. Voxels colored by cluster membership

It's clear that the learned clusters recapitulate certain elements of zebrafish brain anatomy. If the original data were high resolution enough to resolve subcellular structures, we could first perform clustering of the voxels with k equal to an estimate of the number of neurons in the imaged volume. This would allow us to effectively map out the entire neuron cell bodies. We would then define time series for each neuron, which could be used for clustering again to determine different functional categories.

Where to Go from Here

Thunder is still a new project, but already includes a pretty rich set of functionality. In addition to statistics on time series and clustering, it has modules for matrix factorizations, regression/classification, and tools for visualization. It has fantastic documentation and tutorials covering a large array of its functionality. To see Thunder in action, see the recent article (*http://bit.ly/186YPqi*) by Thunder authors in *Nature Methods* (July 2014).

Deeper into Spark

Sandy Ryza

Understanding Spark at the level of transformations, actions, and RDDs is vital for writing Spark programs. Understanding Spark's underlying execution model is vital for writing *good* Spark programs—for making sense of their performance characteristics, for debugging failures and slowness, and for interpreting the user interface.

A Spark application consists of a *driver* process, which in `spark-shell`'s case, is the process that the user is interacting with, and a set of *executor* processes scattered across nodes on the cluster. The driver is in charge of the high-level control flow of work that needs to be done. The executor processes are responsible for executing this work, in the form of *tasks*, as well as for storing any data that the user chooses to *cache*. Both the driver and the executors typically stick around for the entire time the application is running. A single executor has a number of slots for running tasks, and will run many concurrently throughout its lifetime.

At the top of the execution model are *jobs*. Invoking an action inside a Spark application triggers the launch of a Spark job to fulfill it. To decide what this job looks like, Spark examines the graph of RDDs that the action depends on and formulates an execution plan that starts with computing the farthest back RDDs and culminates in the RDDs required to produce the action's results. The execution plan consists of assembling the job's transformations into *stages*. A stage corresponds to a collection of *tasks* that all execute the same code, each on a different partition of the data. Each stage contains a sequence of transformations that can be completed without shuffling the full data.

What determines whether data needs to be shuffled? For the RDDs returned by so-called *narrow* transformations like `map`, the data required to compute a single partition resides in a single partition in the parent RDD. Each object is only dependent on a single object in the parent. However, Spark also supports transformations with *wide* dependencies like groupByKey and reduceByKey. In these, the data required to compute a single partition may reside in many partitions of the parent RDD. All of the tuples with the same key must end up in the same partition. To satisfy these operations, Spark must execute a *shuffle*, which transfers data around the cluster and results in a new stage with a new set of partitions.

For example, the following code would execute in a single stage, because none of the outputs of these three operations depend on data that can come from different partitions than their inputs:

```
sc.textFile("someFile.txt").
  map(mapFunc).
  flatMap(flatMapFunc).
  filter(filterFunc).
  count()
```

The following code, which finds how many times each character appears in all the words that appear more than 1,000 times in a text file, would break down into three stages. The reduceByKey operations result in stage boundaries, because computing their outputs requires repartitioning the data by keys:

```
val tokenized = sc.textFile(args(0)).flatMap(_.split(' '))
val wordCounts = tokenized.map((_, 1)).reduceByKey(_ + _)
val filtered = wordCounts.filter(_._2 >= 1000)
val charCounts = filtered.flatMap(_._1.toCharArray).map((_, 1)).
  reduceByKey(_ + _)
charCounts.collect()
```

At each stage boundary, data is written to disk by tasks in the *parent* stage and then fetched over the network by tasks in the *child* stage. Thus, stage boundaries can be expensive and should be avoided when possible. The number of data partitions in the parent stage may be different than the number of partitions in the child stage. Transformations that may trigger a stage boundary typically accept a numPartitions argument that determines how many partitions to split the data into in the child stage. Just as the number of reducers is an important parameter in tuning MapReduce jobs, tuning the number of partitions at stage boundaries can often make or break an application's performance. Choosing too few partitions can result in slowness when each task is forced to handle too much data. The amount of time it takes a task to complete often increases nonlinearly with the size of the data assigned to it, because aggregation operations must spill to disk when their data does not fit in memory. On the other side, a large number of partitions leads to increased overhead in tasks on the parent side when sorting records by their target partition, as well as more of the overhead associated with scheduling and launching each task on the child side.

Serialization

As a distributed system, Spark often needs to serialize the raw Java objects it operates on. When data is cached in a serialized format, transferred over the network for a shuffle, Spark needs a byte stream representation of RDD contents. Spark accepts a pluggable `Serializer` for defining this serialization and deserialization. By default, Spark uses Java Object Serialization, which can serialize any Java object that implements the `Serializable` interface. Nearly always, Spark should be configured to instead use *Kryo* serialization. Kryo defines a more compact format that serializes and deserializes far faster. The "catch" is that, to get this efficiency, Kryo requires *registering* any custom classes defined in the application up front. Kryo will still work without registering the classes, but the serialization will take up more space and time because the class name must be written out before each record. Turning on Kryo and registering classes in code looks like:

```
val conf = new SparkConf().setAppName("MyApp")
conf.registerKryoClasses(
  Array(classOf[MyCustomClass1], classOf[MyCustomClass2]))
```

We can also register classes with Kryo through configuration. When you're using `spark-shell`, this is the only way to do so. Something like the following can be placed in *spark-defaults.conf*:

```
spark.kryo.classesToRegister=org.myorg.MyCustomClass1,org.myorg.MyCustomClass2
spark.serializer=org.apache.spark.serializer.KryoSerializer
```

Spark libraries like GraphX and MLlib may have their own set of custom classes, with a utility method for registering them all:

```
GraphXUtils.registerKryoClasses(conf)
```

Accumulators

Accumulators are a Spark construct that allow collecting some statistics "on the side" while a job is running. The code executing in each task can add to the accumulator, and the driver can access its value. Accumulators are useful in situations like counting the number of bad records a job encounters or computing the summed error during a stage of an optimization process.

For example, Spark MLlib's K-means clustering implementation uses accumulators for the latter. Each iteration of the algorithm starts with a set of cluster centers, assigns each point in the data set to its closest center, and then uses the assignment to compute a new set of cluster centers. The *cost* of a clustering, which the algorithm is attempting to optimize, is the sum of distances from each point to its closest cluster center. To know when the algorithm should terminate, it is useful to compute this cost after assigning points to their clusters:

```
var prevCost = Double.MaxValue
var cost = 0.0
var clusterCenters = initialCenters(k)
while (prevCost - cost > THRESHOLD) {
  val costAccum = sc.accumulator(0, "Cost")
  clusterCenters = dataset.map {
    // Find the closest center to the point and the distance from
    // that center
    val (newCenter, distance) = closestCenterAndDistance(_,
      clusterCenters)
    costAccum += distance
    (newCenter, _)
  }.aggregate( /* average the points assigned to each center */ )

  prevCost = cost
  cost = costAccum.value
}
```

This example defines the accumulator's add function as integer addition, but accumulators can also support other associative functions like set unions.

Accumulators have some behavioral quirks. In particular, their behavior under failure situations depends on whether they are updated from inside tasks that run in the terminal stage of a job, or whether they run inside an intermediate stage. If a task in an intermediate stage updates an accumulator, but its outputs are lots and it needs to be rerun, it will increment the accumulator again, possibly resulting in double-counting. For tasks in result stages, accumulators will only be incremented the first time the task runs. These strange semantics make accumulators difficult to deal with, and a poor choice for many situations.

Accumulators are an optimization in the sense that, instead, the RDD could be cached and a separate action run over it to calculate the same results. Accumulators allow this to be achieved much more efficiently by avoiding caching the data and avoiding executing another job.

Spark and the Data Scientist's Workflow

A few of Spark's transformations and actions are particularly useful when you're exploring and trying to get a feel for a new data set. Some of these operators employ randomness. These operators use a seed to ensure determinism in the cases that task results are lost and need to be recomputed or multiple actions take advantage of the same uncached RDD.

take enables inexpensively looking at the first few elements of an RDD. If there are no operations preceding it that require shuffles, it only requires computing the elements in the first partition:

```
myFirstRdd.take(2)
14/09/29 12:09:13 INFO SparkContext: Starting job: take ...
14/09/29 12:09:13 INFO SparkContext: Job finished: take ...
res1: Array[Int] = Array(1, 2)
```

takeSample is useful for pulling a representative sample of the data into the driver for charting, playing with locally, or exporting for nondistributed analysis in a different environment like R. Its first argument withReplacement determines whether the sample may contain multiple copies of the same record:

```
myFirstRdd.takeSample(true, 3)
14/09/29 12:14:18 INFO SparkContext: Starting job: takeSample ...
14/09/29 12:14:18 INFO SparkContext: Job finished: takeSample ...
res11: Array[Int] = Array(2, 1, 1)

myFirstRdd.takeSample(true, 5)
14/09/29 12:14:18 INFO SparkContext: Starting job: takeSample ...
14/09/29 12:14:18 INFO SparkContext: Job finished: takeSample ...
res11: Array[Int] = Array(2, 1, 1, 2, 4)

myFirstRdd.takeSample(false, 3)
14/09/29 12:14:18 INFO SparkContext: Starting job: takeSample ...
14/09/29 12:14:18 INFO SparkContext: Job finished: takeSample ...
res11: Array[Int] = Array(2, 1, 4)
```

top collects the k largest records in a data set according to a given Ordering. It is useful in a variety of situations, such as, after giving each record a score, examining the records with the highest scores. Its opposite is takeOrdered, which finds the smallest records. The following snippet generates random numbers between 0 and 100 and finds the ones that occur most and least often:

```
import scala.util.Random

val randNums = Seq.fill(10000)(Random.nextInt(100))
val numberCounts = sc.parallelize(randNums).map(x => (x, 1)).
  reduceByKey(_ + _)

numCounts.top(3)(Ordering.by(_._2))
14/09/30 23:38:42 INFO SparkContext: Starting job: top ...
14/09/30 23:38:42 INFO SparkContext: Job finished: top ...
res6: Array[(Int, Int)] = Array((58,127), (25,120), (28,120))

numCounts.takeOrdered(3)(Ordering.by(_._2))
14/09/30 23:39:54 INFO SparkContext: Starting job: takeOrdered ...
14/09/30 23:39:54 INFO SparkContext: Job finished: takeOrdered ...
res7: Array[(Int, Int)] = Array((74,78), (92,79), (8,80))
```

top functions by first finding the k largest values within each partition in a distributed fashion, pulling these onto the driver, and then finding the largest k among all of them. This works well when k is small, but ends up pulling the entire data set onto the driver when k is as large or larger than the size of data in a single partition.

For these cases, it is wiser to sort the full data set in a distributed manner using `sort ByKey` and then `take` the first *k* elements:

```
numberCounts.map(_.swap).sortByKey().map(_.swap).take(5)  ❶
14/10/06 13:19:08 INFO SparkContext: Starting job: sortByKey ...
14/10/06 13:19:08 INFO DAGScheduler: Job 2 finished: take ...
res3: Array[(Int, Int)] = Array((87,73), (19,76), (75,76), (25,81), (22,81))
```

❶ Swap the order of the tuples to sort on the numbers instead of the counts

This code pulls data into the driver, but often sampling is useful for creating distributed data sets as a step in a pipeline. `sample` creates an RDD by sampling its parent RDD. Like `takeSample`, it can function with and without replacement. It accepts an argument that determines the number of elements to sample as a fraction of the size of the parent RDD. When sampling with replacement, Spark accepts a value greater than one, which is useful for blowing up the size of a data set to stress-test a pipeline. `sample` is also useful for permuting data, which is good practice before running online algorithms over it like stochastic gradient descent:

```
val bootstrapSample = rdd.sample(true, .6)

val permuted = rdd.sample(false, 1.0)
```

`randomSplit` returns multiple RDDs that, combined, would make up their parent. It is particularly useful for tasks like splitting data into train and test sets:

```
fullData.cache()
val Array(train, test) = fullData.randomSplit(Array(0.6, 0.4))
```

File Formats

Spark examples commonly employ `textFile`, but it is usually recommended to store large data sets in binary formats, both to take up less space and to enforce typing. *Avro* and *Parquet* files are the standard row and columnar formats respectively used to store data on Hadoop clusters. *Avro* also refers to an in-memory representation of on-disk data from both of these formats.

The following example demonstrates reading Avro fields with `name` and `favor ite_color` fields:

```
import org.apache.hadoop.io.NullWritable
import org.apache.hadoop.mapreduce.Job
import org.apache.hadoop.mapreduce.lib.input.FileInputFormat
import org.apache.avro.generic.GenericRecord
import org.apache.avro.mapred.AvroKey
import org.apache.avro.mapreduce.AvroKeyInputFormat

val conf = new Job()
FileInputFormat.setInputPaths(conf, inPaths)
```

```
val records = sc.newAPIHadoopRDD(conf.getConfiguration,
  classOf[AvroKeyInputFormat[GenericRecord]],
  classOf[AvroKey[GenericRecord]],
  classOf[NullWritable]).map(_._1.datum)

val namesAndColors = records.map(x =>
  (x.get("name"), x.get("favorite_color")))
```

Similarly, for Parquet:

```
import org.apache.hadoop.mapreduce.Job
import org.apache.hadoop.mapreduce.lib.input.FileInputFormat
import org.apache.avro.generic.GenericRecord
import parquet.hadoop.ParquetInputFormat

val conf = new Job()
FileInputFormat.setInputPaths(conf, inPaths)
val records = sc.newAPIHadoopRDD(conf.getConfiguration,
  classOf[ParquetInputFormat],
  classOf[Void],
  classOf[GenericRecord]).map(_._2)

val namesAndColors = records.map(x =>
  (x.get("name"), x.get("favorite_color")))
```

Note that Avro supports two kinds of in-memory representation:

- Avro *generics* represent records as a map from `String` keys to `Object` values. They are the easiest to get started with when you're exploring a new data set, but they suffer from some inefficiencies, such as the need to wrap primitive types in objects.
- Avro *specifics* use code generation to create Java classes that correspond to the Avro types. They are omitted here for the sake of brevity, but the GitHub repository associated with this book includes an example.

Spark Subprojects

Spark Core refers to Spark's distributed execution engine and the core Spark APIs. In addition to Spark Core, Spark contains a gaggle of subprojects that offer functionality on top of its engine. These subprojects, detailed in the following sections, lie at different stages of development. While the core Spark APIs will remain stable and maintain compatibility, the APIs of subprojects marked alpha or beta are subject to change.

MLlib

MLlib provides a set of machine learning algorithms written on top of Spark. The project aims for high-quality implementations of standard algorithms, focusing on maintainability and consistency over breadth. At the time of this writing, MLlib supports the algorithms listed in Table A-1.

Table A-1. MLlib algorithms

	Discrete	Continuous
Supervised	Decision Forests, Naive Bayes, Linear Support Vector Machines, Logistic Regression and Regularized Variants	Linear Regression, and Regularized Variants (Ridge/L2, LASSO/L1), Decision Forests
Unsupervised	K-means Clustering	Singular Value Decomposition, UV Decomposition through Alternating Least Squares

MLlib represents data as `Vector` objects, which may be sparse or dense. It contains some light linear algebra functionality for operating on `Matrix` objects, which represent local matrices, and `RowMatrix` objects, which represent distributed collections of vectors. For laying out and manipulating data under the covers, it relies on *Breeze*, a Scala linear algebra library.

At the time of this book's writing, MLlib is a beta component, meaning that some APIs may change in future releases.

Several chapters in this book make use of MLlib's algorithms:

- Chapter 3 uses MLlib's alternating least squares implementation for making recommendations.
- Chapter 4 uses MLlib's random decision forests implementation for classification.
- Chapter 5 uses MLlib's K-means clustering implementation for anomaly detection.
- Chapter 6 uses MLlib's singular value decomposition implementation for text analysis.

Spark Streaming

Spark Streaming purposes the Spark execution engine for processing data continuously. Where Spark's typical batch processing executes jobs over large data sets at once, Spark Streaming aims for low-latency (in the hundreds of milliseconds): as data becomes available, it needs to be transformed and dealt with in near real time. Spark Streaming functions by running jobs over the small batches of data that accumulate in small time intervals. It is useful for rapid alerting, for supplying dashboards with up-to-date information, as well as for cases that require more complex analytics. For example, a common use case in anomaly detection is to run K-means clustering on batches of data, and to trigger a warning if the cluster centers deviate from what is normal.

Spark SQL

Spark SQL uses the Spark engine to execute SQL queries—either on data sets stored persistently in HDFS or on existing RDDs. It enables manipulating data with SQL statements *within* a Spark program:

```
import org.apache.spark.sql.hive.HiveContext

val sqlContext = HiveContext(sc)

val schemaRdd = sqlContext.sql("FROM sometable SELECT column1, column2, column3")
schemaRdd.collect().foreach(println)
```

Spark SQL's core data structure is a `SchemaRDD`, an RDD with Schema information that gives a name and type for each column. You can create a `SchemaRDD` by programmatically annotating existing RDDs with type information, or by accessing already Schema'd data stored in Hive, as shown in the preceding example.

At the time of this book's writing, Spark SQL is an alpha component, meaning that some of its APIs may change in future releases.

GraphX

Spark contains a subproject called GraphX that leverages its engine for graph processing. In computer science, the word *graph* refers to a structure consisting of a set of *vertices* connected by a set of *edges*. Graph algorithms are useful for tasks like examining the connections between users in a social network, understanding the importance of pages on the Internet based on what pages link to them, or running any analyses that depend on the connectivity structure between entities. GraphX represents graphs with a pair of RDDs—an RDD of vertices and an RDD of edges. It exposes an API similar to that of Google's *Pregel* graph processing system, and can express common algorithms like PageRank in only a handful of lines of code.

At the time of this book's writing, GraphX is an alpha component, meaning that some of its APIs may change in future releases. Chapter 6 makes use of a variety of GraphX's capabilities for analyzing citation graphs.

Upcoming MLlib Pipelines API

Sean Owen

The Spark project moves fast. When we started writing in August 2014, version 1.1.0 was nearing release. As this book goes to print in April 2015, Spark 1.2.1 is hot off the presses. In this version alone, almost 1,000 improvements and fixes were added.

The project carefully maintains binary and source compatibility for stable APIs in minor releases, and most of MLlib is considered stable. The examples in the book should therefore continue to work with Spark 1.3.0 and future 1.x releases; those implementations won't be going anywhere. However, new releases often add or change experimental or developer-only APIs, which are still evolving.

Spark MLlib has, of course, featured prominently in these chapters, and a book covering Spark 1.2.1 would not be complete without mentioning a significant new direction for MLlib that appears, in part, as an experimental API: the "Pipelines" API.

It's officially only a month or so old, subject to change, and not nearly complete, and so it has not been possible to build the book around it. However, it's worth knowing about, having already seen what MLlib offers today.

This appendix will give a quick look at the new Pipelines API, the result of work discussed in SPARK-3530 (*https://issues.apache.org/jira/browse/SPARK-3530*) in the Spark project issue tracker.

Beyond Mere Modeling

In purpose and scope, the current MLlib resembles other machine learning libraries. It provides an implementation of machine learning algorithms, and just the core implementation. Each takes preprocessed input as an RDD of `LabeledPoint` or `Rat ing` objects, for example, and returns some representation of the resulting model.

That's all. This is quite useful, but solving a real-world machine learning problem requires more than just running an algorithm.

You may have noticed that in each chapter of the book, most of the source code exists to prepare features from raw input, transform the features, and evaluate the model in some way. Calling an MLlib algorithm is just a small, easy part in the middle.

These additional tasks are common to just about any machine learning problem. In fact, a real production machine learning deployment probably involves many more tasks:

1. Parse raw data into features
2. Transform features into other features
3. Build a model
4. Evaluate a model
5. Tune model hyperparameters
6. Rebuild and deploy a model, continuously
7. Update a model in real time
8. Answer queries from the model in real time

Viewed this way, MLlib provides only a small part: #3. The new Pipelines API begins to expand MLlib so that it's a framework for tackling tasks #1 through #5. These are the very tasks that we have had to complete by hand in different ways throughout the book.

The rest is important, but likely out of scope for MLlib. These aspects may be implemented with a combination of tools like Spark Streaming, JPMML (*https:// github.com/jpmml*), REST (*http://en.wikipedia.org/wiki/Representational_state_trans fer*) APIs, Apache Kafka (*http://kafka.apache.org/*), and so on.

The Pipelines API

The new Pipelines API encapsulates a simple, tidy view of these machine learning tasks: at each stage, data is turned into other data, and eventually turned into a model, which is itself an entity that just creates data (predictions) from other data too (input).

Data, here, is always represented by a specialized RDD borrowed from Spark SQL, the `org.apache.spark.sql.SchemaRDD` class. As its name implies, it contains table-like data, wherein each element is a `Row`. Each `Row` has the same "columns," whose schema is known, including name, type, and so on.

This enables convenient SQL-like operations to transform, project, filter, and join this data. Along with the rest of Spark's APIs, this mostly answers task #1 in the previous list.

More importantly, the existence of schema information means that the machine learning algorithms can more correctly and automatically distinguish between numeric and categorical features. Input is no longer just an array of `Double` values, where the caller is responsible for communicating which are actually categorical.

The rest of the new Pipelines API, or at least the portions already released for preview as experimental APIs, lives under the `org.apache.spark.ml` package—compare with the current stable APIs in the `org.apache.spark.mllib` package.

The `Transformer` abstraction represents logic that can transform data into other data —a `SchemaRDD` into another `SchemaRDD`. An `Estimator` represents logic that can build a machine learning model, or `Model`, from a `SchemaRDD`. And a `Model` is itself a `Transformer`.

`org.apache.spark.ml.feature` contains some helpful implementations like `HashingTF` for computing term frequencies in TF-IDF, or `Tokenizer` for simple parsing. In this way, the new API helps support task #2.

The `Pipeline` abstraction then represents a series of `Transformer` and `Estimator` objects, which may be applied in sequence to an input `SchemaRDD` in order to output a `Model`. `Pipeline` itself is therefore an `Estimator`, because it produces a `Model`!

This design allows for some interesting combinations. Because a `Pipeline` may contain an `Estimator`, it means it may internally build a `Model`, which is then used as a `Transformer`. That is, the `Pipeline` may build and use the predictions of an algorithm internally as part of a larger flow. In fact, this also means that `Pipeline` can contain other `Pipeline` instances inside.

To answer task #3, there is already a simple implementation of at least one actual model-building algorithm in this new experimental API, `org.apache.spark.ml.clas sification.LogisticRegression`. While it's possible to wrap existing `org.apache.spark.mllib` implementations as an `Estimator`, the new API already provides a rewritten implementation of logistic regression for us, for example.

The `Evaluator` abstraction supports evaluation of model predictions. It is in turn used in the `CrossValidator` class in `org.apache.spark.ml.tuning` to create and evaluate many `Model` instances from a `SchemaRDD`—so, it is also an `Estimator`. Supporting APIs in `org.apache.spark.ml.params` define hyperparameters and grid search parameters for use with `CrossValidator`. These packages help with tasks #4 and #5, then—evaluating and tuning models as part of a larger pipeline.

Text Classification Example Walkthrough

The Spark Examples module contains a simple example of the new API in action, in the `org.apache.spark.examples.ml.SimpleTextClassificationPipeline` class. Its action is illustrated in Figure B-1.

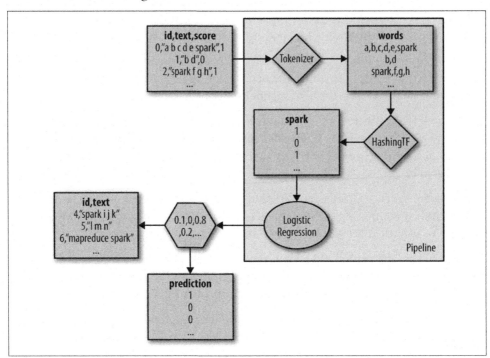

Figure B-1. A simple text classification Pipeline

The input are objects representing documents, with an ID, text, and score (label). Although `training` is not a `SchemaRDD`, it will be implicitly converted later:

```
val training = sparkContext.parallelize(Seq(
  LabeledDocument(0L, "a b c d e spark", 1.0),
  LabeledDocument(1L, "b d", 0.0),
  LabeledDocument(2L, "spark f g h", 1.0),
  LabeledDocument(3L, "hadoop mapreduce", 0.0)))
```

The `Pipeline` applies two `Transformer` implementations. First, `Tokenizer` separates text into words by space. Then, `HashingTF` computes term frequencies for each word. Finally, `LogisticRegression` creates a classifier using these term frequencies as input features:

```
val tokenizer = new Tokenizer().
  setInputCol("text").
  setOutputCol("words")
```

```
val hashingTF = new HashingTF().
  setNumFeatures(1000).
  setInputCol(tokenizer.getOutputCol).
  setOutputCol("features")
val lr = new LogisticRegression().
  setMaxIter(10).
  setRegParam(0.01)
```

These operations are combined into a `Pipeline` that actually creates a model from the training input:

```
val pipeline = new Pipeline().
  setStages(Array(tokenizer, hashingTF, lr))
val model = pipeline.fit(training) ❶
```

❶ Implicit conversion to SchemaRDD

Finally, this model can be used to classify new documents. Note that `model` is really a `Pipeline` containing all the transformation logic, not just a call to a classifier model:

```
val test = sparkContext.parallelize(Seq(
  Document(4L, "spark i j k"),
  Document(5L, "l m n"),
  Document(6L, "mapreduce spark"),
  Document(7L, "apache hadoop")))
model.transform(test).
  select('id, 'text, 'score, 'prediction). ❶
  collect().
  foreach(println)
```

❶ Not strings; syntax for Expressions

The code for an entire pipeline is simpler, better organized, and more reusable compared to the handwritten code that is currently necessary to implement the same functionality around MLlib.

Look forward to more additions, and change, in the new `org.apache.spark.ml` Pipeline API in Spark 1.3.0 and beyond.

Index

Symbols

invoking actions on, 19
K-means clustering and, 86
parallelize method, 16
persisting data in, 27
reusable code, 31-36
ROC (Receiver Operating Characteristic)
curve, 51
row-major data layout, 204
RPC frameworks, 197

S

sampling
in financial risk simulation, 183
multivariate normal distribution, 186
saveAsTextFile action, 19
Scala
aggregations, 28
anonymous function support, 21
benefits of, 10
collection types in, 29
declaring functions in, 21
histogram creation, 29
reusable code, 31-36
structuring data, 23-27
XML library, 125
scores, standard, 91
search indexes, 99
sequence feature, 196
serialization frameworks
Apache Avro, 196
compatible with Spark, 239
types available, 197
sessionization, 167-171
setEpsilon(), 89
setRuns(), 89
shuffles, 237
Silhouette coefficient, 98
singular value decomposition (SVD), 90, 100,
107, 119
sliding method, 181
small-world networks
cliques and clustering coefficients, 143
common properties of, 142
computing average path length, 144
real vs. idealized, 142
sortBy function, 30
span() method, 45
Spark
advanced operations

accumulators, 239
file formats, 242
serialization, 239
underlying execution model, 237
workflow in data science, 240
basic operations
aggregations, 28
bringing data to the client, 18-22
histogram creation, 29
interactive shell vs. compilation, 18
programming overview, 11
record linkage, 11
reusable code, 31-36
shipping code from client, 22
Spark Shell/SparkContext, 13-18
benefits of, ix, 4-6
benefits of for Monte Carlo simulation, 173
benefits of using Scala with, 10
directed acyclic graph of operators, 5
enhanced development with, 5
in-memory processing, 5
interfacing with Adam, 198
Python API, 218
sessionization in, 167-171
subprojects of, 243
temporal and geospatial data in, 153
version 1.2.1, 247
vs. MapReduce, 4
Spark Core, 243
Spark SQL, 245
Spark Streaming, 97, 244
Spray, 157
stacks, 224
stages, 237
standard scores, 91
Stanford Core NLP project, 104
stats() method, 44
stemming, 104
stop words, 104
StorageLevel values, 27
StringOps class, 24
strings, parsing into structured format, 23-27
summary statistics, 30-36
supervised learning, 60, 80, 81
(see also machine learning)
syntax, abbreviated, 22

T

take method, 19

About the Authors

Sandy Ryza is a Senior Data Scientist at Cloudera and active contributor to the Apache Spark project. He recently led Spark development at Cloudera and now spends his time helping customers with a variety of analytic use cases on Spark. He is also a member of the Hadoop Project Management Committee.

Uri Laserson is a Senior Data Scientist at Cloudera, where he focuses on Python in the Hadoop ecosystem. He also helps customers deploy Hadoop on a wide range of problems, focusing on life sciences and health care. Previously, Uri cofounded Good Start Genetics, a next-generation diagnostics company while working toward a PhD in biomedical engineering at MIT.

Sean Owen is Director of Data Science for EMEA at Cloudera. He has been a committer and significant contributor to the Apache Mahout machine learning project, and authored its "Taste" recommender framework. Sean is an Apache Spark committer. He created the Oryx (formerly Myrrix) project for real-time large-scale learning on Hadoop, built on Spark, Spark Streaming, and Kafka.

Josh Wills is Senior Director of Data Science at Cloudera, working with customers and engineers to develop Hadoop-based solutions across a wide range of industries. He is the founder and VP of the Apache Crunch project for creating optimized MapReduce and Spark pipelines in Java. Prior to joining Cloudera, Josh worked at Google, where he worked on the ad auction system and then led the development of the analytics infrastructure used in Google+.

Colophon

The animal on the cover of *Advanced Analytics with Spark* is a peregrine falcon (*Falco peregrinus*); these falcons are among the world's most common birds of prey and live on all continents except Antarctica. They can survive in a wide variety of habitats including urban cities, the tropics, deserts, and the tundra. Some migrate long distances from their wintering areas to their summer nesting areas.

Peregrine falcons are the fastest-flying birds in the world—they are able to dive at 200 miles per hour. They eat other birds such as songbirds and ducks, as well as bats, and they catch their prey in mid-air.

Adults have blue-gray wings, dark brown backs, a buff colored underside with brown spots, and white faces with a black tear stripe on their cheeks. They have a hooked beak and strong talons. Their name comes from the Latin word *peregrinus*, which means "to wander." Peregrines are favored by falconers, and have been used in that sport for many centuries.

Many of the animals on O'Reilly covers are endangered; all of them are important to the world. To learn more about how you can help, go to *animals.oreilly.com*.

The cover image is from Lydekker's *Royal Natural History*. The cover fonts are URW Typewriter and Guardian Sans. The text font is Adobe Minion Pro; the heading font is Adobe Myriad Condensed; and the code font is Dalton Maag's Ubuntu Mono.

Get even more for your money.

Join the O'Reilly Community, and register the O'Reilly books you own. It's free, and you'll get:

- $4.99 ebook upgrade offer
- 40% upgrade offer on O'Reilly print books
- Membership discounts on books and events
- Free lifetime updates to ebooks and videos
- Multiple ebook formats, DRM FREE
- Participation in the O'Reilly community
- Newsletters
- Account management
- 100% Satisfaction Guarantee

Signing up is easy:
1. Go to: oreilly.com/go/register
2. Create an O'Reilly login.
3. Provide your address.
4. Register your books.

Note: English-language books only

To order books online:
oreilly.com/store

For questions about products or an order:
orders@oreilly.com

To sign up to get topic-specific email announcements and/or news about upcoming books, conferences, special offers, and new technologies:
elists@oreilly.com

For technical questions about book content:
booktech@oreilly.com

To submit new book proposals to our editors:
proposals@oreilly.com

O'Reilly books are available in multiple DRM-free ebook formats. For more information:
oreilly.com/ebooks

CPSIA information can be obtained
at www.ICGtesting.com
Printed in the USA
BVOW04s1556281216
472062BV00010B/62/P